D0085319

Adventures in Speech

University of Pennsylvania Press
MIDDLE AGES SERIES
Edited by

Ruth Mazo Karras,
Temple University

Edward Peters,
University of Pennsylvania

A listing of the available books in the series appears
at the back of this volume

Adventures in Speech

Rhetoric and Narration in Boccaccio's *Decameron*

Pier Massimo Forni

PENN

University of Pennsylvania Press

Philadelphia

Forni, Pier Massimo.
   Adventures in speech : rhetoric and narration in Boccaccio's
Decameron / Pier Massimo Forni.
     p. cm. — (Middle Ages series)
   Parts of this work were previously published in Italian.
   Includes bibliographical references and index.
   ISBN 0-8122-3338-7 (alk.paper)
   1. Boccaccio, Giovanni, 1313—1375. Decamerone. 2. Boccaccio,
Giovanni, 1313-1375 — Style. 3. Narration (Rhetoric) I. Title.
II. Series.
PQ4295.F67 1996
853'.1—dc20   95-43882
                                                     CIP

To V.

Votre tres naturel et clair
Rire d'enfant qui charme l'air

Contents

Preface

THIS BOOK DEVELOPED both logically and methodologically from my book of Boccaccian interest entitled *Forme complesse nel Decameron*. Once again I have focused on questions of *provenance* and *work*, that is, the identification of sources, and discussion of modes of authorial intervention on sources. Once again, I have tried to probe the puzzling complexity of Boccaccio's operations of *inventio*. *Adventures in Speech*, however, is a substantially different book from *Forme complesse*. In my first study, concerns about intersections of rhetoric and narrative surfaced sporadically in the course of a comprehensive reading of only one *novella* (IV 1, the famous story of Tancredi and Ghismonda). This new work, on the other hand, uses the notion of rhetoric as a guiding principle for a critical assessment of the entire *Decameron*. When I return here to issues discussed in *Forme complesse*, I present new critical acquisitions, which sometimes strengthen my original argument and sometimes shed a new light on those issues.

In this study, the term "rhetoric" refers to the toolkit of discursive strategies and techniques available to any given author at any given time. With reference to Boccaccio, it is meant to cover, first of all, the range of discursive phenomena displayed by the ten young inhabitants (the *brigata*) of the *Decameron*'s frame-story. The title *Adventures in Speech* brings together the narrative and discursive components of the verbal ritual enacted by the *brigata*. The title is intentionally ambiguous. On the one hand, it alludes to the fact that narrative production in the frame-story is rooted in a discursive context (the narrative situation in the *Decameron* allows for comment upon narration by the narrators themselves). On the other, it points to the Boccaccian habit of exploring the narrative potential of rhetorical forms. This book's founding critical premise is that in the *Decameron* non-narrative discourse and narration constantly gloss each other. Its broadest objective is to begin to map the complexity of such interactions. Readers of *Forme complesse* were given only a sense of the importance, in Boccaccio's *inventio*, of what could be called rhetorical imagination. Now that insight is pursued analytically.

Chapter 1 examines salient aspects of the discursive morphology that emerges in the course of the remarkable verbal interaction taking place in the frame-story. In Chapter 2 the issue of narrative pleasure (one discussed by the narrators themselves) is brought to the fore in connection with an analysis of the two main types of narrative response (explicit and allusive) practiced by the narrators. At the core of Chapter 3 is an attempt at defining, structurally and rhetorically, how the stories in the *Decameron* begin. The first part of Chapter 4 posits in general terms the problem of instances of narrative production thriving on the imaginative use of rhetorical stimuli. The second part of the chapter concerns itself with a number of Boccaccian stories featuring an exploitation of narrative possibilities present in speech. Chapter 5 offers an analytic reading of *Decameron* III 5, a story that relies on rhetorical imagination. Here I try to show, among other things, how intricate the processes of intertextual weaving can be in a story tradition-ally considered of little critical interest. Recent studies have made apparent that a parodic stance is often at the core of Boccaccio's stories. One aim of Chapters 4 and 5 is to identify typical Boccaccian methods for engaging in parodic dialogue with often unexpected sources. Finally, in the Appendix I return to a proposal regarding the *inventio* of *Decameron* IV 1 which I first discussed in *Forme complesse*. My goal here is to develop and strengthen my original arguments, relying on the substantial addition of new evidence.

A concern for the fundamental issue of Boccaccian realism runs throughout the book. I have relinquished the traditional descriptive approach to this central and vexing question, in favor of a functional one. I have looked at realism (what traditionally has been conceived as real-ism), not simply as a product of ideology or an accessory to poetics, but as a functional element of the narrative machine. But (as I strive to show in Chapters 4 and 5) a new approach to the problem of realism also en-tails going beyond the traditional notion, in order to consider one in which the elaboration, the concretization, the *realization* of rhetorical material is in full view.

A Note on the Composition of the Book

In parts of this book I draw freely from works of mine which have been published in Italian but have never appeared in English. Chapters 2 and 3 are, essentially, English versions of two essays entitled "Appunti sull'intrat-tenimento decameroniano" and "Come cominciano le novelle del *Decame-ron*." They were written for symposia organized by the journal *Filologia e*

Critica and the Centro Pio Rajna, and appear in the proceedings of those symposia. Thanks are in order to Professor Enrico Malato of the Università della Tuscia for the permission to use the material. Chapter 5 has its remote origin in a brief essay entitled "Zima sermocinante (*Decameron* III 5)," which was published in the *Giornale Storico della Letteratura Italiana*. The long chapter bears little resemblance to what was originally little more than a note. I am pleased, however, to thank the editors of the *GSLI* for allowing me to take all that I needed from those pages of their journal. Finally, my gratitude goes to the publisher Bollati Boringhieri of Turin, since I have inserted in Chapters 1 and 4 and in the Appendix the translation of a few pages of my essay "Realtà/Verità," which is one of the entries of their *Lessico critico decameroniano*. Complete bibliographical references regarding all the aforementioned works appear in the Works Consulted section at the end of the book.

A Note on the Use of Primary and Secondary Sources

The Italian text of the *Decameron* is quoted from the critical edition established by Vittore Branca: Giovanni Boccaccio, *Decameron*, ed. Vittore Branca (Torino: Einaudi, 1980). Roman numerals identify the Days and Arabic numerals the *novelle* and paragraphs. References to the commentary in the Einaudi edition bear the name of Branca and the page and note numbers. For the English translation I chose Giovanni Boccaccio, *The Decameron*, trans. G. H. McWilliam (Harmondsworth: Penguin, 1982). Reference to this text is made by page number. All other works by Boccaccio, with the exception of the *Genealogia* (for which see the Works Consulted section), are quoted in the original from *Tutte le opere di Giovanni Boccaccio*, gen. ed. Vittore Branca, 10 vols. (Milano: Mondadori, 1964-). The translations used for these works and from other primary sources are listed in the Works Consulted section. When no page number appears after a quotation, the translation is mine. Unless otherwise specified, translations from secondary sources are mine.

Acknowledgments

THIS BOOK COULD NOT have been written without years of intellectual exchange with colleagues and students in the United States and Italy. I owe a special debt of gratitude to my beloved and brilliant *maestro*, the late Fredi Chiappelli, in whose California workshop I learned the ropes of professional reading. His insight was instrumental in pointing me in the right rhetorical direction as I tackled the enigmatic text examined in Chapter 5.

This is not the first time that I am pleased to thank my colleagues and friends Renzo Bragantini, Eduardo Saccone, and Giuseppe Velli for being kind enough to comment on a manuscript of mine. Competent support came as well from Victoria Kirkham, Claude Cazalé, Christopher Kleinhenz, Paolo Valesio, and Matteo Palumbo. In the very last phases of writing I had the good fortune to enjoy the expert and generous advice of Jackson Cope. I hope I managed to take full advantage of his painstakingly close readings of each chapter. Clorinda Donato and Kathy Bosi provided English rough drafts of parts of the book originally in Italian. The English benefited throughout from the keen editorial eye of Virginia Drake. My assistant Sara Brann did meticulous and enlightened work on the page proofs.

I worked on this project in 1993–1994 while holding a fellowship at Villa I Tatti, the Harvard University Center for Italian Renaissance Studies in Florence. I wish to express my warmest thanks to Director Walter Kaiser and the whole I Tatti community for maintaining and fashioning an ideal environment in which to produce scholarly work. On my return to the United States from Florence, I received through I Tatti a Lila Wallace–Reader's Digest Publication Subsidy, which facilitated considerably the transition of my work into print. Heartfelt thanks thus must also go to the Lila Wallace–Reader's Digest Endowment Fund.

Working with Jerome Singerman, Acquisitions Editor at the University of Pennsylvania Press, has been both a priviledge and a pleasure. I will remember his admirable competence, urbanity, and professionalism long after the completion of this project. Together with Jerome, I wish to thank all the other staff members of the Press who worked on this book, in particular Managing Editor Alison Anderson. I am also grateful to Copyeditor

Christina Sharpe, whose work was invaluable, and to Professor Edward Peters, who kindly included *Adventures in Speech* in his Middle Ages Series.

Finally, I am pleased to acknowledge my genial and cooperative colleagues at Johns Hopkins. Chairmen Harry Sieber, Noël Valis, and Eduardo Saccone were very effective in their administrative efforts on my behalf. As he leaves Hopkins for a post in Europe, I wish to thank Eduardo for being first among my interlocutors and closest among my colleagues on campus for the past ten years.

PART ONE

THE RHETORIC OF SELECTION AND RESPONSE

I

Configurations of Discourse

AN EPOCH-MAKING EVENT in the development of early Italian narrative is the canonization, thanks to the astounding success of Boccaccio's *Decameron*, of the *cornice*, the framing device. The formula of the *novelliere aperto*, the loosely structured anthology of stories (such as the *Novellino*), becomes secondary to that of the *novelliere chiuso*, in which a meta-story encompasses all others. In contemporary developments within the genre of lyric poetry, the fragmentary collection evolves into the *prosimetrum* (Dante's *Vita nuova*) and the *canzoniere* (Petrarch's *Rime*). In order to monitor the progress of literary forms out of the archaic period, one must focus on the development of innovative modes of collection, structuring, and closure. Italian literature marks its prime by mastering the art of what semiologists call the macrotext.[1]

Boccaccio's work finds a natural antecedent in the *Novellino*, whose stories were assembled around 1280–1300. The cultural universe of reference in the *Decameron* is, in part, that of the earlier collection. The initial rubric of the *Novellino* could be employed to begin to describe Boccaccio's material: "Questo libro tratta d'alquanti fiori di parlare, di belle cortesie e di be' risposi e di belle valentie e doni, secondo che per lo tempo passato hanno fatti molti valenti uomini" (797); "This book contains a choice of verbal pleasantries, acts of courtliness, witty repartees, and brave and liberal deeds done in the past by many virtuous men." Indeed, a small number of *Novellino* stories reappear in the *Decameron*. Here, however, the similarities end. The Boccaccian stories show degrees of sophistication and complexity (structural and psychological, for instance) unknown to those of the earlier collection, which in this respect may strike the modern reader as quaint narrative archaisms. The major structural difference is between a text which is more or less the sum of its texts, and one in which each fragment maintains its identity as it builds a superior unity—a macrotext. This unity is made possible by the frame-story of the ten young Florentines who during the plague of 1348 find shelter in the countryside, where they entertain themselves by narrating pleasant and instructive stories.

Boccaccio's narrative formula has been seen as a merging of the *topos* of the narration in the presence of a mortal peril (*Libro dei sette savi*, *Le mille e una notte*) with that of the "novellare nel giardino," the aristocratic activity of narration which takes place in a garden (Battaglia Ricci 1987: 42). The mortal peril in the framed narratives of oriental origin, however, is rather different from the one the Florentine group (the *brigata*) is trying to forget (the plague in the city).[2] Of essence is, instead, the structural element of the "novellare nel giardino," which must be connected with the cultural ritual of the Court of Love, one very dear to Boccaccio since his Neapolitan years (Battaglia 1965: 625–44). One of the most famous episodes of his *Filocolo* is Fiammetta's Court of Love in Book IV. It is well known that Boccaccio not only patterned the verbal ritual in the *Decameron* on the general rhetorical structure of the Court of Love, but transformed two of the questions discussed in the Neapolitan Court into stories of Day X in the *Decameron*. One aspect of this operation will be examined later in this chapter.

A thorough investigation of the activities in the *cornice* as a form of Court of Love leads inevitably to jurisprudence, a primary field in Boccaccio's education. It is clear that what happens in the *cornice* is, to a certain extent, related to the pattern of discussion of the juridical case, a pattern that combines narration and deliberation. Boccaccio could find in the tradition of juridical writing and pedagogical practice not only the rhetorical combination of story and gloss, but also the elementary ordering devices that divide material according to topics.[3]

In recent years a good amount of work has been done on the feature of the framing device in the *Decameron*, but we are still far from a satisfactory assessment of the different layers of complexity which it brings to the work.[4] Part of this complexity has to do with metatextual concerns. The *Decameron* is a narrative account of a gathering in which narration takes place. Narration takes place in a context which allows for comment on narration. The work is, among other things, about narrative, a book of narrative poetics. Its discursive sphere essentially has to do with provenance (*inventio*), intention, and response. The young narrators remark on the origin of their stories and the reasons for their choice. They also respond to each other's stories, in several ways, and not always overtly. In this chapter we will begin to examine a number of aspects of the discursive morphology and textual strategy of this verbal ritual. A close investigation of the processes of gloss and response which take place in the *cornice* will help define the complexity of the work's rhetorical construction.

A preliminary note of caution is in order, regarding a crucial concept used throughout this book. When we speak of *inventio* with respect to a work such as the *Decameron*, the word of course assumes a meaning partially different from that found in classical rhetoric. We will not see the concept within the complex set of rhetorical strategies enabling the orator to argue a case successfully, be it epideictic, deliberative, or judicial; adapted to modern critical needs, the discourse on *inventio* becomes one that has to do with the *provenance* and *production* of texts. Where does the author *find* the *novella*? How? How does he retrieve it from the storehouses of written or oral traditions? To what extent can we say that the story was *invented* by him? The attending problems are complicated by the fact that we are working on a macrotext. As I have shown elsewhere, the task of determining how one particular Boccaccian *novella* was born or put together, often cannot be separated from the investigation of how and why it was *put together with other novelle*. In other words, to speak of *inventio* in the *Decameron* means also to speak of *dispositio* — a connection, this, to which we will return often.[5]

There is one instance in the book of the use of the term *inventore*. It occurs in the epilogue, where, while defending his work from hypothetical accusations, the author denies, one more time, that he is the creator of the tales. He sustains the fiction according to which he is the mere scribe of texts produced by the *brigata* at the time of the plague: "Ma se pur proproppor si volesse che io fossi stato di quelle e lo 'nventore e lo scrittore, che non fui" (Concl. Aut., 17); "But even if one could assume that I was the inventor as well as the scribe of these stories (which was not the case)" (831). Even for Boccaccio, therefore, it was possible to think of an *inventare* which did not coincide perfectly with that of Cicero and Quintilian. If it is true that for our purposes the term *inventio* presents drawbacks, it still seems preferable to alternatives such as *invention* or *creativity*. Primarily it makes it easier to conceive of the creative process as one of both retrieval and imaginative intervention. Authorial *inventio* should mean (we will it to mean) to find something that was *already there*, to find again, to bring to the fore, but also to find *something else* in what was already there, to detach a fragment of *novum* from a body of *notum*.

Upon entering the realm of Decameronian *inventio* a distinction must be established between two possible levels of inquiry: 1) the level of the text

commenting on itself (documenting explicitly its own *inventio*), and 2) the
level of our comment on the text (one that relies on data not immediately
and explicitly supplied by the text). We situate ourselves on the first level if
we focus on statements such as the one with which Filostrato introduces
his story in Day IV: "Dovete adunque sapere che, *secondo che raccontano i
provenzali*, in Provenza furon già due nobili cavalieri, de' quali ciascuno e
castella e vassalli aveva sotto di sé" (IV 9, 4); "You must know, then, that
according to the Provençals, there once lived in Provence two noble knights,
each of whom owned several castles and had a number of dependants" (388;
emphasis added). "According to the Provençals": the possibilities of *variatio* in *exordium* allow for the explicit mention of sources. When Filostrato
tells us where he *found* his story, the famous story of the eaten heart—he
opens a small window on the realm of *inventio*.

If, on the other hand, we try to determine what happens to the motif
of the severed head found in the Provençal source but not in Boccaccio's
version, we operate at the second level. In our search we may stumble upon
the severed head in Lisabetta da Messina's story, the fifth on Day IV, and
consider the possibility of genetic links between the two stories.[6] Indeed, it
is not uncommon for Boccaccio to work as a *bricoleur*, to put to good use
residual material lying about his laboratory. It is a recurring, rewarding
experience, that work on the *inventio* of one story will allow precious in-
sights on the *inventio* of another.

Ever conscious of the dictates of rhetorical primers and ready to raise
at strategic junctures the stylistic intonation of his purportedly humble vernacular work, the author introduces the *Decameron* to his readers relying
on the solemnity of a resonant sententious expression:

Umana cosa è aver compassione degli afflitti: e come che a ciascuna persona stea
bene, a coloro è massimamente richesto li quali già hanno di conforto avuto mesti-
ere e hannol trovato in alcuni; (Pr. 2)

To take pity on people in distress is a human quality which every man and woman
should possess, but is especially requisite in those who have once needed comfort,
and found it in others. (45)[7]

The very first words of the book are inspired by a philosophy of humani-
tarian concern which pagan antiquity amply rehearsed and which lies at the
core of the message of Christianity. From the general, sweeping first statement it follows naturally that to be compassionate, to offer succor to fellow

human beings in need and distress, is a particularly compelling duty for
those who have experienced the need of comfort and the charity of the well-
intentioned. The author hastens to reveal that he is one of them. In his
youth he burned with a fierce and uncontrollable love, one that all but oblit-
erated his rational powers and left him close to death. He was lucky enough
to be rescued by the consoling, agreeable words of his friends. They helped
sustain him until he came to his senses and the maddening power of love
lost its grip on him. Having so weathered those stormy times, he feels that
he ought to do something in return. He will show his gratitude by providing solace and amusement to the love-smitten who have fewer opportuni-
ties to take heart and entertain themselves. It is in this way that he finally
comes to identify a female audience for his book.

Having evoked the readership of fragile and oppressed ladies, he proceeds to give a sketchy account of the structure and content of his work. He
will record the one hundred *novelle* ("o favole o parabole o istorie che dire
le vogliamo"; Pr. 13; "or fables or parables or histories or whatever you
choose to call them"; 47) which a group of seven ladies and three young
men narrated during ten days of the recent plague. In turn, the audience of
women in love will be amused by the stories (which will include "piacevoli
e aspri casi d'amore e altri fortunati avvenimenti"; Pr. 14; "love adventures,
bitter as well as pleasing, and other exciting incidents"; 47), so that their
suffering will be lessened. Again following the norms of ancient and medieval rhetoric and poetics, he couples *docere* with *delectare* and defines the
merits of the tales:

[. . .] delle quali le già dette donne, che queste leggeranno, parimente *diletto* delle
sollazzevoli cose in quelle mostrate e *utile consiglio* potranno pigliare, in quanto potranno cognoscere quello che sia da fuggire e che sia similmente da seguitare: le
quali cose senza passamento di noia non credo che possano intervenire. (Pr. 14)

In reading them, the aforesaid ladies will be able to derive, not only *pleasure* from
the entertaining matters therein set forth, but also some *useful advice*. For they will
learn to recognize what should be avoided and likewise what should be pursued,
and these things can only lead, in my opinion, to the removal of their affliction.
(47; emphasis added)[8]

A didactic, eudaemonistic program informs the project. This is a book
that will address serious concerns with the intention of bettering the mental
state of its readers. The degree of its purported seriousness may be measured

with respect to the allusions to death. It will suffice to connect the *noia* of the just quoted *passamento di noia* to the fatal *noia* which appeared in the background autobiographical outline: "Nella qual noia tanto rifrigerio già mi porsero i piacevoli ragionamenti d'alcuno amico e le sue laudevoli consolazioni, che io porto fermissima opinione per quelle essere avenuto che io non sia morto" (Pr. 4); "But in my anguish I have on occasion derived much relief from the agreeable conversation and the admirable expressions of sympathy offered by friends, without which I am firmly convinced that I should have perished" (45).[9]

It is the devoted follower of Ovid who speaks here, the *vir ovidianus* who saw in the ancient poet not only an unsurpassed storyteller and master of style, but also an inspiring psychologist and philosopher. Following in his idol's footsteps, he never forgets that 1) love can kill, and 2) something can or should be done about that fact.[10] The rhetorical, or more precisely sophistic, nimbleness of the Latin poet who wrote first an *Ars Amatoria* and then *Remedia Amoris*, was not wasted on Boccaccio:

Ad mea, decepti iuvenes, praecepta venite,
　Quos suus ex omni parte fefellit amor.
Discite sanari, per quem didicistis amare:
　Una manus vobis vulnus opemque feret.
Terra salutares herbas, eademque nocentes
　Nutrit, et urticae proxima saepe rosa est; (*Rem. Am.* 41–46)

Come, hearken to my precepts, slighted youths, ye whom your love has utterly betrayed. Learn healing from him through whom ye learnt to love: one hand alike will wound and succour. The same earth fosters healing herbs and noxious, and oft is the nettle nearest to the rose; (181)

We are far from having assessed the impact of such rhetorical-philosophical posturing on Boccaccio.[11] Within his ambitious project, he collapses the stances for and against love which he found in Ovid's poetic tracts. If there are good reasons to envision the *Decameron* as an *ars amatoria* for modern times, it is also legitimate to think of it as a *remedium amoris* of sorts. Certainly, it is a book of love, a splendid and lavish *triumphus cupidinis*, but its stories are also cautionary. Perhaps its readers are expected to learn from them how to go about reaching their erotic goals, or how to find fulfillment in love, but they are also abundantly supplied with warnings about the potential for baneful outcome. The author claims to offer lessons in the difficult art of living. He admonishes the reader to pay attention, for it may turn out to be, for him and in particular for *her*, a matter of life and death. Nothing in the preface, however, prepares us for the unconventionality and jocularity with which ethical issues will be treated during the ten days of narration. The continuous shift between the serious and the jocular, between earnestness and parody, is an essential, if puzzling, feature of Boccaccio's book. This shifting is one of the features which has thwarted, and presumably will continue to thwart, attempts to reach persuasive conclusions about authorial intent.

The main narrator's moral posturing at the opening of the book sets the tone for the moralizing (*moralisatio*) which is attached to the narration of the single stories. The task of the ten young narrators who comprise the *brigata* goes beyond story-telling. They engage in an edifying verbal ritual of mutual validation of principle and experience, of essence and circumstance. They explicitly treat their stories as *exempla*, at times more seriously than others. The other guiding authorial principle, pleasure, is also endlessly asserted. We now turn to this discourse surrounding narration, to this multi-layered background rhetoric from which the stories are brought forward with more or less effort as the case may be.

A primary responsibility of the queen or king of the Day is to select the *materia* (the term is Boccaccio's [12]) of narration, and it is incumbent on the subjects to conform even when they disagree. Controversy, however, is rare, confined to Days IV and VII.[13] The only narrator not bound by the rule of topic is Dioneo, who is granted this privilege by Filomena at the end of Day I.[14] Dioneo's eccentric role is defined not only by his freedom of topic selection for his tales, but also, as we will see, by his unorthodox behavior in the topic selection for his Day of reign.

Filomena's ruling on Dioneo's request for narrative freedom is one of many instances in which the members of the *brigata* exchange opinions about the opportune ways of shaping their discursive and narrative ritual. There is always reasoning on the choice of topic; there is continuous justification and rationalization, among the narrators. Sometimes they insist on the relevance of the topic itself, while at other times it is the connection of the new topic to what has been discussed that acquires relevance. Only Filostrato will connect his choice to strictly personal reasons (Day IV). A rhetorical movement of the first kind (absolute relevance) is Filomena's. She makes her choice for Day II within the traditional context (classical and medieval) of the meditation on Fortune's role in human affairs: "con ciò sia cosa che dal principio del mondo gli uomini sieno stati da diversi casi della fortuna menati, e saranno infino al fine, ciascun debba dire sopra questo: chi, da diverse cose infestato, sia oltre alla speranza riuscito a lieto fine" (I Concl., 10–11); "Ever since the the world began, men have been subject to various tricks of Fortune, and it will ever be thus until the end. Let each of us, then, if you have no objection, make it our purpose to take as our theme *those who after suffering a series of misfortunes are brought to a state of unexpected happiness*" (112).

On the other hand, Neifile, queen of the following Day, opts for variation on Filomena's topic rather than embracing radical change: "di chi alcuna cosa molto disiderata con industria acquistasse o la perduta recuperasse" (II Concl., 9); "*People who by dint of their efforts have achieved an object they greatly desired or recovered a thing previously lost*" (229). The device of the variation on the theme informs narrative choice in the *Decameron* not only at the level of topics for the Days, but at that of the individual stories as well.

Another context-based choice is Elissa's for Day VI. Prompt and witty repartees had enlivened Day I, and Elissa explicitly roots her choice in that already rehearsed *materia*. For the last Day of narration, Panfilo chooses instead the lofty theme of deeds of liberality, one new to the gathering. This is certainly not a fortuitous choice, but rather one which is intended to be the most appropriate to bring the exquisite experience of the *brigata* to completion: "Queste cose e dicendo e faccendo senza alcun dubbio gli animi vostri ben disposti a valorosamente adoperare accenderà: ché la vita nostra, che altro che brieve esser non può nel mortal corpo, si perpetuerà nella laudevole fama; il che ciascuno che al ventre solamente, a guisa che le bestie fanno, non serve, dee non solamente desiderare ma con ogni studio cercare e operare" (IX Concl., 5); "The telling and the hearing of such things will assuredly fill you with a burning desire, well disposed as you already are in spirit, to comport yourselves valorously. And thus our lives, which cannot be other than brief in these our mortal bodies, will be preserved by the fame of our achievements — a goal which every man who does not simply attend to his belly, like an animal, should not only desire but most zealously pursue and strive to attain" (731).

In no other instance does a sovereign couch choice of topic in such grandiloquence. The reader immediately perceives both choice and justification as crucial movements in a ritual of closure. The mention of animal-like behavior recalls the book's vivid opening scenes depicting the collapse of civic life and human decency in plague-stricken Florence. Panfilo and his companions were able to respond to the public crisis with a splendid escape into sanity, salubrity, and sodality. For the past fifteen days they have kept degeneracy and death at bay, but now the gilded interlude, the time away from history, is coming to an end. That is why, at Panfilo's mention of the brevity of human life, one perceives, within rhetorical grandeur, a dim note of Christian elegy. Meditation on mortality is certainly relevant for the young Florentines who will soon return to the wounded and perilous city.

From the point of view of the dynamics of topic selection, the most interesting cases are Days IV–V and VII–VIII.

—Amorose donne, per la mia disaventura, poscia che io ben da mal conobbi, sempre per la bellezza d'alcuna di voi stato sono a Amor subgetto, né l'essere umile né l'essere ubidente né il seguirlo in ciò che per me s'è conosciuto alla seconda in tutti i suoi costumi m'è valuto, che io prima per altro abandonato e poi non sia sempre di male in peggio andato; e cosí credo che io andrò di qui alla morte. E per ciò non d'altra materia domane mi piace che si ragioni se non di quello che a' miei fatti è piú conforme, cioè di coloro li cui amori ebbero infelice fine, per ciò che io a lungo andar l'aspetto infelicissimo, né per altro il nome, per lo quale voi mi chiamate, da tale che seppe ben che si dire mi fu imposto—; (III Concl., 5–6)

'Charming ladies, ever since I was able to distinguish good from evil, it has been my unhappy lot, owing to the beauty of one of your number, to find myself perpetually enslaved to Love. I have humbly and obediently followed all of his rules to the very best of my ability, only to find that I have invariably been forsaken to make way for another. Things have gone from bad to worse for me, and I do not suppose they will improve to my dying day. I therefore decree that the subject of our discussion for the morrow should be none other than the one which applies most closely to myself, namely, *those whose love ended unhappily*. For my part, I expect my own love to have a thoroughly unhappy ending, nor was it for any other reason that I was given (by one who knew what he was talking about) the name by which you address me.' (320)

Filostrato bases his choice for Day IV neither on the principle of general relevance, nor on that of the variation on topics already broached: for once, the urgency of a personal plight prevails. This is hardly in harmony with the ideal of pleasant entertainment which informs the program of communal life in the edenic retreat, and Fiammetta will be the first to express perplexity and dissent.[15] Authoritative Pampinea, in turn, finds a way to show her disagreement: with the help of Friar Alberto's shenanigans (IV 2) she inserts a note of lightheartedness between Fiammetta's and Lauretta's horrific stories.[16]

On this dismal and gruesome Day we expect Dioneo to take advantage of his privilege and choose merriment over tragedy. This he does and more, by turning his choice into a message for the future sovereign. His humorous tale, he hopes, will provide guidelines for the topic of the following Day. Filostrato himself repeats his suggestion at the crowning of Fiammetta, after having made his final excuses for his grim choice: "Io pongo a te questa corona sí come a colei la quale meglio dell'aspra giornata d'oggi, che alcuna altra, con quella di domane queste nostre compagne racconsolar saprai" (IV Concl. 3); "I now bequeath you this crown, knowing that you are better able than any other to restore the spirits of our fair companions tomorrow after the rigours of the present day's proceedings" (401). And of course, Fiammetta will be more than happy to meet her companions' wishes: "Filostrato, e io la prendo volentieri; e acciò che meglio t'aveggi di quel che fatto hai, infino a ora voglio e comando che ciascun s'apparecchi di dover doman ragionare di ciò che a alcuno amante, dopo alcuni fieri o sventurati accidenti, felicemente avvenisse" (IV Concl., 5); "I accept with pleasure, Filostrato; and so that you may the more keenly appreciate the error of your ways, I desire and decree forthwith that each of us should be ready on the morrow to recount *the adventures of lovers who survived calamities or misfortunes and attained a state of happiness*" (402). Topic selection may be context-based not only in the sense that the sovereigns exercise their right to *inventio* by resorting to topics already discussed; it is also the case that selection, while still officially entrusted to the king or queen of the Day, may be the result of a collective elaboration, the guided response to a unanimous need.

In only one instance does dissatisfaction with a selected topic induce the women to try to have it changed. The unseemly *materia* is proposed by Dioneo for Day VII:

— Valorose donne, in diverse maniere ci s'è della umana industria e de' casi varii ragionato tanto, che, se donna Licisca non fosse poco avanti qui venuta, la quale con le sue parole m'ha trovata materia a' futuri ragionamenti di domane, io dubito che io non avessi gran pezza penato a trovar tema da ragionare. Ella, come voi udiste, disse che vicina non aveva che pulcella ne fosse andata a marito e sogiunse che ben sapeva quante e quali beffe le maritate ancora facessero a' mariti. Ma lasciando stare la prima parte, che è opera fanciullesca, reputo che la seconda debbia esser piacevole a ragionarne, e perciò voglio che la domane si dica, poi che donna Licisca data ce n'ha cagione, delle beffe le quali o per amore o per salvamento di loro le donne hanno già fatte a' lor mariti, senza essersene essi o avveduti o no. (VI Concl., 4–6)

'Worthy ladies, our discussions have ranged so widely over the field of human endeavor, and touched upon such a variety of incidents, that if Mistress Licisca had not come here a short while ago and said something which offered me a subject for our deliberations on the morrow, I suspect I should have had a hard job to find a suitable theme. As you will have heard, she told us that none of the girls in her neighbourhood had gone to her husband a virgin; and she added that she knew all about the many clever tricks played by married women on their husbands. But leaving aside the first part, which even a child could have told you, I reckon that the second would make an ageeable subject for discussion; and hence, taking our cue from Mistress Licisca, I should like us to talk tomorrow about *the tricks which, either in the cause of love or for motives of self-preservation, women have played upon their husbands, irrespective of whether or not they were found out.*' (514–15)

At the beginning of Day VI, the row between Tindaro and Licisca, Filostrato's and Filomena's servants, brought an element of colorful commotion into the orderly and restrained routines of everyday life in the *cornice*. The dispute delighted everyone because of its paradoxical edge. Tindaro dared to contend that a certain Sicofante's wife had lost her virginity only on her wedding night—a preposterous notion to entertain, according to Licisca. With plebeian vehemence she defended and praised the sisterhood of women using the very arguments traditionally employed by men to prove the wickedness and baseness of the second sex. In her unabashed transformation of an ethical issue into one of pure expediency, loss of virginity before marriage became a point of merit. Even cheating on one's husband was condoned and indeed extolled as a sign of shrewdness and of a healthy spirit of initiative.[17] Acting as a jurist or as a king in a mock Court of Love, Dioneo had ruled in Licisca's favor: "Madonna, la sentenzia è data senza udirne altro: e dico che la Licisca ha ragione, e credo che cosí sia come ella dice, e Tindaro è una bestia" (VI Intr. 13); "'Madam,' Dioneo swiftly replied, 'the last word has already been spoken. In my opinion, Licisca is right. I believe it is just as she says; and Tindaro is a fool'" (482–83).[18]

There is more to this hilarious interlude than immediately meets the eye. It is instrumental in providing Dioneo with the topic of his Day. Of the women's reaction to his choice, we know only that they deem it unsuitable. On the other hand, we are treated to Dioneo's rather lengthy and eloquent defense of it. He argues that in a time of moral collapse men and women can talk about anything they please, provided that laxity in speech does not turn into dishonest conduct. He reminds his companions that their behavior has remained impeccable throughout their days of communal life. The women's honesty, he adds, is well known to everybody: it is such that terror of death could not make it waver, let alone a few silly tales. In fact, their refusing to speak of these escapades may make one suspect that they have something to hide. Finally, just as he has been an obedient subject on the previous days, he expects his authority to be respected now that they have made him king.[19]

It is impossible to gain full understanding of the women's objection to Dioneo's topic from this exchange alone. The reader is left with the impression that they simply resist the presentation of scabrous material. Only at the end of the Day, when it is time to choose a new topic, will the situation acquire clearer contours. Lauretta, newly elected queen of Day VIII, feels compelled to respond to Dioneo's choice:

—Dioneo volle ieri che oggi si ragionasse delle beffe che le donne fanno a' mariti; e, se non fosse che io non voglio mostrare d'essere di schiatta di can botolo che incontanente si vuol vendicare, io direi che domane si dovesse ragionare delle beffe che gli uomini fanno alle lor mogli. Ma lasciando star questo, dico che ciascun pensi di dire di quelle beffe che tutto il giorno o donna a uomo o uomo a donna o l'uno uomo all'altro si fanno; e credo che in questo sarà non meno di piacevole ragionare che stato sia questo giorno—; (VII Concl., 3–4)

'Yesterday, Dioneo insisted that we should talk, today, about the tricks played upon husbands by their wives; and but for the fact that I do not wish it to be thought that I belong to that breed of snapping curs who immediately turn round and retaliate, I should oblige you, on the morrow, to talk about the tricks played on wives by their husbands. But instead of doing that, I should like each of you to think of a story about *the tricks that people in general, men and women alike, are forever playing upon one another*. This, I feel sure, will be no less agreeable a topic than the one to which we have today been addressing ourselves.' (583)

Here Lauretta exposes Dioneo's exploitation of Licisca's outburst—she exposes, that is, the somewhat hostile implications of his topic selection. She steers the *brigata* away from Licisca's paradoxical philosophy and back to conventional wisdom. Within conventional moral bounds, to dwell on the tricks played by women upon their husbands is to feed misogynous prejudice. We are now in a better position to understand why the women had deemed Dioneo's topic unsuitable. Regardless of whether there is an intentional misogynous edge to Dioneo's choice, misogyny does pervade the fabric of these sections of the book. In order to see this more clearly, one has to move away from the narrators' statements about their *inventio* and toward the covert operations of authorial *inventio*.

It is only against the backdrop of Juvenal's Satire VI that the introduction to Day VI and the contents of Day VII, which originate in Licisca and

Tindaro's altercation found in that introduction, can be fully appraised. Conceived in the form of an attempt to dissuade a certain Postumus from getting married, this text contains a vitriolic indictment of the behavior of contemporary Roman women. They are depicted both as product and cause of a monstrously corrupted society: rapaciously greedy, inordinately vain and arrogant, whimsically cruel, domineering, not only adulterous but profligate, shameless in the pursuit of pleasure and social advancement. In the first part of Juvenal's long and congested poem, a series of tableaux of unfaithful wives culminates in a longer sequence regarding Messalina's depravity:

Quid privata domus, quid fecerit Eppia, curas?
respice rivales divorum, Claudius audi
quae tulerit. dormire virum cum senserat uxor.
ausa Palatino tegetem praeferre cubili,
sumere nocturnos meretrix Augusta cucullos
linquebat comite ancilla non amplius una.
set nigrum flavo crinem abscondente galero
intravit calidum veteri centone lupanar
et cellam vacuam atque suam; tunc nuda papillis
prostitit auratis titulum mentita Lyciscae
ostenditque tuum, generose Britannice, ventrem. (VI, 114–24)

Do the concerns of a private household and the doings of Eppia affect you? Then look at those who rival the Gods, and hear what Claudius endured. As soon as his wife perceived that her husband was asleep, this august harlot was shameless enough to prefer a common mat to the imperial couch. Assuming a night-cowl, and attended by a single maid, she issued forth; then, having concealed her raven locks under a light-coloured peruque, she took her place in a brothel reeking with long-used coverlets. Entering an empty cell reserved for herself, she there took her stand, under the feigned name of Lycisca, her nipples bare and gilded, and exposed to view the womb that bore thee, O nobly-born Britannicus! (93)

According to Juvenal, then, Licisca was the name under which Messalina would hide her identity when visiting the brothel in the vain attempt to satisfy her sexual cravings. What are we to make of this coincidence of names which brings together a Roman emperor's wife and Filomena's servant? We may be satisfied pointing out that Licisca in the *Decameron cornice* proposes for everybody's meditation at the beginning of Day VI, the themes of female sexual appetite and female infidelity which are at the core of Juvenal's Satire VI. I suggest, however, that we take a step further. Just as Licisca embodies in Juvenal the oxymoron of the *meretrix Augusta*, Licisca embodies in Boccaccio that of the *serva regina*. She provides, unintentionally to be sure, the topic for a Day (Day VII), a royal task, as we well know. In a way, it is as though she were coopted by king Dioneo to share his throne at the moment of his choice of topic at the end of Day VI.[20] One should bear in mind that the topic of Day VIII also proceeds from Licisca's brief appearance on the scene.

Juvenal's misogynous text may have played a role in the *inventio* of the last story of Day V (Pietro di Vinciolo) as well. This is a rewriting of an episode found in book IX of Apuleius's *Metamorphoses* — a section of the work with a strong misogynistic strain.[21] But while in Apuleius the lover hides under an "alveus ligneus" (IX 23), a "wooden tub" (169), when the husband returns home unexpectedly, in the parallel scene of *Decameron* V 10 it is a "cesta da polli" (V 10, 28), a "chicken-coop," which shelters him, before the ass steps on his hand. I suggest that the direct antecedent of the Boccaccian "cesta" may be the "cista" mentioned by Juvenal in the same section of Satire VI which culminates with the Licisca episode. This is the "cista" in which the mime Latinus hides when impersonating the adulterer on the stage (44).

Dioneo had proposed a similar imaginative nucleus in IV 10, where the adulterous woman and her servant hide the drugged lover (believed dead) in an "arca," a "chest." In that case, though, another Latin moralizing text may have been of service: Horace's Satire II vii. In the Horatian text a "servus" named Davus dares to give a lesson in morality to his master due to the exceptional regime of freedom allowed by the Saturnalia. Harshly reprehending him for his immoral and undignified behavior, he recalls his master hiding in an "*arca*" in pursuit of an adulterous adventure.[22] The "*arca*" motif aside, Horace's Satire II vii is still of interest for the introduction to Day VI. Just as the Horatian "servus" takes advantage of the rare opportunity of the Saturnalia to present his opinions to his master, so the Boccaccian "fante" is allowed to present her masters with her view of the world — the first and the last time that something of this sort happens in the life of the *brigata*.[23] Licisca's shrill lesson in unorthodox and subversive morality can be seen as a parody of Davus's earnest recourse to the tenets of the established stoic moral system of his times. We encounter, here, a vital point of Boccaccian poetics. Any critical discourse on meaning in the *Decameron* must take into consideration its massive recourse to overt or covert parodic techniques of appropriation. A complex case of parody (and self-parody) presented by the story of Zima (III 5) will be examined in Chapter 5.

When Dioneo announces the topic for Day VII, he declares that he would have had trouble finding a good one had Licisca not come to the rescue with her unintentional suggestion. This may indeed be the case. However, the selected topic seems to derive quite naturally from a number of stories he has narrated up to that point, for example II 10, IV 10, and V 10. Just as in II 10, in IV 10 a young woman married to an older man takes a lover when she realizes that her husband is unable to satisfy her. In V 10, the husband is unable to satisfy the wife not because he is old, but because of his homosexual inclinations. Once again the wife looks for a lover capable of giving her what her husband wrongly denies her. In each case the starting point is a deficiency of the man, and in each case the woman explicitly addresses the rightfulness of her demand for sexual satisfaction. If, in these tales, women sin against traditional morality, they do so in a context which affords them a justification.[24] This is a pattern that reappears in a number of tales in Days VII and VIII. Sometimes the male's deficiency, the behavior that justifies adultery, will be jealousy. This is the case of VII 4, the tale of Tofano and Ghita, which loses in Boccaccio's version at least part of the mysogynous connotations of the original (which appears in the *Disciplina clericalis*). In VII 2, Filostrato's retelling of Apuleius's tale of the tub, the blunting of the misogynous edge does not happen so much within the story as it does outside it, in the narrator's *exordium*.[25] Of course, one can emphasize that for all of the attenuations and the disclaimers, the fact remains that a good number of stories present misogynous connotations. This is one of the many instances when the reader of the *Decameron* is left to ponder the essential ambiguity of the moral construction of the book.

Marcel Janssens, one of the very first critics to have studied in some detail the rules of reception within the frame-story, concisely posits the fundamental question of the connection among selected stories:

In the authorial narrative structure of the *Decameron* the reader's role has not only the status of a motif, but also of a theme. This theme shows two aspects, of which we could give lots of examples from our hundred stories: in one case only the way the reader responds to a tale is described; in the other case the reader's response influences the production of other tales. It appears that in the *Decameron* both aspects are closely intertwined. The reception proves to be productive and creative in that it influences the making of other narratives. Reception and production are connected in a circular process which constitutes the making of the *Decameron*. (1977: 136–37)

Elissa's *exordium* in Day VII represents one of the starkest articulations of the device: "Piacevoli donne, lo 'ncantar della fantasima d'Emilia m'ha fatto tornare alla memoria una novella d'un'altra incantagione, la quale, quantunque cosí bella non sia come fu quella, per ciò che alla nostra materia non me ne occorre al presente, la racconterò" (VII 3, 3); "Winsome ladies, Emilia's exorcizing of the werewolf has reminded me of a story about another incantation, and although it is not so fine a tale as hers, it is the only one I can think of for the moment that is relevant to our theme, and I shall therefore relate it to you" (532). Here a motif in the previous story happens to jog the memory of the narrator who would otherwise be unable to perform her duty. No other consideration plays a role, no other reason is given. The coupling of the weak justification and the admission of the weakness of the story itself, make this *exordium* eccentric.[26] It is much more common in the *Decameron* to find the members of the *brigata* engaged in the attempt to highlight the beauty, the entertaining aspects and the pedagogical import of their stories. In fact, their habit of bringing attention to their ability in storytelling assumes at times — most notably in Day X — the character of a competition.

Connections such as the one documented above are disarmingly simple. Essentially, it is the absence of interpretative effort and structural subtlety which makes them so stark and elementary. Let us see, on the other hand, the discursive apparatus that Neifile appends to her story of Abraham and Jehannot of Chevigny in Day I:

— Mostrato n'ha Panfilo nel suo novellare la benignità di Dio non guardare a' nostri errori quando da cosa che per noi veder non si possa procedano: e io nel mio intendo di dimostrarvi quanto questa medesima benignità, sostenendo pazientemente i difetti di coloro li quali d'essa ne deono dare e con l'opere e con le parole vera testimonianza, il contrario operando, di sé argomento d'infallibile verità ne dimostri, acciò che quello che noi crediamo con piú fermezza d'animo seguitiamo. (I 2, 3)

Panfilo has shown us in his tale that God's loving kindness is unaffected by our errors, when they proceed from some cause which it is impossible for us to detect; and I in mine propose to demonstrate to you how this same loving kindness, by patiently enduring the shortcomings of those who in word and in deed ought to be its living witness and yet behave in a precisely contrary fashion, gives us the proof of its unerring rightness; my purpose being that of strengthening our conviction in what we believe. (82)

This is not a simple recording of a jogging of memory, but a well thought out and argued selection based on a summary gloss of the previous text. Panfilo's point, illustrated by Ciappelletto's story, was that God is so good that he is willing to heed the needs of his children even when their advocate is less than honorable. Neifile goes a step further, using the wickedness, corruption, and profligacy of the religious as proof of divine goodness and of the rightness of the Christian religion. That the best *exordia* convey a sense of progression, a narrative discourse flowing naturally from one story to the next, can be clearly assessed when we move from I 2 to I 3:

Poi che, commendata da tutti la novella di Neifile, ella si tacque, come alla reina piacque Filomena cosí cominciò a parlare: — La novella da Neifile detta mi ritorna a memoria il dubbioso caso già avvenuto a un giudeo. Per ciò che già e di Dio e della verità della nostra fede è assai bene stato detto, il discendere oggimai agli avveni-menti e agli atti degli uomini non si dovrà disdire: a narrarvi quella verrò, la quale udita, forse piú caute diverrete nelle risposte alle quistioni che fatte vi fossero. (I 3, 2–3)

Neifile's story was well received by all the company, and when she fell silent, Filo-mena began at the queen's behest to address them as follows: The story told by Neifile reminds me of the parlous state in which a Jew once found himself. Now that we have heard such fine things said concerning God and the truth of our reli-gion, it will not seem inappropriate to descend at this juncture to the deeds and adventures of men. So I shall tell you a story which, when you have heard it, will possibly make you more cautious in answering questions addressed to you. (86)

Here the perspective shifts as the narrator purports to leave the realm of things divine and take on things human. The previous stories clearly sup-ported fine theological points, but it is time now for practical advice. Filo-mena's story will teach caution in answering questions, and that good judgment is a sure road to happiness. This is certainly a legitimate reading of the story of the three rings. It is based, however, on an obliteration of its prominent theological component. Filomena could easily argue that her story is about God and religion, as are the two preceding ones. The essen-tial difference is that while in I 1 and I 2 doubt concerning the truth of the Christian faith was somehow dispelled (in a serious-jocular way), here the question of truth is left in abeyance.

A narrator's perspective on the nature of content may or may not be shared by fellow narrators. In this Day, it is Dioneo who follows Filomena, with the story of the abbot and the young monk. Dioneo's *exordium* is eloquent proof that the *cornice* is a place for interpretation and reinterpretation. Before anything else, he reminds his audience of the festive nature of their gathering: they should not forget that narration is supposed to be a pleasant activity, that *diletto* should be paramount. He then pays homage to the previous stories while loosely placing his in reference to them:

> — Amorose donne, se io ho bene la 'ntenzione di tutte compresa, noi siamo qui per dovere a noi medesimi novellando piacere; e per ciò, solamente che contro a questo non si faccia, estimo a ciascuno dovere esser licito (e cosí ne disse la nostra reina, poco avanti, che fosse) quella novella dire che piú crede che possa dilettare: per che, avendo udito che per li buoni consigli di Giannoto di Civigní Abraam aver l'anima salvata e Melchisedech per lo suo senno avere le sue ricchezze dagli aguati del Saladino difese, senza riprensione attender da voi intendo di raccontar brievemente con che cautela un monaco il suo corpo di gravissima pena liberasse. (I 4, 3)

> Sweet ladies, if I have properly understood your unanimous intention, we are here in order to bring pleasure to each other with our storytelling. I therefore contend that each must be allowed (as our queen agreed just now that we might) to tell whatever story we think most likely to amuse. So having heard how Abraham's soul was saved through the good advice of Jehannot de Chevigny, and how Melchizedek employed his wisdom in defending his riches from the wily manoeuvres of Saladin, I intend, without fear of your disapproval, to give you a brief account of the clever way in which a monk saved his body from very severe punishment. (89)

According to Neifile, her story was about the truth of the Christian religion as it is confirmed by the loving kindness of God, who puts to good use even the scandalous behavior of his men of the cloth. In Dioneo's reading, on the other hand, the story becomes that of a man's salvation and of his friend's crucial assistance in the process. Dioneo wants to establish a connection between his and the two preceding stories, hence the partial vision, the carving of the opportune theme out of Neifile's: "how Abraham's soul was saved through the good advice of Jehannot de Chevigny." This is not, however, the only possible reconstruction of his reinterpretation. The declared theme of Filomena's story (a man who saves himself, who cleverly escapes a danger), while making him think of his story of a different escape (how "a monk saved his body from severe punishment"), may also make him see the theme of salvation in Neifile's story.

The complexities of *variatio* in *exordium* are well represented also by Fiammetta's response to her fellow narrators' response to the story of the scholar and the widow (VIII 7). Yes, the women agree there, the treacherous widow should have been punished for what she did to the scholar, but the punishment which he eventually inflicts upon her is excessive and cruel:

—Piacevoli donne, per ciò che mi pare che alquanto trafitte v'abbia la severità dell'offeso scolare, estimo che convenevole sia con alcuna cosa piú dilettevole ramorbidare gl'innacerbiti spiriti; e per ciò intendo di dirvi una novelletta d'un giovane, il quale con piú mansueto animo una ingiuria ricevette e quella con piú moderata operazion vendicò; per la quale potrete comprendere che assai dee bastare a ciascuno se quale asino dà in parete tal riceve, senza volere, soprabondando oltre la convenevolezza della vendetta, ingiuriare, dove l'uomo si mette alla ricevuta ingiuria vendicare. (VIII 8, 3)

Charming ladies, since you appear to have been somewhat stricken by the harshness of the offended scholar, I consider this a suitable moment at which to soothe your outraged feelings with something slightly more entertaining; and I therefore propose to tell you a little tale about a young man who took a more charitable view of an injury he received, and devised a more harmless way of avenging himself. You will thereby be enabled to apprehend, that when a man seeks to avenge an injury, it should be quite sufficient for him to render an eye for an eye and a tooth for a tooth, without wanting to inflict a punishment out of all proportion to the original offence. (645)

Fiammetta's prompt intervention is particularly opportune because the issue had the potential to create a split in the serene society of men and women.[27] Wanting to be entertaining and soothing, she maintains Pampinea's controversial theme. Her story of Spinelloccio and Zeppa is still about revenge, but a revenge characterized by more acceptable connotations. VIII 7 and VIII 8, thus, become two halves of a unit which is meant to give a sense of structural and instructional completion. Pampinea's is a dark, serious, almost tragic treatment of the theme of revenge; Fiammetta's is lighthearted, optimistic, and outright comic. The disposition of the material in oppositional and complementary patterns is typical of the organizing and ideological strategy of the book. It is a strategy rooted in the sophistic principle of dual argumentation, and connected to the ambition (which parallels that of Dante's *Comedy*) to apprehend the world in its totality. Oppositional and complementary patterns are the product of the book's multiple perspective. In the *Decameron*, the so-called human comedy which responds to the divine one, a democratic vision — the different perspectives of the ten narrators — replaces the tyranny of the Dantean eye. Of course, the innumerable aspects of reality cannot all be recorded in a book, but a book can give the impression of touching reality in all its forms, can convey the *sense* of totality. This the *Decameron* does, relying both on its major structures, the topics of the Days, and the minor ones, the topics of the stories, as in the case of the coupling of VIII 7 and VIII 8.[28]

Some attention must be given to the moral component of Fiammetta's choice. Moral advice in the *Decameron* is not always presented in a straight-forward manner. Dioneo's outrageous illustration of the pious duty of put-ting the Devil back in Hell is a case in point (III 10). We could also mention, among numerous other examples, Emilia's jocular teaching of the prayer to keep the *fantasima* at bay (VII 1). Fiammetta, on the contrary, has a genu-ine ethical principle to promote, that of moderation in retribution, and that she manages to do. To be sure, the narrative vector of such a principle is comic in nature, and what the characters do is clearly objectionable in terms of conventional morality. Perhaps because it is presented against the back-ground of the deadly serious story of the widow and the scholar, however, the principle maintains its moral efficacy. It cannot be completely undercut by the playfulness of the *exemplum* which purports to sustain it.

The first response to appear at the end of a story is a collective one. Usually given by the main narrator (rather than a member of the *brigata*) in very synthetic terms, it proves unanimously favorable in most circum-stances (see, for instance, I 3, 2; V 3, 2). At times the recorded unanimous reaction can be other than verbal (laughter or weeping, such as in IV 2, 2; V 5, 2). The feelings of the whole *brigata* can also be summarized by one of the narrators (III 9, 3). A non-unanimous collective response usually entails a division of sexual difference (IX 10, 2; V Concl., 1). Finally, in rare circum-stances the report is analytical rather than synthetic:

Chi potrebbe pienamente raccontare i varii ragionamenti tralle donne stati, qual maggior liberalità usasse, o Giliberto o messer Ansaldo o il nigromante, intorno a' fatti di madonna Dianora? Troppo sarebbe lungo. (X 6, 2)

It would take far too long to recount in full the various discussions that now took place amongst the ladies as to whether Gilberto or Messer Ansaldo or the magician had displayed the greater liberality in the affair of Madonna Dianora. (762)

This passage documents an exceptional use of source. Madonna Dianora's adventure has a history which goes back to Boccaccio's early novel, the *Filocolo*. There it had taken the guise of a question of love at the Court of Love convened in Naples under the rule of Fiammetta (IV 31). The transformation of that old *questione d'amore* into a *novella*, requires that the *novella* be treated as a *questione*. The verbal ritual of the Florentine *brigata* assumes thus, if only briefly, a clear connotation of Court of Love. Disputing, however, is not a fitting activity for the present gathering. Not surprisingly, it is Fiammetta who intervenes (at Panfilo's behest): "Splendide donne, io fui sempre in opinione che nelle brigate, come la nostra è, si dovesse sí largamente ragionare, che la troppa strettezza della intenzion delle cose dette non fosse altrui materia di disputare: il che molto piú si conviene nelle scuole tra gli studianti che tra noi, le quali appena alla rocca e al fuso bastiamo" (X 6, 3); "Illustrious ladies, I have always been of the opinion that in a gathering such as ours, we should talk in such general terms that the meaning of what we say should never give rise to argument among us through being too narrowly defined. Such arguments as these are better conducted among scholars in seats of learning than among ourselves, who have quite enough to do in coping with our distaffs and our spindles" (762).

The game of covert reference is enlivened by a number of subtleties. Having evoked the aristocratic world of the Neapolitan Court of Love, Boccaccio has the Florentine namesake of the Neapolitan queen connect the current dispute not to that courtly entertainment, but to scholarly practice. Furthermore, he has her ironically state that she and her companions have enough to do with their distaffs and spindles. Fiammetta proceeds, however, to introduce a story in which the protagonist will be a king, and a king of Naples to boot. In selecting her story she is influenced by the response which the *brigata* gave to the previous one: "E per ciò io, che in animo alcuna cosa dubbiosa forse avea, veggendovi per le già dette alla mischia, quella lascerò stare e una ne dirò non mica d'uomo di poco affare ma d'un valoroso re, quello che egli cavallerescamente operasse in nulla movendo il suo onore" (X 6, 4); "And therefore, since the story I was going to tell you is possibly a little ambiguous and I see you squabbling over those we have already heard, I shall abandon it and tell you another, concerning the chivalrous action, not of any insignificant man, but of a valiant king, whose reputation was in no way diminished in consequence" (762). The tranquil gathering must not be disturbed. Even a genteel dispute similar to those held in the Courts of Love is unacceptable. These passages belong to the realm of individual response, for the narrator responds to her fellow narrators' response, rather than responding to a specific story.

Another exceptional analytic response follows the story of Lisabetta da Messina and her lover Lorenzo (IV 5). There is no expression of compassion for the protagonists' tragic fate. The story is highly appreciated for a

reason which has nothing to do with its human interest. Filomena had put
an end to it observing that it had provided the inspiration for a well-known
popular song:

La giovane non restando di piagnere e pure il suo testo adimandando, piagnendo si
morí, e cosí il suo disaventurato amore ebbe termine. Ma poi a certo tempo divenuta
questa cosa manifesta a molti, fu alcun che compuose quella canzone la quale ancora
oggi si canta, cioè:

> Qual esso fu lo malo cristiano,
> che mi furò la grasta, *et cetera*. (IV 5, 23–24)

The girl went on weeping and demanding her pot of basil, until eventually she cried
herself to death, thus bringing her ill-fated love to an end. But after due process of
time, many people came to know of the affair, and one of them composed the song
which can still be heard to this day:

> Whoever it was,
> Whoever the villain
> That stole my pot of herbs, etc. (369–70)

It is this very connection which the *brigata* finds exceedingly intriguing:
"Quella novella che Filomena aveva detta fu alle donne carissima, per ciò
che assai volte avevano quella canzone udita cantare né mai avean potuto,
per domandarne, sapere qual si fosse la cagione per che fosse stata fatta"
(IV 6, 2); "The story related by Filomena was much appreciated by the
ladies, for they had heard this song on a number of occasions without ever
succeeding, for all their inquiries, in discovering why it had been written"
(370). Our interest in these passages lies in the emphasis on the identification of sources. Boccaccio's game of gloss entails a displacement: the focus
is not on the sources of the story, but on the story as source. We are being
told how the song was born of the story, or, more precisely, of the events
contained in it. This strategy leaves the reader wondering about the origin
of the story itself. We cannot help entertaining the possibility that the declared creative sequence from story to song must be reversed in order to
begin to understand the story's processes of *inventio*. It is certainly plausible
that the song as a whole, and in particular the lines quoted by Filomena,
may have furnished Boccaccio's imagination with essential stimuli for the
narrative configuration of IV 5 (cf. Branca 532, n. 3).

Similar considerations are relevant for III 10, the story with which

Dioneo playfully instructs his companions how to put the Devil back in Hell. Narrating the adventures of Rustico and Alibech he not only accomplishes that practical goal, but also provides the "historical" data on the origin of an expression they may have heard hundreds of times. First Alibech learns from Rustico how one puts the Devil back in Hell. Then the women of Capsa hear with much delight about that crucial skill from Alibech:

Poi l'una all'altra per la città ridicendolo, vi ridussono in volgar motto che il più piacevol servigio che a Dio si facesse era rimettere il diavolo in inferno: il qual motto, passato di qua da mare, ancora dura. (III 10, 35)

The story was repeated throughout the town, being passed from one woman to the next, and they coined a proverbial saying there to the effect that the most agreeable way of serving God was to put the devil back in Hell. The dictum later crossed the sea to Italy, where it survives to this day. (319)

Again, as in Lisabetta's story, the sequence must be reversed. Within the context of the authorial processes of *inventio* it is not the dictum which follows the story, but the opposite. Boccaccio has taken a widely used common expression, one often repeated in popular piety, and endowed it with a jocular historical origin and a scabrous meaning. The story has, in other words, a phraseological origin, or at least a phraseological elemental narrative component (which does not mean that other components do not contribute to its *inventio*).

The issue of verbal or phraseological imagination in general, and in the *Decameron* in particular, will be discussed in Chapters 4 and 5. For the time being, it will suffice to establish that the discourse of gloss and response which takes place in the *cornice* is connected with the seminal issue of truthfulness in storytelling. When Filomena identifies the story of Lisabetta as her source of the song, not only does she infuse reality into the contents of the song (she treats them as events which really happened) but she also gives a certification of sorts to the reality of the events in Lisabetta's story. By explicitly linking her story to the song, she is implicitly asserting the factual truth of the story itself. Of course, one could emphasize the irony of two texts, both fictional, each claiming reality relying on the reality of the other.

This is a good story, this is a story for the common good, the narrators never tire of repeating. What makes a story supportive of the common good is evidently its functioning as an *exemplum*, its adaptability as a vehicle for wisdom and morality. It is an intuitive truth—and one exploited by medieval writers and users of *exempla*—that an exemplary story which happens to be true, or presented as such, will be more effective. It is also a tenet of classical and medieval rhetoric that a good story (one capable of yielding narrative pleasure) must be true, or at least have an appearance of truth. Horace's teaching could not be clearer on this point: "ficta voluptatis causa sint proxima veris" (*De Arte Poetica* 338); "Fictions meant to please should be close to the real" (479). Elsewhere I have tried to provide a comprehensive critical assessment of the notions of truth and reality in the discursive parts of the *Decameron* (Forni 1995). Here, I would like to offer a few examples of the concern for truth in storytelling among the members of the *brigata*. My goal is to show how this concern fits within the general rhetorical context of the frame-story.

The problem of truthfulness presents itself explicitly several times in the moralizing introductions to the single stories. Lauretta in Day III says that she will tell "una verità che ha, troppo piú di quello che ella fu, di menzogna sembianza" (III 8, 3); "a true story, [. . .] which sounds far more fictitious than was actually the case" (294), of Ferondo's apparent death. Also unbelievable, although in a different way, is Madonna Beritola's story, with its trials, tribulations, and recognitions, that Emilia in turn must insist on the truthfulness of the events: "una novella non meno vera che pietosa" (II 6, 4); "a story, no less true than touching" (155). As " una novelletta non men vera che piacevole" (VIII 3, 3); "a little story of mine, which is no less true than entertaining" (596), Elissa presents the adventure of Calandrino and the heliotrope, her assertion of its truthfulness perhaps linked to the incredible stupidity of the protagonist. Dioneo relates another unlikely episode in his story about Tingoccio who returns from Purgatory to speak with his friend Meuccio: a "novelletta [. . .] la quale, ancora che in sé abbia assai di quello che creder non si dee, nondimeno sarà in parte piacevole a ascoltare" (VII 10 7); "a little tale [. . .] which, albeit much of it will strain your credulity, should nevertheless prove entertaining in parts" (579–80). Filostrato invokes truth as well, when recounting the unlikely story of Nathan and Mitridanes, which is set in the Far East. He asserts that it is most certain that there lived in Cathay a nabob called Nathan—most certain, that is, "se fede si può dare alle parole d'alcuni genovesi e d'altri uomini che in quelle contrade stati sono" (X 3, 4); "if the word of various Genoese and of others who have been to those parts may be trusted" (743). It is one of the many cases in the *Decameron* in which the narrator refers to his source in order to enhance the aura of narrative truthfulness. It may be possible, of course, to apply to the narrators in the *Decameron* what Cesare Segre observed speaking of storytellers in general:

It is a fact that they multiply historical points of reference, that they often base themselves on authorities which do not exist, that their authoritative sources are often made up, that they introduce into their texts the (false) traces of a history of previous editions; it is a fact, too, that such efforts are multiplied when the subject matter breaks free of the real and the possible. We should also note that these authentications are often brought forward in undisguised bad faith where playfulness invites amiable complicity. Reflections of unreality are made to play upon simulations of the real. (1988: 189–90)

As far as the *Decameron* is concerned, however, it would be a mistake to neglect these claims on account of their being mere instances of conventional literary truth-play. In fact, they can point to covert seminal levels of meaning. Let us turn to Fiammetta's introduction to the fourth and last novella of Calandrino's cycle. The problem which she faces (and it is not by chance that it is the eminently authoritative and subtle Fiammetta who is given this charge) is that of justifying the return to the already amply utilized lore of the practical jokes inflicted upon the poor Florentine dauber. She resolves this dilemma by observing that there is no subject among those that have been discussed at length that could not be proposed again with success "dove il tempo e il luogo che quella cotal cosa richiede si sappi per colui che parlar ne vuole debitamente eleggere" (IX 5, 3); "provided the person by whom it is broached selects the appropriate time and place" (701). Since the *brigata* convened "per aver festa e buon tempo" (IX 5, 4); "for no other purpose than to rejoice and be merry" (p. 701), it would be thoroughly suitable to seek pleasure once more in the adventures of a character who has already been a source of amusement. Having thus justified her choice, Fiammetta concludes with a unique clarification:

[. . .] la quale [novella], se io dalla verità del fatto mi fossi scostare voluta o volessi, avrei ben saputo e saprei sotto altri nomi comporla e raccontarla; ma per ciò che il partirsi dalla verità delle cose state nel novellare è gran diminuire di diletto negl'intendenti, in propria forma, dalla ragion di sopra detta aiutata, la vi dirò. (IX 5, 5)

I could easily have told it in some other way, using fictitious names, had I wished to do so; but since by departing from the truth of what actually happened, the storyteller greatly diminishes the pleasure of his listeners, I shall turn for support to my opening remarks, and tell it in its proper form. (701)

Fiammetta seems to say that in storytelling one must remain faithful to the facts which have become story, that the integrity of the story containing the facts must be respected at all costs if the narrative act is to achieve a complete success. This is a general, superficial meaning (superficial and yet interesting in and of itself) to which we must add a specific, less obvious one.

Fiammetta's words are to be connected, that is, to the particular discursive situation in which the *novella* is being presented. Though it possesses a certain degree of autonomy, this story, like every other story in the *Decameron*, is a tessera in a series of discursive and narrative mosaics. The smallest mosaic in which it finds a place is the cycle of four stories that have Calandrino as their protagonist: Calandrino and the heliotrope (VIII 3), Calandrino and the stolen pig (VIII 6), Calandrino pregnant (IX 3), Calandrino in love (IX 5). Fiammetta's story can be seen as a reply to those that Elissa, Filomena and Filostrato have already told, not only because of the choice of protagonist, but also because elements from these previous stories are put to use in its configuration. Presenting a novella that ends with Tessa beating Calandrino, Fiammetta is obeying a structural need. In this final story of the cycle the wife can finally take revenge for the unwarranted beating that she received from her husband in the opening one. Nello, the relative who informs Tessa of Calandrino's affair, makes explicit reference to that beating when exhorting her to take revenge (IX 5, 51–52). Later Tessa, having seen "la Niccolosa addosso a Calandrino" (IX 5, 62); "Calandrino lying there on his back, straddled by Niccolosa" (708), exclaims: "Alla fé di Dio, egli non era ora la Tessa quella che t'impregnava" (IX 5, 64); "God's faith, it wasn't your wife who was getting you with child this time" (708). This is a reference to the preposterous notion at the core of Filostrato's story in this same Day (IX 3). It is apparent that Fiammetta, the last to speak of Calandrino, delights in using material from the stories that have come before hers. Since the story of the heliotrope has been picked up again, as well as the story of Calandrino's pregnancy, we might wonder what has happened to the story of the stolen pig. It is likely that Tessa is alluding to it when she throws the epithet "ladro piuvico" (IX 5, 53); "false villain" (707) in her husband's face.

Keeping all this in mind, the principle Fiammetta expounds in her introduction — "by departing from the truth of what actually happened, the storyteller greatly diminishes the pleasure of his listeners" (701) — takes on a more precise contour. The *intendenti* of which she speaks are a privileged audience capable of understanding and enjoying the subtleties of narrative response, and the structural harmonies of the macrotext that the narrators are constructing story by story and day by day. Had she composed her novella "under fictitious names" (701) the enjoyment of the rhetorical and structural configuration of response and closure (Calandrino beating his wife in the opening story, Tessa beating her husband in the closing one, etc.) would have been lost, or considerably diminished. Fiammetta's axiom, which seemed merely to pay conventional homage to the classical and medieval convention on truth and verisimilitude in *narratio*, reveals now an unexpected meaning. Why would taking distance from truth in storytelling diminish the pleasure? In this case, in this story, in this cycle of stories, because it would not allow for the full flowering of rhetorical and structural artifice: an exquisite paradox, exquisitely Boccaccian. This reading can be supported with reference to Fiammetta's mention of "tempo" and "luogo." Ostensibly, the "tempo" and "luogo" indicate the general situation of pleasant entertainment in which the *brigata* finds itself: a time and place to be merry. On the other hand, "tempo" and "luogo" might designate the very moment in which Fiammetta is speaking and the very place where the *brigata* finds itself with respect to narration. This is where we are, with the sequence of our stories — Fiammetta seems to be saying. And being where we are, this new Calandrino story will be pleasurable, not *in spite* of our having tapped this source three times before, but *for* that very reason: a fourth the story is needed to complete the cycle.

Just as in stories such as Lisabetta's and Alibech's, Boccaccio plays with the notion of source, he plays here with that of truth. There the offered origin of a popular song and saying was a screen behind which the origin of the story itself could be glimpsed. Here the discourse on factual truth points toward a different truth: an inner truth of the book itself. By doing what he does, by weaving what he weaves, the author tells us covertly, he is being true to the structural requirements of his book. This is textual truth, a highly valued truth for the master story-teller and craftsman, a truth in a way truer than truth. This is truth in rhetorical garb.[29]

Clusters of interrelated stories such as Calandrino's cycle (more on it and the attending notion of *diletto* in the next chapter) are prime evidence of the structural and rhetorical cohesiveness of the *Decameron*. They are a powerful reminder of what we mean exactly when we identify Boccaccio's work as a *novelliere chiuso*. The task of closure is entrusted to the citizens of the frame-story: the *brigata* is an incessant, clever, artful, ironic producer of structure and completion. The notion of irony is of paramount importance. We know very well that openness could be as easily emphasized as a central element of the work. There is no need to review the notion that the *Decameron* is significantly marked by ethical ambiguity, epistemological nonchalance, and refusal of dogmatism.[30] The tension between the exigencies of closure and those of possibility is one of the principal sustaining forces of this remarkably complex textual edifice.

2

Pleasure and Response

ANY PRELIMINARY AND COMPREHENSIVE critical survey of the *Decameron* that confined the notions of play and entertainment to a secondary level of importance would, doubtless, be surprising. The book not only introduces itself to the reader as entertainment, but it is structured as the sum-total of a number of pleasant social gatherings. The pleasure enjoyed by the members of the *brigata* furnishes a pleasurable diversion, particularly to those female readers who are in love and who require the comfort of words (cf. Pr. 14).

The exquisite experience of the young Florentine refugees materializes in light of an ideal which comprises health (physical and moral) and pleasure. The program is clearly articulated by the authoritative Pampinea in the early sequences that take place inside the church of Santa Maria Novella:

[. . .] io giudicherei ottimamente fatto che noi, sí come noi siamo, sí come molti innanzi a noi hanno fatto e fanno, di questa terra uscissimo, e fuggendo come la morte i disonesti essempli degli altri onestamente a' nostri luoghi in contado, de' quali a ciascuna di noi è gran copia, ce ne andassimo a stare, e quivi quella festa, quella allegrezza, quello piacere che noi potessimo, senza trapassare in alcun atto il segno della ragione, prendessimo. (I Intr., 65)

I would think it an excellent idea [. . .] for us all to get away from this city, just as many others have done before us, and as indeed they are doing still. We could go and stay together on one of our various country estates, shunning at all costs the lewd practices of our fellow citizens and feasting and merrymaking as best we may without in any way overstepping the bounds of what is reasonable. (61)

Once the *brigata* reaches its first destination, it is Dioneo who insists on the founding notion of care-free living.[1] At that point, Pampinea takes it upon herself to establish the necessary order in the communal lifestyle. Her suggestion that the *brigata* elect a sovereign is motivated by her concern about the sustenance of pleasure. As soon as she is elected queen, she puts into effect proper forms of insulation to ensure that the enchantment of the place they have chosen — a place immune to the horrors of history — may not be broken.[2]

It is within this strategy of preserving pleasure that the decision to tell stories comes about. Storytelling is presented by the queen as the best choice among other forms of pastime and diversion (such as playing checkerboard games):

Come voi vedete, il sole è alto e il caldo è grande, né altro s'ode che le cicale su per gli ulivi, per che l'andare al presente in alcun luogo sarebbe senza dubbio sciocchezza. Qui è bello e fresco stare, e hacci, come voi vedete, e tavolieri e scacchieri, e puote ciascuno, secondo che all'animo gli è piú di piacere, diletto pigliare. Ma se in questo il mio parer si seguisse, non giucando, nel quale l'animo dell'una delle parti convien che si turbi senza troppo piacere dell'altra o di chi sta a vedere, ma novellando (il che può porgere, dicendo uno, a tutta la compagnia che ascolta diletto) questa calda parte del giorno trapasseremo. Voi non avrete compiuta ciascuno di dire una sua novelletta, che il sole fia declinato e il caldo mancato, e potremo dove piú a grado vi fia andare prendendo diletto: e per ciò, quando questo che io dico vi piaccia, ché disposta sono in ciò di seguire il piacer vostro, facciànlo; e dove non vi piacesse, ciascuno infino all'ora del vespro quello faccia che piú gli piace. (I Intr., 110–12)

'As you can see, the sun is high in the sky, it is very hot, and all is silent except for the cicadas in the olive-trees. For the moment, it would surely be foolish of us to venture abroad, this being such a cool and pleasant spot in which to linger. Besides, as you will observe, there are chessboards and other games here, and so we are free to amuse ourselves in whatever way we please. But if you were to follow my advice, this hotter part of the day would be spent, not in playing games (which inevitably bring anxiety to one of the players, without offering very much pleasure either to his opponent or to the spectators), but in telling stories — an activity that may afford some amusement both to the narrator and to the company at large. By the time each of you has narrated a little tale of his own or her own, the sun will be setting, the heat will have abated, and we shall be able to go and amuse ourselves wherever you choose. Let us, then, if the idea appeals to you, carry this proposal of mine into effect. But I am willing to follow your own wishes in this matter, and if you disagree with my suggestion, let us all go and occupy our time in whatever way we please until the hour of vespers.' (67–68)

Storytelling is regarded as an alternative to games, or as *another type* of game, with a different way of playing. But, if indeed it is a ludic activity, how exactly does it produce pleasure? We may divide our areas of interest into the spheres of *inventio* and *dispositio*. In the first place, storytelling produces pleasure because the individual stories that are told (found, selected: *inventio*) are pleasurable. Laughter and enjoyment are, *simply* and *directly*, a function of their content. The stories contain "sollazzevoli cose" (Pr. 14), "entertaining matters" (47), and are enjoyable in and of themselves. They would be amusing, that is, even had they not been woven into the daily ritual of narration and conversation. Not all the stories, however, lend themselves to being classified in this manner, and the exceptions are certainly not negligible. Thus, the program of pleasurable entertainment unfolds without a hitch over the first three Days, until Filostrato, the love-sick king, proposes as topic love stories with a tragic ending. Amorous Fiammetta protests, but eventually complies. Pampinea, on the other hand, chooses a story that respects the criterion of the tragic ending, but is at odds with the somber spirit of the Day (IV 2). Dioneo exercises his privilege in Day IV by telling a happy story which has an apparent, rather than a real, death at its core and which mocks all of the others.

Dioneo's parodic choice leads us to the second sphere of verbal pleasure we intend to explore, that having to do with *dispositio*. His story of the chest (IV 10) is funny, and it would be amusing even if it were told on a different Day. Its humor, however, assumes a heightened tone by virtue of placement: the additional yield of pleasure depends on its functioning as a response to the other stories of the Day. The notion of play is thus expanded to include structural manipulation. The entertainment of the *brigata does* take place within a complex ritual of narration and conversation, of proposal and response. Narrative content can be seen as the *end* of narration (as giving pleasure to the extent that it is *immediately* pleasurable), or as a *means* (allowing for the achievement of a different type of pleasure). Enjoyment is to be identified in structures as well as in content. At the end of Chapter 1, we shed light upon what seemed *prima facie* a conventional homage to the principle of truthfulness in storytelling. Fiammetta's introduction to IX 5, the last story of the book featuring Calandrino, appeared to convey a covert theorization of structural pleasure. It is to the Calandrino cycle that we may turn again in order to find a prime example of the typical Decameronian synergy between narrative and structural pleasure.

The *brigata* shows an exceptional preference for this anti-hero by telling four of his adventures (VIII 3, VIII 6, IX 3, IX 5). The narrators never tire of drawing attention to the enjoyable quality of the *novelle* in which he is both protagonist and victim:

Bellissime donne, lo scostumato giudice marchigiano, di cui ieri vi novellai, mi trasse di bocca una novella di Calandrino la quale io era per dirvi; e per ciò che ciò che di lui si ragiona non può altro che multiplicar la festa, benché di lui e de' suoi compagni assai ragionato si sia, ancor pur quella che ieri aveva in animo vi dirò. (IX 3, 3)

Lovely ladies, that uncouth fellow from the Marches, the judge of whom I spoke to you yesterday, took from the tip of my tongue a story I was on the point of telling you concerning Calandrino. We have already heard a good deal about Calandrino and his companions, but since anything we may say about him is bound to enhance the gaiety of our proceedings, I shall now proceed to recount the tale I intended to tell you yesterday. (691)

In his introductory passage, Filostrato seems to refer to the pleasure of content. We know, however, that pleasure is produced here in part thanks to a certain number of cohesive elements that allow us to see the series of four stories as a macrotext (cf. Ch. 1, 25–28). Within the macrotext, a rather sophisticated responsive game is played by Elissa, whose story (VIII 6) follows Filomena's (VIII 3). VIII 3 is the famous opening adventure of the cycle, featuring the ill-fated search for the fabulous heliotrope. Bruno and Buffalmacco, having duped and severely punished Calandrino for his simple-mindedness, proceed to make fun of him by accusing him of making fun of them. Says Buffalmacco:

Calandrino, se tu avevi altra ira, tu non ci dovevi per ciò straziare come fatto hai; ché, poi sodotti ci avesti a cercar teco quella pietra preziosa, senza dirci a Dio né a diavolo, a guisa di due becconi nel Mugnon ci lasciasti e venistitene, il che noi abbiamo forte per male; ma per certo questa fia la sezzaia che tu ci farai mai. (VIII 3, 57)

'Look here, Calandrino, you had no right to play such a mean trick on us, just because you were feeling piqued about something or other. You talked us into going with you to look for this magic stone, and then, without so much as bidding us fare you well or fare you badly, you left us standing there along the Mugnone like a pair of boobies, and cleared off home. We're not exactly pleased with the way you've behaved: and you can rest assured that you'll never do this to us again.' (603)

In good faith, Calandrino opposes his own version of the facts to Buffalmacco's interpretation: he believes that he found the precious stone which made him invisible; it was his wife who eventually broke the spell. His persecutors now pretend to believe his version:

Buffalmacco e Bruno, queste cose udendo, facevan vista di maravigliarsi forte e spesso affermavano quello che Calandrino diceva, e avevano sí gran voglia di ridere, che quasi scoppiavano; (VIII 3, 63)

As they listened to Calandrino's tale, Bruno and Buffalmacco feigned great astonishment, and nodded at regular intervals to confirm what he was saying, though it was all they could do to prevent themselves from bursting out laughing. (604)

At this point in the story, Calandrino has already beaten his wife within an inch of her life for having broken the spell. As he gets ready to hit her again, Bruno and Buffalmacco intervene, trying to make him be reasonable. In this last sequence, his version of the adventure is ostensibly accepted as definitive: yes, he found the charmed stone, but he was so stupid as to not make sure that his wife was nowhere in sight when he returned home with it: "il quale avvedimento Idio gli aveva tolto o per ciò che la ventura non doveva esser sua o perché egli aveva in animo d'ingannare i suoi compagni, a' quali, come s'avedeva averla trovata, il dovea palesare" (VIII 3, 64); "Moreover it was God Himself, they argued, who had prevented him from taking this precaution, either because Calandrino was not destined to enjoy this singular piece of good fortune, or because he was intending to deceive his companions, to whom he should have revealed his discovery the moment he realized the stone was in his possession" (604–5). If nothing else, the duped Calandrino is left with the conviction that his friends believe him. His consolation is short-lived. The story of the heliotrope seems to end here, but, as we will see, it remains secretly open.

In VIII 6 (the story of the stolen pig told by Filomena) the perpetrators Bruno and Buffalmacco keep with their tried and true scheme, blame Calandrino for the disappearance of the animal, and accuse him of not wanting to share it with them. Bruno reminds his victim of the events surrounding the search for the heliotrope, and interprets them in the way Buffalmacco had originally explained them in VIII 3:

«[. . .] Tu sí hai apparato a esser beffardo! Tu ci menasti una volta giú per lo Mugnone raccogliendo pietre nere; e quando tu ci avesti messi in galea senza biscotto, e tu te ne venisti e poscia ci volevi far credere che tu l'avessi trovata! e ora similmente ti credi co' tuoi giuramenti far credere altresí che il porco, che tu hai donato o ver venduto, ti sia stato imbolato. Noi sí siamo usi delle tue beffe e conosciamole; tu non ce ne potresti far piú! E per ciò, a dirti il vero, noi ci abbiamo durata fatica in far l'arte, per che noi intendiamo che tu ci doni due paia di capponi, se non che noi diremo a monna Tessa ogni cosa». (VIII 6, 53–55)

You've become quite an expert at fooling people, haven't you? Remember the time you took us along the Mugnone? There we were, collecting those black stones, and as soon as you'd got us stranded up the creek without a paddle, you cleared off home, and then tried to make us believe that you'd found the thing. And now that you've given away the pig, or sold it rather, you think you can persuade us, by uttering a few oaths, that it's been stolen. But you can't fool us any more: we've cottoned on to these tricks of yours. As a matter of fact, that's why we took so much trouble with the spell we cast on the sweets; and unless you give us two brace of capons for our pains, we intend to tell Monna Tessa the whole story.' (620)

What Filomena does here, in VIII 6, is reopen the case of Elissa's VIII 3: we may say that she provides the missing or, perhaps, a second ending. Calandrino must give up. Not only has he failed to persuade his friends of his innocence regarding current events, but he has been found retrospectively guilty. He is now guilty of a misdeed of which he ostensibly had been found innocent at the end of the previous adventure. Will he have the wherewithal to ask himself whether his friends previously had merely pretended to believe him? Or will he simply maintain that the alleged prank of the pig has now prompted them to revise their view of previous events? What if this is not the first time that the original prank has been thrown back in his face? Is it possible that the accusation has become commonplace within the time elapsed between the adventure of the heliotrope and the current one? At times it is difficult to resist the temptation to peer into the unwritten: where are the characters and what do they do when we do not see them?

In the responsive set constituted by VIII 3 and VIII 6 we see one of the clearest challenges to the concept of the Boccaccian *novella* as a unified organism. We may notice a resemblance between what Bruno and Buffalmacco do at the level of content (let us say their scheming) and what Elissa and Filomena do at the level of speech (their structural-narrative cooperation). Because of the association of the two devious friends and the alliance of the two narrators, we perceive Calandrino as doubly victimized. We might say that the borders between narrative play and play within the narrative are blurred, leaving the impression that poor Calandrino really has no chance. He is the victim of persecutors in two worlds: the world of stories and that of the frame-story, or, if you will, the world of narrative and that of meta-narrative. This, too, can be ascribed to entertainment.

An equally or perhaps more sophisticated narrative dialogic exchange involves Fiammetta and Filostrato in Days IV and V. When in Day V, the

Day of happy loves, queen Fiammetta invites unhappy lover Filostrato to speak, in his *exordium* he links his choice of story to the controversy spurred by his choice of topic for the previous Day: "Io sono stato da tante di voi tante volte morso perché io materia da crudeli ragionamenti e da farvi piagner v'imposi, che a me pare, a volere alquanto questa noia ristorare, esser tenuto di dover dire alcuna cosa per la quale io alquanto vi faccia ridere; e per ciò uno amore, non da altra noia che di sospiri e d'una brieve paura con vergogna mescolata a lieto fin pervenuto, in una novelletta assai piccola intendo di raccontarvi" (V 4, 3); "I have been teased so many times, and by so many of you, for obliging you to tell cruel stories and making you weep, that I feel obliged to make some slight amends for the sorrow I caused, and tell you something that will make you laugh a little. Hence I propose to tell you a very brief tale about a love which, apart from one or two sighs and a moment of fear not unmixed with embarrassment, ran a smooth course to its happy conclusion" (431). Filostrato, like everybody else, presents a story with comedic features, (a perilous beginning and a happy ending). His story is intended to provoke laughter—and indeed his audience finds it (the famous story of the nightingale) utterly hilarious. Fiammetta was among those who reprimanded Filostrato in Day IV. She complained about the cruel topic in her *exordium* to IV 1. Even a superficial survey of Filostrato's story in Day V shows that it is not simply a response to the criticism for his choice of topic for Day IV but more precisely a response to IV 1, Fiammetta's story of Tancredi and Ghismonda.

The story of the nightingale, in which Messer Lizio da Valbona discovers his daughter Caterina in bed with her lover Ricciardo, is a lighthearted, comic retelling of that of Prince Tancredi, who witnesses his daughter Ghismonda having intercourse with Guiscardo. While presenting imaginative nuclei essentially linked to those found in IV 1, its set of variations ensures a happy rather than a tragic outcome.[3] Once more, we must distinguish between the pleasure derived from the story itself and that which is a function of response and placement. On the one hand, the enjoyment of this story is essentially connected to the frequent recourse to amusing sexual metaphors centered on the thematic image of the nightingale. On the other hand, a game of more or less covert references to a previously narrated text produces delight of a different nature.

At the beginning of the story, Ricciardo and Caterina, the comedic doubles of Guiscardo and Ghismonda, rehearse commonplace notions of the rhetoric of seduction:

E avendo molte volte avuta voglia di doverle alcuna parole [sic] dire e dubitando taciutosi, pure una, preso tempo e ardire, le disse: «Caterina, io ti priego che tu non mi facci morire amando». La giovane rispose subito: «Volesse Idio che tu non facessi piú morir me!» Questa risposta molto di piacere e d'ardire aggiunse a Ricciardo, e dissele: «Per me non starà mai cosa che a grado ti sia, ma a te sta il trovar modo allo scampo della tua vita e della mia». (V 4, 8–10)

Though frequently seized with the longing to speak to her, he was always too timid to do so until one day, having chosen a suitable moment, he plucked up courage and said to her: 'Caterina, I implore you not to let me die of love for you.' 'Heaven grant,' she promptly replied, 'that you do not allow me to die first for love of you.' Ricciardo was overjoyed by the girl's answer, and, feeling greatly encouraged, he said to her: 'Demand of me anything you please, and I shall do it. But you alone can devise the means of saving us both.' (432)

Against the backdrop of the previous day when lovers really did die for love, the traditional phraseology acquires a parodic connotation. Filostrato is depicting two characters who, feeling dangerously close to that tragic world, question their own placement in the world of the comic. Part of the narrator's strategy is to play a rhetorical game along the borders between the fictional and the structural, to give the characters a ghostly awareness of their own *situation* within the work. Thanks to a daring artifice, we see in Caterina and Ricciardo a reborn Ghismonda and Guiscardo who cast off the shroud of tragedy as they warily cross into the world where love is supposed to end happily. A seemingly conventional courtship sequence turns covertly into an evocation of the threshold between two genres. This reading can be supported by the phraseological choices found in the crucial scene in which Caterina's parents witness the awakening of the young couple:

Né guari dopo queste parole stettero [*scil*. Messer Lizio and his wife], che Ricciardo si svegliò; e veggendo che il giorno era chiaro si tenne morto e chiamò la Caterina dicendo: «Oimè, anima mia, come faremo, che il giorno è venuto e hammi qui colto?» Alle quali parole messer Lizio, venuto oltre e levata la sargia, rispose: «Faren bene». Quando Ricciardo il vide, *parve che gli fosse il cuore del corpo strappato*; e levatosi a sedere in su il letto disse: «Signor mio, io vi cheggio mercé per Dio. Io conosco, sí come disleale e malvagio uomo, aver meritata morte, e per ciò fate di me quello che piú vi piace: ben vi priego io, se esser può, che voi abbiate della mia vita mercé e che io non muoia». (V 4, 40–2)

Nor did they have long to wait before Ricciardo woke up, and on seeing that it was broad daylight, he almost died of fright and called to Caterina, saying: 'Alas, my treasure, the day has come and caught me unawares! What is to happen to us?' At these words, Messer Lizio stepped forward, raised the curtain, and replied: 'What you deserve.' On seeing Messer Lizio, Ricciardo nearly leapt out of his skin [literally: "*he felt as though his heart was being ripped out*"] and sat bolt upright in bed, saying: 'My lord, in God's name have mercy on me. I know that I deserve to die, for I have been wicked and disloyal, and hence you must deal with me as you choose. But I beseech you to spare my life, if that is possible. I implore you not to kill me.' (435–36; emphasis added)

We must focus on the commonplace phrase "parve che gli fosse il cuore del corpo strappato," which has a special resonant literalness for whomever has read the stories of Day IV. Tancredi's actions in IV 1, had an element of savagery that went beyond killing the boy and maiming his corpse. As Millicent Marcus has observed: "When the prince sends his daughter the token of her lover's excised heart, he has literalized the central metaphor of courtly love. [. . .] By making Guiscardo's heart visible to 'gli occhi della fronte,' Tancredi has restored the metaphor to its origins in human physiology" (1979b: 58–59).[4]

Filostrato, in his story, reverses the process. He reinstates the heart within the boundaries of metaphorical discourse but, as he does so, he takes us back to the tragic extraction of Guiscardo's heart in Fiammetta's story. Again, we cannot help seeing Guiscardo in Ricciardo. Ricciardo, who seemed wary about his destiny as character at the beginning of the story, feels that the worst may be happening after all. He finds himself thrown back into the world of tragedy: if only for a moment, he is forced to don again the mask of poor Guiscardo.[5] We are now in the position to appreciate fully the responsive game enacted by Filostrato. His story responds to Fiammetta's not only at the level of content, but also at that of rhetorical artifice (the oscillation between the literal and the metaphorical).[6]

Having established that Filostrato, on the Day when Fiammetta is queen, narrates a story which responds to the one told by Fiammetta on the Day when he was king, we may in turn wonder whether Fiammetta's choice in her own Day is of dialogic nature as well. Indeed, she narrates in Day V a story which is connected, at least through a central imaginative nucleus, to that narrated by Filostrato in his. In Fiammetta's story (V 9), Federigo degli Alberighi feeds his beloved monna Giovanna his falcon, the only precious possession left to him after he has spent his entire patrimony in her pursuit. In Filostrato's story of the previous Day (IV 9), Guillelm de Roussillon feeds his wife her lover's heart. In both stories the female protagonist is unaware of the real nature of the food until the very end of her meal. But, while in IV 9 the final disclosure of the secret causes the woman's suicide, in V 9 it is instrumental in convincing her of her suitor's virtues and in paving the way to the happy ending. It may not be merely accidental that both responsive stories, V 5 and V 9, prominently feature birds (the nightingale and the falcon).[7] It appears that Fiammetta, not satisfied with a mere response to Filostrato's story of Day IV, manages to respond with a fitting flourish of *bravura* by relating the same story (V 9) to Filostrato's own response to her story of Day IV.[8]

The narrators seem to engage in a covert narrative parlor game which reminds us of literary responsive devices such as the "risposta per le rime," and the transformation of the *plazer* in *enueg* or *enueg* in *plazer*. There is no doubt that the notions of parody and self-parody can be invoked in order to give a first critical assessment of the phenomenon. The parodic nature of the *Decameron* as a whole and of its individual stories has been eloquently and persuasively illustrated in recent years by a number of scholars.[9] This does not mean that more work is not warranted. Not only do we need to identify more targets of Boccaccio's parodic writing, we also must determine what models of parodic writing contributed most to the overall configuration of the book.

Some progress on the latter task may be made by focusing on the *corone* of sonnets on the months of the year written by Folgore da San Gimignano and Cenne da la Chitarra between the last decade of the thirteenth century and the first decades the fourteenth. It is not unlikely that the beautifully pleasant communal life of the Boccaccian *brigata* may have been modeled in part on the exquisitely stylized experiences of the *brigata* that appears in Folgore's sonnets. The fact that the latter's range of activities is more varied (Folgore's goal was to list the appropriate pleasant, aristocratic activities for each month of the year) does not preclude the possibility. Michelangelo Picone has highlighted a few interesting (and in some cases, compelling) verbal correspondences between Folgore's and Boccaccio's descriptions of the *locus amoenus* (1988a: 111, 115). It is also of interest that the activities listed by Folgore for the amorous month of May include conversations, and perhaps storytelling, of an amorous nature.

If Boccaccio was familiar with Folgore's *corona* of the months, it is likely that he knew the parodic version of the *corona* penned by the jongleur Cenne da la Chitarra. Cenne's playful transformation of Folgore's *plazer* in *enueg* may have spurred Boccaccio's imagination. The jongleur's rhetorical initiative of burlesque counterpoint may bear a degree of responsibility for the rhetorical nimbleness of the members of the Boccaccian *brigata*, who provide comic versions of texts narrated by fellow narrators. With V 4 Filostrato produces, as it were, the parodic *plazer* version of the story (IV 1) presented as tragic *enueg* by Fiammetta. This is not to say that all the contrapuntal configurations with which Boccaccio enriches his book must be explained with reference to Folgore and Cenne. Nevertheless, we cannot afford to ignore the opportunity for documented understanding provided by texts that must have been extremely appealing to the master storyteller and consummate rhetorician. A sophisticated pleasure for "intendenti" in and outside the frame-story is derived from an appreciation of the text's unhampered and adroit response to undisclosed sources.

PART TWO

THE RHETORIC OF BEGINNINGS

3

Realism and the Needs of the Story

THE SIXTEENTH-CENTURY PIONEER of Boccaccio studies Francesco Bonciani observed from an Aristotelian perspective, that any given *novella* of the *Decameron* can be divided into three parts: a "prolago" (prologue), a "scompiglio" (the knotting of the plot), and a "sviluppo," or "snodamento" (*dénouement*) (1972: 164–65). Of these, the "prolago" is to be regarded as a pre-narrative introduction. It is the part that gives the essential information about characters and facts, and fades into the first stirrings of action. Bonciani's notion of "prolago" coincides approximately with what modern students of fiction call "initial situation," "background," "background and descriptive material," "exposition," or "introduction."[1] As Thomas M. Greene, among many others, has observed, this part of the story offers a picture of stability, even as it brings to the fore premonitions of change: "We begin with an initial equilibrium which has maintained itself for a considerable period of time before the story begins; a pre-narrative indefinite balances the post-narrative indefinite extension. But the initial equilibrium is nonetheless vulnerable by definition, since it is threatened by those forces or events which set the narrative in action" (1968: 300).

In the opening tension, which leads to what Bonciani calls "scompiglio," we clearly perceive the tension which is at the heart of the story, that which makes a story a story. Maurice Valency's definition of the *novella* aptly captures the nature of the genre:

The word *nuovo*, from which *novella* is derived, had in its day a variety of connotations. Primarily it meant *new*; it could mean *young, fresh, strange*, or *extraordinary*. The word *novella* therefore carried the idea not only of something new—a piece of news—but also of something remarkable, something worth telling. This something worth telling was usually advanced as fact, and the resulting literary genre was by nature realistic, and could be distinguished from the *fiaba* which was fantastic. (1960: 1)

Thus, as Walter R. Davis has remarked:

Central to the effect of a *novella* [. . .] is a kind of double relation to its audience's lives. On the one hand, the *novella* is introduced by a narrator in direct rapport with his audience (as if he were an oral storyteller) almost as if it were part of their lives: this really happened in such-and-such a time and place, it is real, it is true, the narrator keeps insisting. On the other hand, it is also something arresting that will take them out of their lives into the realm of the unusual, the strange, the wonderful. The *novella*, like many a modern "news" story, dwells on the "strange but true," and is constantly insisting, as it were, on the fictional quality of everyday life. Hence, for instance, its frequent employment of violent dramatic reversal. (1981: 3)

Every *novella* stages a number of transitions from the *notum* to the *novum*: from flows of continuity to their fraction, from the well-known to the new, and from the ordinary to the extraordinary. This simple, structural truth is the point of departure for the considerations assembled in the following pages.

This chapter's general subject will be a crucial zone in the rhetoric of narration of the Boccaccian storytellers: the zone of inception. The opening of a story is a privileged space, one that lends itself to a critical discourse which transcends mere questions of narrative sequence and goes to the heart of the narrative act. In particular, our focus will be on phenomena of *contextualization*. A typical opening procedure used by the narrators in the *Decameron* is that of evoking a context of conformity around their narrative contents. Viktor Shklovsky eloquently showed how in literary texts decontextualization is often at work, how the reader is made to see the object as for the first time (1990: 1–14). But the narrators at times employ the inverse strategy, that of showing the object as if for the thousandth time, relegating it to the realm of the ordinary and the indistinct. This narrative necessity of mentioning the unmarked, of rehearsing the unremarkable, constitutes the fundamental interest of the present pages.

The Boccaccian *brigata*'s narrative discourse is marked by the recurrence of conversive segments which situate the content of the stories within a context of normalcy.[2] Let us turn, for example, to the premise of the book's first story. Musciatto Franzesi, finding himself with a great amount of unfinished business in France which requires immediate attention, chooses a number of agents — Ciappelletto is one of them — who will act on his behalf. As Panfilo presents the initial situation, he discreetly underlies the normality of the occurrence:

[. . .] sentendo egli li fatti suoi, *sí come le più volte son quegli de' mercatanti*, molto intralciati in qua e in là [. . .] (I 1, 7)

But finding that his affairs, *as is usually the case with merchants*, were entangled here, there, and everywhere [. . .] (69; emphasis added)

In like fashion, Filomena will observe, in Day V, that what happens to the young, unmarried and noble Nastagio degli Onesti should not be surprising: "*sí come de' giovani avviene*, essendo senza moglie s'innamorò" (V 8, 5); "Being as yet unmarried, he fell in love, *as is the way with young men*" (457; emphasis added). And Fiammetta will adhere to the same rhetorical convention in the following story of Federigo degli Alberighi: "Il quale, *sí come il più de' gentili uomini avviene*, d'una gentil donna [. . .] s'innamorò [. . .] *sí come di leggiere adiviene*, le ricchezze mancarono" (V 9, 6−7); "*In the manner of most young men of gentle breeding*, Federigo lost his heart to a noble lady [. . .] Federigo lost his entire fortune *(as can easily happen)*" (463−64; emphasis added).

A merchant who, by the way, is a historical figure (cf. Branca 51, n.5) finds himself in circumstances seen as typical to all merchants, whether they are to be encountered inside the stories as characters or outside in real life. A young man (we do not know whether he is recognized by the audience as a historical character, but he is presented as such by the narrator) is portrayed in a similar way, surrounded by the evoked chorus of all the young people burning with love just as he does. We are asked to view the contents of the story in light of what happens every day in real life. Rather than true information, this is a kind of pseudo-information. These are fragments of a rhetoric of the *notum*: we are told what we already know, we are reminded that *that's the way life is*.

The colloquial segments, connecting fictional events with the extra-textual world, and situating them within the sphere of the ordinary, not only project a light of verisimilitude on the stories and color them realistically, but assume a significant function in the texture of narrative discourse as well. To begin to see that in detail, let us go back to the opening passage of the novella of Ser Ciappelletto:

Ragionasi adunque che essendo Musciatto Franzesi di ricchissimo e gran mercatante in Francia cavalier divenuto e dovendone in Toscana venire con messer Carlo Senzaterra, fratello del re di Francia, da papa Bonifazio addomandato e al venir promosso, sentendo egli li fatti suoi, sí come le piú volte son quegli de' mercatanti, molto intralciati in qua e in là e non potersi di leggiere né subitamente stralciare, pensò quegli commettere a piú persone [. . .] (I 1, 7)

It is said, then, that Musciatto Franzesi, having become a fine gentleman after ac-quiring enormous wealth and fame as a merchant in France, was obliged to come to Tuscany with the brother of the French king, the Lord Charles Stateless, who had been urged and encouraged by Pope Boniface. But finding that his affairs, as is usu-ally the case with merchants, were entangled here, there, and everywhere, and being unable quickly or easily to unravel them, he decided to place them in the hands of a number of different people. (69)

The reference to the universe of the *notum* — "sí come le piú volte son quegli de' mercatanti" — supports the circumstantial contexture ("essendo [. . .] e dovendone [. . .] sentendo [. . .]") out of which the first significant event will eventually coalesce ("pensò"). The listener is asked to dwell on the ter-rain of the usual and unremarkable, as the contents that *make* the story, that make it unusual, and therefore memorable, inch closer. The momentary grounding in conformity primes us for the crucial deviation. The story is told *because* of the unusual, but *through* the usual. The unheard of must emerge from that which is known, the perception of difference can only be produced from within the perception of the norm.

Emphasis on the ordinary often entails formulas hinging upon "veg-giamo": "avvenne, *sí come noi veggiamo* talvolta di state avvenire, che subi-tamente il cielo si chiuse d'oscuri nuvoli" (V 7, 11); "they suddenly found that the sky had become overcast with thick dark clouds, *such as we occasion-ally observe* in the course of the summer" (450). "*Sí come noi tutto il giorno veggiamo* per cammino avvenir de' signori" (II 3, 20); "*in the style regularly to be observed* in gentlemen of quality when they are travelling" (130). "E veggendo molti uomini nella corte del padre usare, gentili e altri, *sí come noi veggiamo* nelle corti" (IV 1, 6); "In her father's court, she encountered many people *of the kind to be found in any princely household*, of whom some were nobly bred and others not" (332–33; emphasis added).

At other times an explicit reference is made to the habits of the com-munity to which the *brigata* belongs: "Elena, vestita di nero *sí come le nostre vedove vanno*" (VIII 7, 6); "Elena, who was dressed (*as our widows usually are*) in black" (621). "E essendosene [. . .] andata, *come nostro costume è di state*, a stare a una sua bellissima possessione in contado" (VII 6, 7); "But having gone to stay, *as we Florentines are apt to do in the summer*, at her beautiful country villa" (551). "*come usanza è delle nostre donne*, l'anno di state

[. . .] se n'andava in contado a una sua possessione" (V 9, 10); "every summer, *in accordance with Florentine custom*, she went away with her son to a country estate of theirs" (464; emphasis added).

"When I come across even the most trivial statements in a narrative," observes Gerald Prince," I (may) feel — or know — that the triviality is only superficial and temporary because it is oriented, because it is meaningful in terms of what is to come" (1982: 157). What do we feel in our bland, inno-cent, trivial statements? Quite simply, we feel that the story is beginning — or that it is beginning again, since the sense of a beginning is not limited only to the opening sequences. A story begins again every time a sense of stability is reestablished. Rhythms of inertia, contextures of lull, continue to appear throughout the course of a story. There is a continual need for a background from which a new event will eventually arise.

Aside from the rubrics, it is the expository preludes to narration, what we have called *exordia*, which provide the first mention of the events of each story. Emilia's *exordium* on Day I promises something memorable: "Né io altressí tacerò un morso dato da un valente uomo secolare a uno avaro reli-gioso con un motto non meno da ridere che da commendare" (I 6, 3); "I likewise will describe a stinging rebuke, but one which was administered by an honest layman to a grasping friar, with a gibe no less amusing than it was laudable" (96). Having created an expectation for the jibe,[3] Emilia be-gins the story by resorting to a leisurely parenthetic cadence. She situates the action in the recent past, in the most familiar of places, and remarks upon well-known customs:

Fu dunque, o care giovani, *non è ancora gran tempo, nella nostra città* un frate minore inquisitore della eretica pravità, il quale, come che molto s'ingegnasse di parer santo e tenero amatore della cristiana fede, *sí come tutti fanno*, era non meno buono inves-tigatore di chi piena aveva la borsa che di chi di scemo nella fede sentisse. (I 6, 4)

Not long ago then, dear young ladies, there was *in our city* a Franciscan, an inquisitor on the look-out for filthy heretics, who whilst trying very hard, *as they all do*, to preserve an appearance of saintly and tender devotion to the Christian faith, was no less expert at tracking down people with bulging purses than at seeking out those whom he deemed to be lacking in faith. (96; emphasis added)

What does Emilia accomplish here by insisting on the closeness of the nar-rated reality to the *brigata*, and by emphasizing the ordinariness of her premise ("sí come tutti fanno")? She rouses the audience's attention as she winds up the narrative mechanism. The *brevitas* of the *exordium* was directed at explaining the essence and novelty of the story. Now the *prolago* proposes a minimal elaboration of the circumstances, in which the *notum* has a prominent position. The value of the apparently banal statement "sì come tutti fanno," then, is to be assessed not only by looking ahead, toward the fracture in the continuity which is just around the corner, but also by paying attention to what came before, that is, to the *exordium*, where a sense of the infraction of a norm (essentially: "I am about to tell you something remarkable") has already been planted. A statement that seems negligible, instead must be seen as a cogwheel in a rather sophisticated narrative-discursive mechanism.

The *exordium* of VI 4 is more elaborate than that of I 6:

Quantunque il pronto ingegno, amorose donne, spesso parole presti e utili e belle, secondo gli accidenti, a' dicitori, la fortuna ancora, alcuna volta aiutatrice de' paurosi, sopra la lor lingua subitamente di quelle pone che mai a animo riposato per lo dicitore si sareber saputo trovare: il che io per la mia novella intendo di dimostrarvi. (VI 4, 3)

Amorous ladies, whilst a ready wit will often bring a swift phrase, apposite and neatly turned, to the lips of the speaker, it sometimes happens that Fortune herself will come to the aid of people in distress by suddenly putting words into their mouths that they would never have been capable of formulating when their minds were at ease; which is what I propose to show you with this story of mine. (491)

Nonetheless, the passage from the promise of the unusual to the arrangement of a picture containing references to common knowledge is repeated. The following *prolago* responds to the preceding *exordium*:

Currado Gianfigliazzi, *sí come ciascuna di voi e udito e veduto puote avere*, sempre della nostra città è stato notabile cittadino, liberale e magnifico, e vita cavalleresca tenendo continuamente in cani e in uccelli s'è dilettato, le sue opere maggiori al presente lasciando stare. (VI 4, 4)

As all of you will have heard and seen for yourselves, Currado Gianfigliazzi has always played a notable part in the affairs of our city. Generous and hospitable, he lived the life of a true gentleman, and, to say nothing for the moment of his more important activities, he took a constant delight in hunting and hawking. (491; emphasis added)

As a further example, let us take the *exordium* of VIII 5:

Dilettose donne, il giovane che Elissa poco avanti nominò, cioè Maso del Saggio, mi farà lasciare stare una novella la quale io di dire intendeva, per dirne una di lui e d'alcuni suoi compagni: la quale ancora che disonesta non sia per ciò che vocaboli in essa s'usano che voi d'usar vi vergognate, *nondimeno è ella tanto da ridere che io la pur dirò*. (VIII 5, 3)

Delectable ladies, after hearing Elissa referring just now to the young man called Maso del Saggio, I have been prompted to discard the tale I was intending to relate in order to tell you one about Maso and some of his companions, which, though not improper, contains certain words that you ladies would hesitate to use. *But since it is highly amusing, I am sure you would like to hear it.* (610–11; emphasis added)

And let us place beside it the ensuing reference to the *notum*:

Come voi tutte potete avere udito, nella nostra città vegnono molto spesso rettori mar-chigiani, li quali generalmente sono uomini di povero cuore e di vita tanto strema e tanto misera, che altro non pare ogni lor fatto che una pidocchieria. (VIII 5, 4)

As all of you will doubtless have heard, the chief magistrates of our city very often come from the Marches, and tend as a rule to be mean-hearted men, who lead such a frugal and beggarly sort of life that anyone would think they hadn't a penny to bless themselves with. (611; emphasis added)

The rhetoric of beginnings relies on the repetition of knowledge shared by the community: "Sí come ciascuna di voi e udito e veduto puote avere"; "Come voi tutte potete avere udito." The object of this common knowledge is inscribed in the realm of the usual: "Currado Gianfigliazzi [. . .] *sempre* della nostra città *è stato* notabile cittadino;" "nella nostra città *vengono molto spesso* rettori marchigiani, li quali *generalmente*." As they begin to tell the story (which means: surprising, amusing, never heard before deeds and words *are expected*) the narrators declare that they are not saying *anything new*. Insistence upon the impression of the "nothing out of the ordinary," helps establish the equilibrium, the "uneventfulness" (of the pre-narrative time when, as it were, everything *is* and nothing *happens*), out of which the event will emerge. Let us see this actualizing of the narrative potential in our last two beginnings:

Il quale [Currado Gianfigliazzi] con un suo falcone *un dí presso a Peretola una gru ammazzata* [. . .] (VI 4, 5)

One day, having killed a crane with one of his falcons in the vicinity of Peretola [. . .] (491)

Ora, essendovene venuto *uno* per podestà, tra gli altri molti giudici che seco menò, ne menò *uno* il quale si facea chiamare messer Niccola da San Lepidio [. . .] (VIII 5, 5)

Now, *one of these March-men* came here once to take up his appointment as *podestà*, and among the numerous judges he brought with him, *there was one* called Messer Niccola da San Lepidio [. . .] (611; emphasis added)

The polarization of *exordium* and *prolago* is particularly evident in the story of Ferondo:

Carissime donne, a me si para davanti a doversi far raccontare *una verità che ha, troppo più che di quello che ella fu, di menzogna sembianza*; e quella nella mente m'ha ritornata l'avere udito un per un altro essere stato pianto e sepellito. *Dirò adunque come un vivo per morto sepellito fosse, e come poi per risuscitato, e non per vivo, egli stesso e molti altri lui credessero essere della sepoltura uscito, colui di ciò essendo per santo adorato che come colpevole ne dovea più tosto essere condannato.* Fu adunque in Toscana una badia, *e ancora è, posta, sí come noi ne veggiam molte*, in luogo non
troppo frequentato dagli uomini, nella quale fu fatto abbate un monaco [. . .] (III 8, 3–4)

Dearest ladies, I find myself confronted by *a true story, demanding to be told, which sounds far more fictitious than was actually the case*, and of which I was reminded when I heard of the man who was buried and mourned in mistake for another. *My story, then, is about a living man who was buried for dead, and who later, on emerging from his tomb, was convinced that he had truly died and been resurrected — a belief that was shared by many other people, who consequently venerated him as a Saint when they should have been condemning him as a fool.* In Tuscany, then, there was *and still is* a certain abbey, situated, *as so many of them are*, a little off the beaten track. Its newly-appointed abbot [. . .] (294–95; emphasis added)

The dark and congested initial digest, marked by the unusual and the bizarre, turns into a narrative beginning made somewhat soothing and tranquil through the allusions to the everyday ("e ancora è," "sí come noi ne veggiam molte"). It is as though the story were reluctant to coalesce into its narrative core. As it yields to the coaxing of the narrator who calls it to life, it resists ever so slightly by voicing claims of normalcy.

Is it sufficient to go back to the *exordia* in order to assess the narrative yield of these allusions to the everyday? When we witness the departure for Cyprus of Landolfo Rufolo, the wealthy merchant from Ravello, we are reassured, in the usual manner, of the normalcy of his actions:

Costui adunque, *sí come usanza suole esser de' mercatanti*, fatti suoi avvisi, comperò un grandissimo legno e quello tutto, di suoi denari, caricò di varie mercatantie e andonne con esse in Cipri. (II 4 6)

This Rufolo, then, *having made the sort of preliminary calculations that merchants normally make*, purchased a very large ship, loaded it with a mixed cargo of goods paid for entirely out of his own pocket, and sailed with them to Cyprus. (136; emphasis added)

Landolfo is presented as a merchant like any other, one who does what all merchants do, one safely moving in the realm of the ordinary. We, the audience, however, sense and know that unusual events will follow, that this is not just any other trip, taken by just any other merchant. How do we know that we are about to encounter events that are anything but ordinary? We know it by virtue of what was stated in the previous sentence of the *prolago*:

Tralle quali cittadette n'è una chiamata Ravello, nella quale, come che oggi v'abbia di ricchi uomini, ve n'ebbe già uno il quale fu ricchissimo, chiamato Landolfo Rufolo; *al quale non bastando la sua ricchezza, disiderando di radoppiarla, venne presso che fatto di perder con tutta quella se stesso.* (II 4, 5)

In one of these little towns, called Ravello, there once lived a certain Landolfo Rufolo, and although Ravello still has its quota of rich men, this Rufolo was a very rich man indeed. *But being dissatisfied with his fortune, he sought to double it, and as a result he nearly lost every penny he possessed, and his life too.* (136; emphasis added)

We are also aware of it because of what Lauretta said in the *exordium*:

Graziosissime donne, niuno atto della fortuna, secondo il mio giudicio, si può veder maggiore che *vedere uno d'infima miseria a stato reale elevare, come la novella di Pampinea n'ha mostrato essere al suo Alessandro adivenuto.* E per ciò che a qualunque della proposta materia da quinci innanzi novellerà converrà che infra questi termini dica, non me vergognerò io di dire *una novella, la quale, ancora che miserie maggiori in sé contenga, non per ciò abbia cosí splendida riuscita.* Ben so che, pure a quella avendo riguardo, con minor diligenzia fia la mia udita: ma altro non potendo sarò scusata." (II 4, 3–4)

Fairest ladies, it is in my opinion impossible to envisage a more striking act of Fortune than the spectacle *of a person being raised from the depths of poverty to regal status, which is what happened, as we have been shown by Pampinea's story, in the case of her Alessandro.* And since, from now on, nobody telling a story on the prescribed subject can possibly exceed those limits, I shall not blush to narrate *a tale which, whilst it contains greater misfortunes, does not however possess so magnificent an ending.* I realize of course, when I think of the previous story, that my own will be followed less attentively. But since it is the best I can manage, I trust that I shall be forgiven. (136; emphasis added)

Though it may pale in comparison with Pampinea's, Lauretta's story is, of course, of the same type (it follows the pattern given by queen Filomena). The members of the *brigata* were asked to tell stories on "chi da diverse cose infestato, sia oltre alla speranza riuscito a lieto fine" (I Concl., 11); "those who after suffering a series of misfortunes are brought to a state of unexpected happiness" (112). And continuing backwards we would arrive at the main narrator's Proem: "Nelle quali novelle piacevoli e aspri casi d'amore e altri fortunati avvenimenti si vederanno cosí ne' moderni tempi avvenuti come negli antichi" (Pr. 14); "In these tales will be found a variety of love adventures, bitter as well as pleasing, and other exciting incidents, which took place in both ancient and modern times" (47).

Our expectation of the extraordinary, then, is deeply rooted in the act that is being performed. A story is being told, and "we tell stories when we know something unusual" (Weinrich 1978: 163). Every assertion of normalcy ("sí come usanza suole esser de' mercatanti") must work in the presence of a primary psychological disposition that regulates our sharing in the ritual of narration: that of the expectation of something that breaks with the norm. Any normalization, any enhancement of the ordinary, is suspicious. Or, in other words, it follows the rules of the game. By tracing the contour of the usual with parenthetical ease, the narrator sets up the character for his future as a character, while at the same time setting us up for our role as co-protagonists in the narrative act. He changes positions, makes himself more comfortable in his seat, and tells us: pay attention, a story is about to begin. In the beginning of the story we can read the story of the beginning, of all beginnings.

These realistic, normalizing, colloquial segments bring an evasive element to the narrative flow. While telling about his characters Musciatto, Landolfo, Nastagio, and Federigo the narrator takes leave of them for a moment to cast an eye upon all other merchants or all other young people. This moment is marked by the limits of the parenthesis. The parenthetical rhythm is the rule in the *Decameron*'s areas of inception:

In Ravenna, antichissima città di Romagna, furon già assai nobili e gentili uomini [. . .] (V 8, 4)

In Ravenna, a city of great antiquity in Romagna, there once used to live a great many nobles and men of property [. . .] (457)

Nella nostra città, la qual sempre di varie maniere e di nuove genti è stata abondevole, fu, ancora non è gran tempo, un dipintore chiamato Calandrino, uom semplice e di nuovi costumi. (VIII 3, 4)

Not long ago, there lived in our city, where there has never been any lack of unusual customs and bizarre people, a painter called Calandrino, a simple, unconventional sort of fellow [. . .] (596)

Dovete dunque sapere che, secondo che raccontano i provenzali, in Provenza furon già due nobili cavalieri [. . .] (IV 9, 4)

You must know, then, that according to the Provençals, there once lived in Provence two noble knights [. . .] (388)

Ghino di Tacco, per la sua fierezza e per le sue ruberie uomo assai famoso, essendo di Siena cacciato e nimico de' conti di Santafiore, ribellò Radicofani alla Chiesa di Roma [. . .] (X 2, 5)

Ghino di Tacco, whose feats of daring and brigandage brought him great notoriety after being banished from Siena and incurring the enmity of the Counts of Santa Fiore, staged a rebellion of Radicofani against the Church of Rome; (738)

These are typically Boccaccian configurations of discursive and narrative ease, in which the narrator, having taken the first step, leisurely marks the time. The parenthetical clause, however, far from appearing solely at the beginning of the stories, is one of the stylistic traits that most characterizes the prose of the *Decameron* in its entirety. We should take an interest not only in the notional contents of our realistic segments, but in their syntactical rhythms as well. The parenthetical clause is a fascinating token of reluctance to proceed, a minimal detour, a leisurely glance cast around on the threshold of the event. It is a rhetorical device which provides a momentary shelter from the pressing demands of teleological purpose. Everything we have said about the role of the banal statements could be re-examined profitably within the context of a study of the role of the parenthetical clause in the *Decameron* as a whole.

Are parenthetical statements devices of *captatio benevolentiae*? Is there something concessive or conciliatory about them? To what degree do they contribute to the program of non-aggressive communication that is at work among the young narrators? There seems to be little doubt that this realistic, parenthetic pseudo-information promotes a sort of innocent complicity between narrator and listener. The latter is blandished, cajoled by the presentation of a shared reality. Not only is the difference between what is recounted and what belongs to the real world minimized, but that among the protagonists of the narrative act as well. A form of momentary evasion that offers cover from sequential and teleological rigor, the parenthesis represents one of the great architectural themes of the book. It echoes, within the syntactical music of the page, the theme of a flight from the flow of history (the plague in the city, the destiny of everyone), followed by the refuge in an unscathed zone of recreation (the edenic retreat in the countryside), and ultimately followed by a return to the eventful and perilous flow of life.

PART THREE

RHETORIC AND IMAGINATION

4

The Poetics of Realization

THE MAIN CONCERN OF THIS CHAPTER is the investigation of cognitive processes which entail, to use an expression by Luigi Meneghello, a "tracing back from words to facts" (1975: 60). We will see that in Boccaccio there are textual configurations made possible by the discovery of a material side within a metaphorical context, by a practice of actualization, of *realization* of phraseological abstractions. Before directly addressing the evidence of this phenomenon in the *Decameron*, I would like to touch upon its theoretical contours, with the help of analogues found in texts that cover a wide chronological span.

Let us consider firstly a minor classic of twentieth-century Italian literature such as Massimo Bontempelli. Part of his production connects him to writers such as Landolfi, Buzzati, Calvino, and Morovich, writers who have given life to many non-realistic renditions of reality. They have produced novels and short stories touched by manifold manifestations of magic. In their fiction, charmed and shaped by myth, romance, tall tale, fairy tale and fable, we find prime examples of what we can call de-metaphorization or realization. In Bontempelli's story *Quinto viaggio* the restless protagonist, after being exhorted by his great-grandmother to "andare a zonzo" (an idiom meaning to gallivant, to gad about), goes immediately to the train station and buys a ticket for Zonzo. During the journey he happens to see a village on a hill-top. When an impatient conductor "manda a quel paese" (literally: "sends to that village" or "to that land," a common Italian injunction to "get lost") the protagonist and his travel companion Cristopazio have not the slightest hesitation in assuming that the village in question is the one to be seen from the window. They get off the train and make their way there, but, once arrived, they realize that they must be in the wrong village because a beggar greets them with the words:

"Benvenuti in questo paese" (451); "Welcome to this village." "*Questo* paese," obviously, cannot be "*quel* paese." Therefore they take up their march again, only to be greeted in the same way when they reach the next village. There they hear that the village is called Ramengo:

A questo punto ci si presentò un piú grave problema. Perché eravamo andati a Ramengo? e che cosa dovevamo fare, una volta che il destino ci aveva spinti colà? (452)

At this point a more serious problem presented itself. Why did we go to Ramengo? And what were we supposed to do once destiny had brought us there?

"Andare a ramengo" is a colloquial version of "andare ramingo," the original meaning of which being: "to move aimlessly from place to place," like a bird from branch (*ramo*) to branch. In the vulgarized form, the idiom is almost always used with a strong negative connotation: "to go to the dogs," "to finish badly," "to end up ruined." The injunction "va' ramengo" or "va' a ramengo" is the equivalent of the English "get lost," or "go to Hell." Once again, what interests us here is the phraseological imagination from which the text springs. The story rests upon the exploitation of narrative potentials latent in colorless linguistic commonplaces. The writer time and again forces the metaphoric cliché, raising it onto an outlandish plane of narrative reality. He makes it somewhat "real" — he realizes it.

In another buoyant story by Bontempelli, *Il buon vento*, the transformation of the metaphoric into the literal is not simply an action-making procedure, as in the case of *Quinto viaggio*, but an object of reflection within the narrative context. It is the imaginative procedure itself that the author explicitly presents as his principal theme. "Circa dodici anni fa avevo messo su per mio divertimento una specie di gabinetto di chimica, ove mi appassionavo a tentare esperienze col secreto proposito di trovare la sostanza di contatto tra il mondo fisico e il mondo spirituale" (722); "About twelve years ago I had built for fun a kind of chemical laboratory, where I loved trying experiments with the secret aim of finding the substance which connects the physical and the spiritual world." This is the premise of the story, in the course of which the protagonist Massimo will discover that very substance, and will be able to test its efficacy. He need only to keep the strange powder in his pocket for extraordinary effects to take place. Massimo hopes that a mister Bartolo will finance his research, but when they meet in a restaurant, the man denies him the money, affecting consternation: "Le giuro che nel farle questo rifiuto il cuore mi sanguina" (723); "I swear that

my heart bleeds to have to refuse you." Right there and then, his words
acquire a prodigious power:

E scòrsi che dal suo petto, dalla parte sinistra, sotto la tasca del fazzoletto, sulla tela
bianca del vestito c'era una piccola macchia rossa. Pensavo d'insistere. Ma mi avvidi
che la macchiolina era fresca, e s'allargava. Stavo allora per avvertirlo, quando egli
riprese a parlare:
— Il cuore mi sanguina — ripeté — e io mi compiaccio di spiegarle . . . (724)

And I saw that on his chest, on the left side, under the pocket of his handkerchief,
on the white cloth of his suit there was a little red stain. I thought I should ask
again. But I noticed that the little stain was fresh, and that it was spreading. I was
about to mention it to him, when he began to speak again:
"My heart bleeds, he repeated," "and I would like to explain . . ."

Massimo realizes that, for whomever is within the powder's action range, a
passage is created between the real world and that of the imagination:

[. . .] la mia polvere SERVE A REALIZZARE LE IMMAGINI: le immagini di
cui fanno uso gli uomini parlando. *Il cuore mi sanguina*, egli aveva detto, e ripetuto.
E il disgraziato . . . (724)

[. . .] my powder CAN MAKE IMAGES REAL: the images that men use when
they speak. *My heart bleeds*, he said, and said again. And the poor wretch . . .

This is only the first miracle of realization caused by the powder. Bartolo's
wife and daughter will be affected as well, and then the waiter who tries to
remember the name of a rich man who might finance Massimo's chemical
experiments: "Aspetti. Il nome ce l'ho sulla punta della lingua. — Bravo.
Mostratemi la lingua. — Che dice? — Mostrate, súbito. Ero cosí imperioso
che lui ubbidí. Cacciò fuori la lingua. M'accostai, lessi forte: — Com-men-
da-tor Bar-ba. — Appunto! Come lo sa? — L'avevate sulla punta della lingua"
(725–26); "'Wait. I've got his name on the tip of my tongue.' 'Good. Show
me your tongue.' 'What?' 'Show it to me at once.' I was so imperative that
he obeyed. He stuck out his tongue. I drew close and read out aloud: 'Com-
men-da-tor Bar-ba.' 'Precisely! How did you know?' 'You had it on the tip
of your tongue.'" Unable to pay for his lunch, Massimo later gets himself
out of the predicament by crying out to the waiter: "Siete un asino" (726);
"You are an ass." This brings about the expected metamorphosis, perhaps
reminiscent of Apuleius's wonder-filled pages.

The free lunch is the only concrete gain that this bourgeois King Midas of literalization manages to get out of his discovery. Neither the meeting with Commendator Barba (which offers the opportunity for further amusing literalizations), nor the final one with Baldo, the restaurant's rich owner, bring any money to Massimo's pockets. The sequence describing this latter meeting, (on the last page of the story) brings to an enchanting climax the poetics of lightness of these pages:[1]

Verso occidente, il cielo era tutto addobbato di nuvolette a festoni, di fiocchi rosei a ghirlande tra il raso azzurro dell'aria. E da lontano vidi spuntare sul viottolo Baldo. Veniva a passi tranquilli, paffuto e raso, con una curva pancia soave. Fumava un'-avana, e s'avvicinava. Io trepidavo, e tentai di vincermi. Cercavo un bel saluto che lo disponesse a benignità. S'avvicinava. I bocciuoli di rosa dall'alto azzurro piovevano riflessi amorosi sul carneo fiore sbocciato del suo volto. Era a tre passi da me; come mi vide la sua bocca si schiuse a un sorriso sereno. Io mostrai di scorgerlo soltanto in quel momento. — Oh — dissi — oh, signor Baldo, *qual buon vento vi porta?*

E un caro vento spirò dalla terra, un dolce zefiro su mollemente sollevato portava lui, sopra ai prati, sopra alle siepi, sopra alle cime degli alberi. Io alzando a mano a mano la faccia guardavo: Baldo elevavasi morbido sempre piú in alto verso il placido etere; sopra le ali dello zefiro tepido lepido in panciolle se n'andava; fin che il fumo del suo avana si confuse tra le nuvolette, e il fiore sbocciato del suo volto sfumò tra le rose del cielo. (728)

Toward the west, the sky was all arrayed with festoons of clouds, of rosy garlands in the midst of the blue satin of the air. And from far away I saw Baldo appear on the path. He advanced at a tranquil pace, plump and shaven, with a placid curved paunch. He was smoking a havana, and drawing near. I was trembling, and tried to control myself. I searched for a fitting greeting that would dispose him to benignity. He was drawing nearer. The pink rosebuds from the celestial heights showered amorous reflections on the blooming flower of his face. He was three steps away from me. As he saw me his mouth parted in a serene smile. I pretended to have seen him in just that moment. "Oh," I said, "Oh Signor Baldo, *what good wind blows you here?*"

And a precious wind rose from the earth; a sweet zephyr gently rising took him over the fields, over the bushes, over the tree tops. I raised my head slowly, following his flight: Baldo rose softly, ever higher in the serene sky. He departed idling on the wings of the warm, playful zephyr, until the smoke of his havana merged with the smaller clouds, and the blooming flower of his face was lost amongst the celestial roses.

The text is leavened with a grace that brings to mind the levitations and aerial transits in the Franciscan *Fioretti*. Of course, added elements here are a delightful irony (the conventional lyrical praise for the rosy flesh of the beloved applied to a fat restaurant owner, his ascent into celestial heights), and a gentle shuttling between the literal and the metaphoric.[2]

Among those who in recent years have observed the propensity for rhetorical imagination of the literature of the fantastic is Tzvetan Todorov. According to Todorov, the enormous serpents and birds in the tales of Sinbad the Sailor are the result of an extension of hyperbolic language ("*exaggeration* leads to the supernatural"; 1975: 77). Thus, certain fantastic episodes in Beckford's *Vathek* ought to be seen as realizations of figurative expressions. This is the case of the Indian who rolls himself up, thus *looking like* a ball, and eventually *becoming* a ball. In *Véra*, by Villiers de l'Isle-- Adam, the whole narration is nothing other than a literalizing development of the commonplace "love is stronger than death." The point is well argued and, to a certain extent, persuasive. Todorov, however, radicalizes his reading:

> The different relations that we have observed between the fantastic and figurative discourse shed light on each other. If the fantastic constantly makes use of rhetorical figures, it is because it originates in them. The supernatural is born of language, it is both its consequence and its proof: not only do the devil and vampires exist only in words, but language alone enables us to conceive what is always absent: the supernatural. (1975: 81–82)

In order to find quick solutions to complex problems one would like to agree with such sweeping and seductive statements, but simple common sense, of course, prevents one from taking them seriously. Even while refuting a linguistic radicalism of this type, however, it is possible to argue that the study of the connections between metaphor and narration is a productive way of investigating the nature of the fantastic.[3]

A concise and useful reference tool in this respect is Maria Rita Alessandri's *Manuale del fantastico*. The sections entitled "Metaphors" and "Materializations," in particular, contain a wealth of pertinent material. In the first we find an exploit of the idiot of Gotham. Exhorted by his mother to be kind to his betrothed and to "throw at her glances as meek as those of a sheep," he hurries away to buy a handful of sheep's eyes from the butcher, and throws one on the girl's dress with all the kindness that he can summon (Alessandri 1992: 17–18). Within this tradition,

> Even words cease to refer to that which they designate and become themselves reality: the parts of language are transformed into objects. Perrault describes the meta-

morphosis of the words which come out of the mouths of the good child and the bad child after meeting the fairy. With every phrase, two roses, two pearls and two large diamonds come from the mouth of the younger child; two vipers and two toads from the elder's. (Alessandri 1992: 18)

In fairy-tales everything can undergo materialization: moon-beams, pieces of lightning, rainbows, states of mind, dreams:

Tears become pearls, laughter is transformed into roses and nasty words into revolting toads. In a fairy tale from Katmandu, a man forgets a word and searches desperately for it along the road. When a casket made of air is opened, stories fly out of it, and as if by magic, palaces, castles, villages and cities spring up. In the tale "Carnation" by the brothers Grimm, a child has the magic power of transforming all the words that come from his mouth into reality. (Alessandri 1992: 53)

This last example brings us back to the areas of imagination exploited by Bontempelli in *Il buon vento*.[4]

The transformation of the metaphoric into the literal, or the oscillation between the two, not only produces wonder, but also hilarity. Henri Bergson acutely connected these phenomena to one of his fundamental laws on the origins of laughter: "We laugh if our attention is diverted to the physical in a person when it is the moral that is in question" (1984: 135). When applied to language, the physical and the moral become the literal and figural sense:

Most words might be said to have a *physical* and a *moral* meaning, according as they are interpreted literally or figuratively. Every word, indeed, begins by denoting a concrete object or a material action; but by degrees the meaning of the word is refined into an abstract relation or a pure idea. If then the above law holds good here, it should be stated as follows: *"A comic effect is obtained whenever we pretend to take literally an expression which was used figuratively"*; or, *"Once our attention is fixed on the material aspect of a metaphor, the idea expressed becomes comic."* (Bergson 1984: 135)

One of the examples of this verbal comicality presented by Bergson concerns Boufflers, who, having been told that a pretentious personage "is always running after a joke," answers laconically: "I'll back the joke" (1984: 136). Boufflers refuses to become a passive consumer of the commonplace, and obliges the interlocutor to rediscover the metaphor. He awakens it from its stereotyped sleep — to use an image borrowed from the same Bergson and later adopted by Olbrechts-Tyteca in her treatise on the comic (1977: 283–87).[5] Freud himself, following in Bergson's footsteps, identified literal-metaphorical ambiguity as one of the fundamental comic-producing devices of jokes (1963: 36).

Once again, Massimo Bontempelli offers an excellent example of the Bergsonian truth according to which insistence on the material side of metaphor can produce comedy. In an episode of his novel *La vita intensa*, the protagonist Massimo is invited by his friend Florestano to accompany him to the station where a certain Bartoletti is about to arrive. Massimo maintains that he has excellent reasons for refusing to do so:

[. . .] ti dirò che non soltanto io non accetto di accompagnarti alla stazione, ma ho l'intenzione di sconsigliare violentemente anche te dall'andarvi. Un poetucolo celta ha detto una volta che *partir c'est mourir un peu*, frase oltremodo imbecille, tanto che s'è moltiplicata in miliardi d'album, ventagli, cartoline illustrate e lettere d'amore; ma tu sei adattissimo per crederci, e allora devi ammettere — fai bene attenzione alla mia dialettica ferrea — che se *partir c'est mourir un peu*, poiché arrivare è il contrario di partire, logicamente *arriver c'est naître un peu*; e per conseguenza andare a vedere arrivare è come andare a vedere una nascita, anzi un poco di nascita: ha dell'assistenza ostetrica; e l'immagine è cosí poco incitante che basta a far repugnare invincibilmente dal compiere qualunque cosa abbia potuto suscitare l'immagine stessa. A questo proposito potrei ricordare altre comuni immagini dello stesso genere, testimonianze sicure del mal gusto popolare; per esempio quella del «togliersi il pane di bocca» o l'altra del «mangiare la minestra sulla testa di qualcuno» per indicare la prima un atto di benefica sollecitudine e la seconda un atto di proterva insolenza; il pensiero delle quali immagini popolari basta a far sí che nessun uomo di buon gusto possa mai nella vita essere né benefico né insolente verso il suo prossimo. (204)

[. . .] let me tell you that not only will I not accompany you to the station, but I also intend to strongly discourage you from going yourself. A second-rate Celtic poet once said that "partir c'est mourir un peu," an exceedingly imbecile phrase, so much so that it has been reproduced on millions of albums, fans, illustrated postcards and love letters. But you are just the right sort of person to believe it, and therefore you must admit — pay attention to my cast-iron dialectics — that if "partir c'est mourir un peu," since to arrive is the contrary of to leave, logically "arriver c'est naitre un peu." And so consequently to go to watch someone arrive is like witnessing a birth — that is, a bit of a birth. In short, it smacks of obstetrical assistance, and the image is so very uninviting that it is enough to convince one to refrain from doing anything which might conjure up the image itself. With regard to this I could mention other common images of the same type, a veritable testimony to popular bad taste. For example, "taking the bread from one's own mouth," or "eating your soup on someone's head," to indicate in the first case an act of beneficial solicitude and in the second an act of arrogant insolence. The thought of those popular sayings is enough to ensure that no man of good taste will ever in his life be either beneficial or arrogant towards his neighbour. (204)

To simply say that the comic quality of this passage consists of attention being centered on the material side of a number of metaphors, is to explain a lot, but not all. One should speak of the nature and style of this attention and examine the context in which it is found. Even in Bouffler's repartee cited by Bergson, attention is given to the material side of the metaphor, and yet it is evident how much the two texts differ in kind. Even though here, as in *Il buon vento*, we can see metaphors materialize, the whole process remains circumscribed within the realm of language. In Bontempelli's story the metaphor was projected into reality (fictional reality, that is), it created reality: the heart really did bleed. Here, instead, there is nothing beyond a rhetorical realization of rhetoric. There is an anatomy of metaphor that takes us into the field of materialization, but it all remains within the context of the protagonist's sophistic reasoning ("pay attention to my cast-iron dialectics"). In short, if the first text can be defined as fantastic, or incredible, or surreal, the second contains nothing to prevent one from perceiving it as realistic.[6]

Clayton Koelb, in his book *The Incredulous Reader*, coins the term "logomimesis," applying it to narratives which "reproduce or elaborate structures found not in the nonlinguistic world but in the resources of language itself" (1984: 41). One example of logomimetic fiction, of fiction which imitates language, which he presents, concerns Thomas Mann's *Die vertauschten Köpfe* (*The Transposed Heads*). Koelb looks at the action in the story as a dramatization of the German phrase "den Kopf verlieren" ("to lose one's head"):

[. . .] The physical severing of the heads of Schridaman and Nanda is only the last step in a process of "losing their heads" over a girl named Sita. They chanced to observe Sita one day as she went to bathe in the river, and the sight of her naked body was so bewitching, so irresistibly enticing, that both fell in love with her. The complications and frustrations arising from this love triangle eventually bring about the situation in which the young men actually lose their heads in an attempt to settle what reason (which has been lost) cannot. (1984: 51)

Logomimesis is not an invention of modernity. In Koelb's pages on *Ornithes* (*Birds*), one can rediscover that the voyage imagined by Aristophanes can be linked to rhetorical structures. The protagonists Euelpides and Pisthetairos, looking for a better place than Athens to live, end up going *es korakas* ("to the crows" or "to the crows' place"). They literally go to the birds of the title—this being the essential action in the plot. The phrase *es korakas elthein* is a metaphorical commonplace with a meaning similar to

the English "to go to the dogs." (Koelb 1984: 69). There may be no discern-
able genetic link between Aristophanes' *Birds* and Bontempelli's *Quinto
viaggio*. On the basis of the realization of analogous commonplaces, however, the latter's protagonists' literal going "a quel paese" and "a Ramengo,"
can be compared to the voyage of Aristophanes's pair of Athenian
dreamers.

One must also keep in mind that logomimesis is only one type of creative intervention on rhetorical material. In a later study, *Inventions of Reading*, Koelb introduces the notion of "rhetorical construction" (1988: 13–23),
to designate the large range of possibilities within this area of *inventio*.
Kafka's very brief story, *Gibs auf* (*Give it up*), owes its existence (at least in
part, one should add), to the narrative potential of an expression ("to ask
the way") which is very common and open to two interpretations: literal
and metaphoric. The expression can refer to the way to be taken to reach a
physical place, or to a Dantean "diritta via." Whatever the general interpretation one wishes to bestow on Kakfa's text, one must acknowledge that it
is the colloquial fragment which opens up the narrative space. This is a text
which results from an "invention of reading," or a "rhetorical construction." In such inventions the reader is the "author, who by performing an
act of reading upon someone else's language" — in this case a linguistic fragment which belongs to everybody and no one — "is able to invent the language for his or her literary invention" (Koelb 1988: 15).

According to Koelb (and Günther Anders and Walter Sokel before
him), one can talk of rhetorical construction with reference to Kafka's *Die
Vernwandlung* (*The Metamorphosis*), whose origin can be traced to the common insult "Du bist ein Ungeziefer" ("You are a louse"):

Kafka has arranged a situation in which one could properly address Gregor Samsa
with these words in either the literal or the figurative meaning, or in both. Though
no one actually thus addresses him in the story, the existence of the expression as
part of a common stock of similar unremarkable phrases belonging to every speaker
of German acts as a kind of anchor in the known universe for this story partaking
so strongly of the supernatural. (1988: 19)[7]

Kafka's two stories, *Give it up* and *The Metamorphosis*, allow Koelb to establish the distinction between rhetorical construction and logomimesis. Both
texts are elaborations of rhetorical material, but one can speak of logomimesis only regarding the latter, inasmuch as the story "imitates" the equa-
tion of person and insect proposed by common phrases such as "Du bist
ein Ungeziefer." The first story is not exactly the imitation of the phrase "to

ask the way," so much as the dramatization of two possible interpretations of it. "Rhetorical construction," in sum, "is the general phenomenon of which logomimesis is a special (and particularly interesting) case" (Koelb 1988: 20).

A brief section of *Inventions of Reading* is concerned with rhetorical construction and logomimesis in Boccaccio's *Decameron*. Koelb reminds us that in the Epilogue, the main narrator characterizes the acute phase of the Florentine pestilence as a "tempo nel quale andar con le brache in capo per iscampo di sé era alli piú onesti non disdicevole" (Concl. Aut., 7); "a time when even the most respectable people saw nothing unseemly in wearing their breeches over their heads if they thought their lives might thereby be preserved" (830). The metaphorical saying "to wear one's breeches over one's head," allows Boccaccio to state in a spirited way that the Florentine crisis had made acceptable behaviors normally considered unseemly. Although this is the only appearance of the colloquial phrase in the whole *Decameron*, in Day IX we find a story in which a character *really* wears breeches over her head. This character is the Abbess of *novella* 2, who, getting dressed hastily and in the dark, mistakes for her veil the underwear of the priest with whom she has been dallying, and with this unusual headgear goes on her way about the convent. Koelb examines phrase and story within a comprehensive evaluation of the book's moral claims. For our purposes, it will be sufficient to point out the apparent immediate mechanics of *inventio*. This is rhetoric turned narrative: the metaphor is literalized as it is recast in narrative form. The Abbess in the course of the story becomes a metaphor in flesh and blood, she is the trope personified, a stock comic character in a carnival generated by rhetoric.

Among the stories made possible by a realization of sexual metaphors, Koelb mentions VII 2. In it the sexual act, conceived metaphorically as "scraping of the tub," is carried out by Peronella and her lover Giannello Scrignario while her husband is busy cleaning out the real tub, which is the central action-producing object of the story. A similar taste for the shifting between the literal and the metaphoric gives zest to the story of Belcolore and the priest of Varlungo (VIII 3), one not taken into consideration by Koelb. Here it is not a tub but a mortar which becomes central to the action: a real mortar belonging to Belcolore which the priest uses to recover the cloak with which he has paid for her sexual favors. It is the two characters themselves, in this case, who make explicit the connection between the real and metaphorical mortar, the latter being Belcolore's sex organ. A more detailed assessment of these stories will be found later in this chapter.

Also not included in Koelb's survey is I 6—a further illustration of Bergson's law according to which laughter is provoked by the shifting of attention from the moral to the physical. The generating notion-phrase is that of receiving a hundredfold as a reward for one's good actions: the "centuplum accipiet" found in the Gospel of Matthew.[8] In this story, a tipsy Florentine's somewhat blasphemous boasting of the quality of his wine — it is so good "che ne berebbe Cristo" (I 6, 5); "that Christ himself would have drunk it" (96) — is brought to the attention of a corrupt Franciscan inquisitor, who sees in it an opportunity for personal gain. The Florentine, threatened with being burned at the stake as a heretic, gives a goodly sum of money to the friar, who doles out a much milder punishment. The penitent will wear a cross on his clothes, hear mass every morning and present himself to the friar every day at dinner time. The penance proceeds without incident until the day the friar, while having dinner with friends, asks the wretch whether he has heard anything in church which left him in doubt. Made wary by his experience, he replies that he doubts nothing and holds everything to be true. He adds, however, that he heard a phrase which has made him very sorry for the inquisitor and all the friars, thinking of what awaits them in the next world. The phrase is "Voi riceverete per ognun cento" (I 6, 17); "for every one you shall receive an hundredfold" (98). The friar, naturally, wants to know why this disturbed him so much.

«Messer,» rispose il buono uomo «io vel dirò. Poi che io usai qui, ho io ogni dí veduto dar qui di fuori a molta povera gente quando una e quando due grandissime caldaie di broda, la quale a' frati di questo convento e a voi si toglie, sí come soperchia, davanti; per che, se per ognuna cento ve ne fieno rendute, di là voi n'avrete tanta, che voi dentro tutti vi dovrete affogare». (I 6, 19)

'Sir,' the good man replied, 'I will tell you. Every day since I started coming here, I have seen a crowd of poor people standing outside and being given one and sometimes two huge cauldrons of vegetable-water which, being surplus to your needs, is taken away from you and the other friars here in the convent. So if you are going to receive a hundred in the next world for every one you have given, you will have so much of the stuff that you will all drown in it.' (98)

Publicly shamed, the inquisitor not only refrains from inflicting a new penance on the Florentine, but also frees him from any previous obligation. It is surprising that Koelb does not mention this story since he examines a jocular use of the biblical phrase in Rabelais. In *Pantagruel* Panurge, justifying his stealing money in church, states:

[. . .] car les pardonnaires me le donnent quand ilz me disent, en presentant les reliques à baiser: *Centuplum accipies*, que pour un denier j'en prene cent: car *accipies* est dict selon la maniere des Hebreux, qui usent du futur en lieu de l'imperatif, comme vous avez en la loy: *Diliges Dominum* et *dilige*. Ainsi quand le pardonnigere me dict: *Centuplum accipies*, il veut dire: *Centuplum accipe* [. . .] (308–9)

Indeed, the pardoners give it to me when they tell me, as they give me the relics to kiss: *Centuplum accipies* which is tantamount to saying that for one farthing I am to take a hundred. For *accipies* is said according to the custom of the Hebrews, who use the future instead of the imperative, as you find it in the Law: *Diliges Dominum* and *dilige*. So when the seller of pardons said to me: *Centuplum accipies*, he meant *centuplum accipe* [. . .]

Of interest here is not so much the grammatical explanation of the equivalence of the future and the imperative, but the fact that for Panurge, "*centuplum*" no longer refers to a spiritual recompense: it is instead a precise figure which can be applied to a venal profit. Boccaccio's and Rabelais's narrative contexts have very little in common; the comic strategy they enact on the basis of the scriptural phrase, however, is essentially the same.

Because of its eminence within the history of European literature, and the richness and variety of the examples which it can provide, the Boccaccian *novella* is a natural point of reference for whomever wishes to explore the phenomenology of the contacts between *inventio* and *elocutio*. From Manni and Bottari in the eighteenth century to De Sanctis in the nineteenth, up to Auerbach, Petronio, Battaglia, Getto, and Branca, a dominant perspective in the history of criticism of the *Decameron* has seen in the work an ambitious attempt to offer an exhaustive, realistic reflection of human existence. It is true that in the last twenty-five years there has been a broadening of the critical horizon, but this has not authorized a radical reapprisal of the traditional perspective. Even today, it seems impossible to deny Salvatore Battaglia's assertion that the Boccaccian *novella* is profoundly marked by an interest for the "flow of life" (1991: 57). Indeed, one perceives in it what Antony Easthope calls "a sense of the empirical everyday" (1991: 144). For what the notion is worth, the stories in the *Decameron* are undoubtably realistic or, to use another formula by Battaglia, a fusion of "psychology and circumstance" (1991: 58). Nevertheless, one feels compelled to do justice to Boccaccio's work by showing not only how words imitate extratextual reality, but how textual reality imitates words. Alongside the rules of mimesis we must begin to understand those of what Koelb calls rhetorical construction and logomimesis. These mechanisms of *inventio*, found time and again in the *Decameron*, cannot be dismissed as curiosities. In recent years, scholars such as Giuseppe Mazzotta, Millicent Marcus, Francesco Bruni, and Giuseppe Velli, have begun to illustrate the importance of the metaphorical component in Boccaccio's narrative imagination. Thanks to their efforts, and to Koelb's, it is becoming more and more apparent that it is virtually impossible to assess effectively Boccaccio's poetics as a whole without accounting for his poetics of realization. In the next several pages, I will try to give a sense of the complex problems arising in the study Boccaccian stories featuring realizations.

Mental processing of information—poetic and narrative texts included—inevitably entails reduction and condensation. The workshop of human cognition appears to be ruled by ellipsis and synecdoche. One of the ways we make a story ours, is by reducing it to a simplified version of itself, by foregrounding and fixing an image, a character, a sequence or a sentence. We transform the story into an essential construct, we produce its emblematic equivalent. "Fateci dipignere la Cortesia" (I 8, 16); "Let Generosity be painted there" (105), says that splendid courtier, Guiglielmo Borsiere to the tight-fisted Genoese nabob Ermino de' Grimaldi, and we immediately feel that the whole story is contained in the simple, grand, necessary sentence. We think of those heroines of tragic Day IV, Ghismonda and Lisabetta and, before the contours of their vicissitudes surface in our memory, the poetic emblems of their destinies occupy us: a golden cup containing a lover's heart and a pot of basil in which a lover's head is buried.

Then there are Zima's clever monologue (III 5) and Federigo's falcon (V 9), Chichibio's lucky reply to Currado Gianfigliazzi (VI 4) and Simona and Pasquino's fatal sage (IV 7), Masetto's merry vegetable garden (III 1) and Caterina's nightingale (V 4), the Marchioness of Montferrat's chickens (I 5) and Guido Cavalcanti's tombs (VI 9), Calandrino's heliotrope (VIII 3) and Donno Gianni's peculiar tail (IX 10), Peronella's tub (VII 2) and Belcolore's mortar and pestle (VIII 2), and so on, and on. These are the book's memorable thematic objects, the objects which make the stories, the vectors of the *novum* without which there would not be *novella*. They are the elemental images that stand in the reader's mind for the whole stories. We ask them, radiant synecdoches and memorable objective correlatives, to assist us as we look for the genetic secrets of the texts in which they appear.

A few words on terminology and the nature of these formations are in order. A monologue is less obviously an object than a mortar. In a narrative configuration, however, mortar and monologue may be seen as having the same function. In their respective Decameronian stories, they function as story-making devices; of those stories they appear to be natural, memorable synecdoches. I mentioned Masetto's garden, Peronella's tub, and Guido Cavalcanti's tombs, but this is not the only possible way of identifying the thematic objects of those stories. Other readers (or we in a different moment) could conceive of them as the actions of Masetto's tilling of the garden, as the scraping of Peronella's tub, and as Guido Cavalcanti being trapped among the tombs or vaulting over a tomb. The essential nucleus of the same story, therefore, can present itself to us alternatively as an everyday object, as an action involving that object, or simply as an action, verbal or otherwise. In general, it is possible to perceive more than one thematic object in the same story. In the face of these complexities our critical tasks do not vary: we want to investigate the provenance of the story-making devices, and to see how they work within the text.

In very general terms, we can say that Boccaccio plays with his shining synecdoches, and that his play entails at times a shuttling movement between letter and metaphor. A thematic object in VII 9 is the pear tree that allows Lidia to enjoy the embraces of her lover Pirro in the presence of her husband Nicostrato. She contrives to make gullible Nicostrato think that her dallying was imaginary, a hallucination provoked by the enchanted tree, and eventually has Pirro fell it so that "non ne farà mai piú niuna, né a me né a altra donna, di queste vergogne" (VII 9, 77); "[it] will certainly never bring shame upon me or any other woman again" (578). The centrality to the story of the tree and of its felling is highlighted by the curious reaction of the women in the *brigata*: "Restava solamente al re il dover novellare; il quale, poi che vide le donne racchetate, che del pero tagliato che colpa avuta non avea si dolevano, incominciò" (VII 10, 2); "All that now remained was for the king to tell his story, and as soon as he perceived that the ladies had stopped mourning over the fate of the innocent pear-tree, he began" (579). The attentive reader now — if not before — feels compelled to go back to the beginning of the story, realizing that the chopping of the tree had been foreshadowed there in typical Boccaccian phraseological fashion. This happened when, after a failed attempt at seducing Pirro, Lidia decided to try again, because, as she told her servant Lusca: "per lo primo colpo non cade la quercia" (VII 9, 17); "an oak is not felled by a single blow of the axe" (570). If we now check the *Lidia* or *Comedia Lidie*, Boccaccio's source for the story of the pear tree, an enlightning finding awaits us. There, Lidia's philosophical remark is: "Quid facit in silice stilla rotata semel?" (222), which can be translated as: "What dent does a single drop of water make on the rock?" It appears, then, that Boccaccio found the original metaphor

unsatisfactory, and decided—if indeed we can talk of a conscious decision—to substitute for it one thematically fitting. A metaphorical felling of
the tree matches the literal one.

In V 10, the story of Pietro di Vinciolo, the matching metaphor appears in the playful *moralisatio* with which Dioneo seals his narration: "Per
che così vi vo' dire, donne mie care, che chi te la fa, fagliele; e se tu non
puoi, tienloti a mente fin che tu possa, *acciò che quale asino dà in parete tal
riceva* (V 10, 64); "So my advice to you, dear ladies, is this, that you should
always give back as much as you receive; and if you can't do it at once, bear
it in mind till you can, *so that what you lose on the swings, you gain on the
roundabouts*" (478; emphasis added). G. H. McWilliam's translation does
justice to the immediate meaning of the proverbial phrase, but the loss of
the reference to the "asino" (ass) is not negligible. A more literal rendering:
"so that the ass will be smitten by what he smote," would be more satisfactory. The sentence "quale asino dà in parete tal riceva" manages to convey
a clear allusion not only to the sexual give and take central to the story, but
also to the crucial sequence which brings about the dénouement. The
phraseological ass points to the ass (of Apuleian origin: the story follows
rather closely *Metamorphoses* XI 14–28) which steps on the fingers of
Pietro's wife's lover hiding beneath the chicken-coop. The movement, in
this case, is retrospective rather than proleptic: it is the language of closure
that bears a rhetorical trace of the thematic object.

At the beginning of VIII 2, unforgettable Monna Belcolore is presented as "una piacevole e fresca foresozza, brunazza e ben tarchiata *e atta
a meglio saper macinar che alcuna altra*" (VIII 2, 9); "a vigorous and
seductive-looking wench, buxom and brown as a berry, *who seemed better
versed in the grinder's art than any other girl in the village*" (591; emphasis
added). The sexual metaphor of the "macinare" reappears when the priest
of Varlungo, in order to seduce her, boasts of the sexual vigor of the clergy:
"E dicoti piú, che noi facciamo vie miglior lavorio; e sai perché? *perché noi
maciniamo a raccolta*" (VIII 2, 23); "What's more, we do a much better job
of it than other men, and do you know why? It's *because we do our grinding
when the millpond's full*" (593; emphasis added). Given these premises, the
arrival of an actual mortar on the scene (a mortar belonging to Belcolore,
and which the priest uses to recover the cloak with which he has paid for
her sexual favors) will certainly not surprise us. It is the characters themselves, in this case, who dwell, albeit speaking in code, on the connection
between the literal and the metaphorical:

La Belcolore brontolando si levò, e andatasene al soppediano ne trasse il tabarro e diello al cherico e disse: «Dirai cosí al sere da mia parte: 'La Belcolor dice che fa prego a Dio che voi non pesterete mai piú salsa in suo mortaio [. . .]». Il cherico se n'andò col tabarro e fece l'ambasciata al sere; a cui il prete ridendo disse: *«Dira'le, quando tu la vedrai, che s'ella non ci presterà il mortaio, io non presterò a lei il pestello; vada l'un per l'altro».* (VIII 2, 44–45)

Belcolore got up, grumbling and muttering to herself, and went to fetch the cloak, which she had tucked away in a chest at the foot of the bed. And as she handed it over to the sacristan, she said: 'Give the priest this message from me: "Belcolore says that she swears to God you won't be grinding any more of your sauces in her mortar [. . .]." ' The sacristan took the cloak back to the priest and gave him Belcolore's message, whereupon he burst out laughing and said: *'Next time you see her, tell her that if she doesn't lend me her mortar, I shan't let her have my pestle. It's no use having one without the other.'* (595; emphasis added)

It is the kind of speaking in code which one finds in Peronella's story, where the sexual act, conceived metaphorically as "scraping of the tub," is carried out by the woman and her lover Giannello while the husband is kept busy scraping the actual tub, the central action-producing object of the story. Boccaccio's delight in the play of ambiguity is evident in the words with which Giannello assesses the condition of the literal tub:

«Il doglio mi par ben saldo, ma egli mi pare che voi ci abbiate tenuta entro feccia, ché egli è tutto impastricciato di non so che cosa sí secca, che io non ne posso levar con l'unghie, e però io nol torrei se io nol vedessi prima netto». (VII 2, 29)

'The tub seems to be in pretty good shape, but you appear to have left the lees of wine in it, for it's coated all over with some hard substance or other that I can't even scrape off with my nails. I'm not going to take it unless it's cleaned out first.' (530–31)

Once more, checking the source proves productive. The boy lover's assessment of the tub in Apuleius's *Metamorphoses* has quite a different bent:

Nec ille sermoni mulieris defuit, sed exsurgens alacriter "Vis" inquit "verum scire, mater familias? Hoc tibi dolium nimis vetustum est et multifarium rimis hiantibus quassum. "Ad maritumque eius dissimulanter conversus, "Quin tu, quicumque es, homuncio, lucernam" ait "actutum mihi expedis, ut erasis intrinsecus sordibus diligenter aptumne usui possim dinoscere, nisi nos putas aes de malo habere?" (IX 7)

The latter took his cue from the woman's remarks and briskly emerged. "Do you want to know the truth, lady?" he asked. "This jar of yours is very old and badly cracked all over." Then he turned to the husband, pretending not to know who he was. "Hey, fellow, whoever you are," he said, "be quick and hand me a lamp, so that I can scrape off the dirt inside and make quite sure if it is fit for use—unless you think I get money from appletrees." (137)

The Latin narrator is more interested in contriving the mechanics of action than in exploiting the ambiguities of language. Thus, his young lover's statement that the jar is old and badly cracked all over is perfectly adequate to further the plot. But Boccaccio is not satisfied with that. He has Giannello state just the opposite: that the tub is sound ("ben saldo"). For Boccaccio narrative-rhetorical logic requires the tub to be in as good a shape as the sexual organ which it is meant to represent. Peronella is an attractive young woman ("una bella e vaga giovinetta;" VII 2, 7), therefore the tub must be "ben saldo." The only thing wrong with it is the old "feccia," the "secca" substance which encrusts it. Giannello is a wit: deceiving the husband is not sufficient for him, he must also mock him in the presence of his wife with a covert accusation of neglecting his sexual duties. This is a minimal but significant authorial intervention. By fleshing out symbolic implications, and by crafting cleverer verbal play, Boccaccio makes Apuleius's story his. The realization of the cliché in Belcolore's and Peronella's stories is akin to that which we see in stories such as that of the nightingale, of the lustful abbess, and of Masetto di Lamporecchio. In all of them *inventio* entails a rather elementary and straightforward reference to everyday sexual metaphors.

Elsewhere, I showed two instances of proleptic and covert appearance of the thematic object in *Decameron* IV 1 (Forni 1992: 72–79). The first happens at the beginning of the story, when Fiammetta, the narrator, says that Guiscardo had received Ghismonda in his heart ("l'aveva [. . .] nel cuor ricevuta"; IV 1, 6).[9] In the second Ghismonda herself tells her father that, if he considers the principles of things, he will see that the flesh of all humans comes from the same mass of flesh ("tu vedrai noi d'una massa di carne tutti la carne avere"; IV 1, 39), and her lover Guiscardo is as noble as any aristocrat. The two expressions' overt meanings are, of course: Guiscardo fell in love with Ghismonda, and: all humans have the same origin, are of one flesh. Within this particular context, however, the metaphoric mention of the heart entails a secret reference to the story's thematic object, the heart of flesh and blood which will be taken out of Guiscardo's chest. And it is precisely the human organ in its anatomical concreteness which one can glimpse in the mass of flesh of which Ghismonda speaks to her father (still at a moment when the tragedy has not yet been consummated). Ghismonda, that is, seems to be visited by the gift of prophecy: she enigmatically evokes the horror to come ("tu vedrai") in the presence of the cruel perpetrator.

The oscillation between metaphor and letter is explicitly conceptualized at the end of the story, when the heroine talks to her lover's heart contained in the golden cup:

Ahi! dolcissimo albergo di tutti i miei piaceri, maladetta sia la crudeltà di colui che con gli occhi della fronte or mi ti fa vedere! Assai m'era con quegli della mente riguardarti a ciascuna ora. (IV 1, 51)

Ah! dear, sweet vessel of all my joys, cursed be the cruelty of him who has compelled me to see you with the eyes of my body, when it was enough that I should keep you constantly in the eyes of my mind! (340)

It is then that the tragedy clearly becomes a gloss on at least two centuries of erotic literature — in particular on the rhetorical conventions of the courtly love tradition. Boccaccio uses his story to appropriate and contemplate, with manneristic taste, a central thematic object of that tradition. He brings to a breaking point the tension between letter and metaphor which, with reference to the image of the heart, is found in innumerable texts of that tradition. It is not central to our present interests to determine whether we are supposed to see here a response to the Dantean episode of Paolo and Francesca (*Inf.* V), in which the philosophy of courtly love seems to be called into question.[10] It will suffice to add this striking act of realization to our collection. The image of the exposed and bloodied heart stands in stark contrast with the fanciful and seductive cardiac ambiguities of the courtly heritage.[11]

The use of central commonplaces of courtly love rhetoric allows us to establish a link between IV 1 and IV 2. While in the former, as we just saw, the dramatization of those commonplaces is conceived in a tragic mode, in the latter the procedure is comedic. The story of the Agnolo Gabriello entails an elaborate realization of a hyperbole. Lisetta da ca' Quirino, the silly Venetian protagonist, conveys in the following manner her opinion of her beauty to the covetous Friar Alberto:

«Deh, messer lo frate, non avete voi occhi in capo? paionvi le mie bellezze fatte come quelle di queste altre? Troppi n'avrei degli amadori se io ne volessi; ma non son le mie bellezze da lasciare amare da tale né da quale. Quante ce ne vedete voi le cui bellezze sien fatte come le mie? *ché sarei bella nel Paradiso*». (IV 2, 13)

'What, Master Friar?' [. . .] 'Have you no eyes in your head? Does it seem to you that my charms are to be compared to those of these other women? I could have lovers to spare if I wanted them, but my charms are not at the service of every Tom, Dick or Harry who happens to fall in love with them. How often do you come across anyone as beautiful as I? *Why, even if I were in Heaven itself, my charms would be thought exceptional.*' (345; emphasis added)

Beauty defined as celestial, the woman as heavenly creature, as angel: it is a common hyperbole, one belonging to everyday speech, but a cliché which also figures prominently in the linguistic code of the courtly lyrical production from the Provençals to the Stilnovo. The story develops, in part, as a mockery of a poetic language with which Boccaccio was familiar from the early years of his Neapolitan cultural apprenticeship. Friar Alberto's strategy of seduction is based on a transformation of the cliché into literal truth. If monna Lisetta is a celestial beauty, if she is a heavenly creature, then she deserves an angelic lover. He proceeds to don angelic garb — wings and all — and, pretending to be the Archangel Gabriel, easily seduces her. A parodic use of the scriptural references to the annunciation, therefore, becomes an essential element of the story's make-up. In the following sequence the iconography of the encounter between the blessed Virgin and the angel is mentioned:

Madonna baderla allora disse che molto le piaceva se l'agnolo Gabriello l'amava, per ciò che ella amava ben lui, né era mai che una candela d'un mattapan non gli accendesse davanti dove dipinto il vedea; e che, qualora egli volesse a lei venire, egli fosse il ben venuto, ché egli la troverebbe tutta sola nella sua camera: ma con questo patto, che egli non dovesse lasciar lei per la Vergine Maria, ché l'era detto che egli le voleva molto bene, e anche si pareva, ché in ogni luogo che ella il vedeva le stava ginocchione innanzi; (IV 2, 24–25)

Lady Noodle said she was delighted to hear that the Angel Gabriel was in love with her, for she herself was greatly devoted to him and never failed to light a fourpenny candle in his honour whenever she came across a painting in which he was depicted. So far as she was concerned, he would be welcome to visit her whenever he pleased, but only if he promised not to desert her for the Virgin Mary, of whom it was said that he was a great admirer, as seemed to be borne out by the fact that in all the paintings she had seen of him, he was invariably shown kneeling in front of the Virgin. (347)

Saverio Bellomo reminded us that in the traditional iconography of the Annunciation appears a bed, the *thalamus Virginis*, which alludes to the union of the Virgin with God. He also hypothesized a connection with the *Evangelia Apocrypha*. In the gospel of Pseudo-Matthew, when the virgins try to reassure a perturbed Saint Joseph by stating that no man has touched his wife and only the angel of God could be responsible for her pregnancy, Joseph replies:

Ut quid me seducitis ut credam vobis quia angelus domini impraegnavit eam? Potest enim fieri ut quisquam se finxerit angelum domini et deceperit eam. (X)

Why do you want to induce me to believe that the angel of the Lord impregnated her? It could have passed that somebody pretended to be the angel of the Lord and deceived her.[12]

It is evident that here we are witnessing a phenomenon of *inventio* different in nature from those examined so far. We may still speak of realization, but it is a realization which does not entail logomimesis. Boccaccio seems to have given narrative reality to what was only a hypothesis in the passage from the *Apocrypha*. Joseph's *verba* become *res*, transformed, actualized, into a grotesque comedy. The shuttling between the metaphoric and the literal, which we have often documented above is, however, present as well. First we see friar Alberto engaged in metaphoric flights without wings (in lovemaking, that is): "molte volte la notte volò senza ali" (IV 2, 32); "he flew without wings several times before the night was over" (348). Later, pursued by Madonna Lisetta's in-laws, he leaves behind his angelic garb as he escapes jumping from a window into the Grand Canal. Thus, a real flight without wings matches the metaphorical ones: "I cognati [. . .] trovarono che l'agnol Gabriello, quivi avendo lasciate l'ali, se n'era volato" (IV 2, 47); "The lady's in-laws discovered that the Angel Gabriel had flown, leaving his wings behind" (350).[13]

An imaginative reading of the holy scriptures contributes significantly to the *inventio* of VI 9. This is the story of the brief encounter between Messer Betto Brunelleschi's merry *brigata* of Florentine young men and Guido Cavalcanti, the sophisticated poet and natural philosopher who has always refused to join their ranks. Guido is well known by the youngsters not only for the eminence of his intellectual achievements, but also for his alleged lack of faith in God: "e per ciò che egli alquanto tenea della oppinione degli epicuri, si diceva tralla gente volgare che queste sue speculazioni erano solo in cercare se trovar si potesse che Iddio non fosse" (VI 9, 9); "And since he tended to subscribe to the opinions of the Epicureans, it was said among the common herd that these speculations of his were exclusively concerned with whether it could be shown that God did not exist" (504).

The encounter takes place amongst the "arche grandi di marmo [. . .] dintorno a San Giovanni" (VI 9, 10); "those great marble tombs [. . .] and the numerous other graves that lie all around San Giovanni" (504). As soon as Betto and his friends, who are riding on horseback, spot the haughty intellectual, they corner and taunt him: "Guido, tu rifiuti d'esser di nostra brigata; ma ecco, quando tu avrai trovato che Idio non sia, che avrai fatto?" (VI 9, 11); "Guido, you spurn our company; but supposing you find that God doesn't exist, what good will it do you?" (504). Guido's reply is swift, elegant, and enigmatic:

«Signori, voi mi potete dire a casa vostra ciò che vi piace»; (VI 9, 12)

'Gentlemen, in your own house you may say whatever you like to me.' (504)

He then places a hand on the tomb against which he has been pushed and, nimble of body as he is of mind, vaults over the top of it escaping the ambush. The puzzled young Florentines dismiss Guido's parting words as nonsense — he must not be completely *compos mentis* — until their leader provides them with an explanation:

Alli quali messer Betto rivolto, disse: «Gli smemorati siete voi, se voi non l'avete inteso: egli ci ha onestamente e in poche parole detta la maggior villania del mondo, per ciò che, se voi riguarderete bene, queste arche sono le case de' morti, per ciò che in esse si pongono e dimorano i morti; le quali egli dice che son nostra casa, a dimostrarci che noi e gli altri uomini idioti e non letterati siamo, a comparazion di lui e degli altri uomini scienziati, peggio che uomini morti, e per ciò, qui essendo, noi siamo a casa nostra». (VI 9, 14)

But Messer Betto turned to them, and said: 'You're the ones who are out of your minds, if you can't see what he meant. In a few words he has neatly paid us the most back-handed compliment I ever heard, because when you come to consider it, these tombs are the houses of the dead, this being the place where the dead are laid to rest and where they take up their abode. By describing it as our house, he wanted to show us that, by comparison with himself and other men of learning, all men who are as uncouth and unlettered as ourselves are worse off than the dead. So that, being in a graveyard, we are in our own house.' (505)

Key elements of the story can be found in the anecdote about a Florentine Dinus (perhaps the famed physician Dino del Garbo) which Petrarch included in his *Rerum Memorandarum Libri* (II 60). The anecdote, however, was probably a widely known fragment of Florentine lore, and Boccaccio's reference need not be to Petrarch's book. Furthermore, it is far from being the sole source for the *inventio* of Guido's story. In an essay written at the beginning of this century, Ernesto Giacomo Parodi suggested that as Boccaccio was fashioning his portrait of Guido, he must have had in mind Salimbene de Adam's portrait of Frederic II. In his *Cronica* (512), Salimbene argued that the emperor was a follower of Epicurus's doctrines, and was trying to find in the sacred scripture the proof that there is no afterlife. One of the passages perversely used by Frederic was, according to Salimbene: "Et sepulchra eorum domus illorum in aeternum" (*Ps.* 48. 12); "And their sepulchers will be their house forever." Parodi plausibly offers this biblical verse as the archetype of the connection tomb-house upon which Boccaccio builds his story. Parodi himself, however, adds, as an afterthought, that the sepulchres in the *Decameron* must depend first and foremost on the Epicureans' sepulchres of *Inferno* X. Guido's story may thus be read as a response to the Dantean episode in which Guido's father asks the pilgrim poet why his son is not accompanying him on his journey. While Cavalcante Cavalcanti is forever trapped in his fiery sarcophagus in the circle of the Heretics, his son Guido manages, in Boccaccio's story, to deliver himself from the tombs of San Giovanni. Robert Durling has seen in Guido's leap a symbol of resurrection and salvation:

By depicting Guido performing an action that iconographically signifies resurrection, then, Boccaccio has raised the question of Guido's salvation. He has put his finger on what is indeed the central question of *Inferno* X: "Mio figlio ov'è?" ("Where is my son?") In other words, Boccaccio has seen that the question of Guido's salvation literally haunts Dante, and he has seen an essential level of meaning of Dante's last message to Cavalcante, that Guido is still conjoined to the living. For just as the connection *house:tomb* is basic to the interpretation of Guido's retort, and just as that connection inescapably implies the dual sense of *tomb* (burial of the body, burial of the soul), so the phrase *co' vivi congiunto* has two senses. If Guido is still literally alive in April, 1300, he may still be spiritually alive; and when Dante is writing the poem years later, the answer to "Mio figlio ov'è?" may still be the same: Guido may be, and Dante must hope that he is, somewhere other than in Hell. (Durling 1983: 284)

It is of course of exceptional interest that the future commentator of the *Divine Comedy* should insert in his collection a narrative gloss of such a prominent and enigmatic episode of Dante's poem. The Dantean subtext is an addition of primary interest to the palimpsest of the story's *inventio*, but another seminal element has been added recently by Giuseppe Velli (1991). In Seneca's letter 82 to Lucilius we read that: "otium sine litteris mors est et hominis vivi sepultura" (4); "leisure without study is death; it is a tomb for the living man" (243).[14] In letter 60, the Latin moralist again refers to metaphoric death to denounce moral inertia and lack of civic activism:

Hos itaque, ut ait Sallustius, "ventri oboedientes" animalium loco numeremus, non hominum, quosdam vero ne animalium quidem, sed mortuorum. Vivit is qui multis usui est, vivit is, qui se utitur; qui vero latitant et torpent, sic in domo sunt, quomodo in conditivo. Horum licet in limine ipso nomen marmori inscribas, mortem suam antecesserunt. (4)

Therefore those who, as Sallust puts it, "hearken to their bellies," should be numbered among the animals, and not among men; and certain men, indeed, should be numbered, not even among the animals, but among the dead. He really lives who is made use of by many; he really lives who makes use of himself. Those men, however, who creep into a hole and grow torpid are no better off in their homes than if they were in their tombs. Right there on the marble lintel of the house of such a man you may inscribe his name, for he has died before he is dead. (425)

Boccaccio's imagination worked on the Senecan passages in the usual way: tampering with the boundaries between the metaphorical and the literal. The metaphorical tombs of the Latin writer become the real tombs of marble in the Florentine landscape. They are real tombs, but also metaphorical homes, while in Seneca the real homes of the morally and intellectually inert were presented metaphorically as tombs. At the end of IV 1 Ghismonda had conceptualized the oscillation between metaphor and letter with regard to the thematic image of the heart. Here it is Betto Brunelleschi who is assigned the task of glossing the fundamental imaginative component of the story. Only in this case, however, the gloss is endowed with an essential narrative function.[15]

For a final example of procedures of realization, let us turn to the story of Gentile de' Garisendi, one of two rewritings of *questioni* discussed in

Filocolo IV 67 to appear in Day X of the *Decameron*. In the first half of the story, which follows closely the early version, Gentile, a Bolognese gentleman, having been informed of his beloved madonna Catalina's death, rushes to her tomb spurred by erotic intentions. Gentile does not know that the woman, who is the pregnant wife of another Bolognese gentleman, Niccoluccio Caccianimico, is erroneously believed dead. He descends into the tomb, lies by her, and, weeping profusely, proceeds to kiss her. Unable to control his desire, he then begins to touch her breasts, and perceives the faint beating of her heart. Realizing that a spark of life still animates her body, he takes her to his house, where, thanks to his mother's ministrations, she is revived.[16]

Francesco Mazzoni has persuasively shown that these essential elements of the plot must have come to Boccaccio from the *Historia Apollonii regis Tyrii*. In a famous episode of that novel of late antiquity (chapters 25–26), Apollonius's wife, after giving birth to a girl, is believed dead, put in a coffin and abandoned at sea. The coffin is cast ashore and found by an Ephesian doctor who has one of his students prepare the body for the funeral pile. As he pours ointment on the woman's limbs, the young man suspects that she may not be dead. He proceeds to warm the body until the congealed blood flows again. According to Mazzoni, Boccaccio freely utilized the episode, transforming the ministrations of the young physician (his palpations, his touching of the woman's lips with his in order to check her breathing, etc.) into acts of love. It is precisely this transformation which must be investigated.

A stimulus to Boccaccio's imagination could have come from the *Historia Apollonii regis Tyrii* itself. Apollonius repeatedly embraces and kisses the body of his wife before abandoning it to its destiny: "cucurrit Apollonius et vidit coniugem suam iacentem exanimem, scidit a pectore vestes unguibus [. . .] et lacrimis profusis iactavit se super corpusculum et coepit amarissime flere [. . .]. Dedit postremo osculum funeri, effudit super eam lacrimas" (25, 10–25);" "Apollonius came running and saw his wife lying lifeless; he ripped the clothes from his breast with his nails, [. . .] and in a flood of tears threw himself on her slight body. He began to cry most bitterly [. . .]. He kissed the corpse for the last time, and showered it with tears" (139). It is possible that Boccaccio was struck by the vestiges of passion contained in these scenes. We would not be doing justice to the complexity of his *inventio*, however, if we stopped here. In order to reach a more solid ground, we must turn to the rhetorical configuration with which Boccaccio, first in the *Filocolo*, and then in Gentile's story, accounts for his male protagonist's desire and intentions when he is apprised of the woman's death.

Thus speaks the nameless knight in the *Filocolo*:

«Ahi villana morte, maladetta sia la tua potenza! Tu m'hai privato di colei cui io più ch'altra cosa amava,e cui io più disiderava di servire, ben che verso di me la conoscessi crudele. Ma poi che così è avvenuto, quello che amore nella vita di lei non mi volle concedere, ora ch'ella è morta nol mi potrà negare: ché certo, s'io dovessi morire, la faccia, che io tanto viva amai, ora morta converrà che io baci». (IV 67, 4)

"Ah, villainous death, cursed be your power! You have deprived me of her whom I loved more than anything else, and whom I most desired to serve, though as you knew she was cruel to me. But since this has happened, Love cannot deny me, now that she is dead, what he was unwilling to grant me during her life; for indeed, even if I had to die for it, now she is dead I must kiss the face I loved so much when she was alive." (295)

And this is the echo of those words in *Decameron* X 4:

«Ecco, madonna Catalina, tu se' morta: io, mentre che vivesti, mai un solo sguardo da te aver non potei: per che, ora che difender non ti potrai, convien per certo che, cosí morta come tu se', io alcun bascio ti tolga». (X 4, 8).

'So, Madonna Catalina, you are dead! You never accorded me so much as a single glance when you were alive; but now that you are dead, and cannot reject my love, I am determined to steal a kiss or two from you.' (750)

An archetype of these passages can be found in the so called *Elegia di Costanza*, a poetic exercise by young Boccaccio, included in the Zibaldone laurenziano (cod. Laur. XXIX 8, f. 60r–v). In the elegy, Costanza addresses a passerby from her sepulcher recounting the story of her blossoming life destined to an untimely end. She was only fifteen years old when, beautiful, gifted, in love, and looking forward to her wedding day, she died, leaving her betrothed in a state of utter desperation. Now she asks the passerby to persuade her young lover to forgo his tears and live his life fully, so that her spirit may happily enter the realm of the blessed. The passerby, who happens to be her lover, proceeds to respond, giving an account of his plight. Still and forever prey to excruciating sorrow, unable to reconcile himself with his loss, he yearns to join his betrothed in death:

Te si fata michi contraria subripuerunt,
saltim vidisse te morientem dedissent.
Forte dixisses: morior, carissime, vale!
Set non dederunt; utinam te mortuam darent
ut videre possem, et quos michi vita negavit
mors daret amplexus: ora pallentia sepe
rigando lacrimis oscula dando piis,
o possem tumulo tecum recumbere tuo,
ut quos iunxit amor mors iungeret una sepulcro. (91–99)

If only the adverse fate which stole you from me had allowed me to see you as you
were dying! You could have said: "I am dying, dearest one, fare well." But no, that
was not allowed. Oh, to see you dead, and to receive from death the embraces that
life denied. I wish I could cover with pious tears and kisses your pale face and lie
beside you in your tomb, so that one death united in the sepulchre those whom love
united.

It is likely that this formulation about receiving from death the embraces
denied by life, is, at least in part, responsible for those found in the *Filocolo*
and the *Decameron*. The similarities between this and the passages in the
story of the violation of the tomb are undeniable. The optative movement
in the elegy, however, is far from being a plan of literally entering the tomb
with erotic intentions. The contemplated kisses and embraces are of an essentially rhetorical nature.[17] The union, entailing an almost complete tran-
scendence of sexuality, is of the kind which we find, for instance, in the
Ovidian story of Pyramus and Thisbe, a text which echoes in the elegy:

quique a me morte revelli
heu sola poteras, poteris nec morte revelli.
hoc tamen amborum verbis estote rogati,
o multum miseri meus illiusque parentes,
ut, quos certus amor, quos hora novissima iunxit,
conponi tumulo non invideatis eodem; (*Metam.* IV 152–57)

Whom death alone had power to part from me, not even death shall have the power
to part from me. O wretched parents, mine and his, be ye entreated of this by the
prayers of us both, that you begrudge us not that we, whom faithful love, whom
the hour of death has joined, should be laid together in the same tomb. (189)[18]

Like Thisbe, Costanza's betrothed expresses the intention to die in order to
be reunited with the beloved in the tomb and in the netherworld. In the
Filocolo, the male protagonist contemplates death only as an accident which

could happen during his incursion into the tomb: "ché certo, s'io dovessi morire, la faccia, che io tanto viva amai, ora morta converrà che io baci." When the story is rewritten for inclusion in the *Decameron*, even this mention of death as a possibility disappears. A rhetorical construct has been actualized as narrative action.

It is not easy to place, with a high degree of precision, the poetics of realization within the context of Boccaccio's culture. I will present here a few suggestions, well aware of the preliminary nature of the attempt. In *Paradiso* XXIX, as Dante pronounces one of his invectives against the corruption of the clergy, an intriguing instance of rewriting Scripture occurs:

Non disse Cristo al suo primo convento:
'Andate e predicate al mondo ciance';
ma diede lor verace fondamento;
e quel tanto sonò ne le sue guance,
sì ch'a pugnar per accender la fede
de l'Evangelio fero scudo e lance. (109–14; emphasis added)

Christ did not say to his first company, 'Go and preach idle stories to the world,' but he gave to them the true foundation; and that alone sounded on their lips, so that to fight for kindling of the faith they made shield and lance of the Gospel. (331)

The modification of Mark's text ("Et dixit eis: Euntes in mundum universum praedicate Evangelium omni creaturae"; 16.15) is not an irreverent parody, of course, but a rhetorical device in the service of a moral argument. The rectitude and holiness of the evangelical message is presented here in sharp contrast to the degraded behavior of present-day men of the cloth:

Ora si va *con motti e con iscede*
a predicare, e pur che ben si rida,
gonfia il cappuccio e più non si richiede. (115–17; emphasis added)

Now men go forth to preach with jests and with buffooneries, and so there be only a good laugh, the cowl puffs up and nothing more is asked. (331)

Dante uses a jest in order to condemn the buffonery and corruption of the ministers of the faith who should be serious in words and irreproachable in deeds. Boccaccio seems to have had this Dantean passage in mind when, towards the end of the epilogue, he justifies his own recourse to the ridicule:

Io confesso d'esser pesato e molte volte de' miei dí esser stato; e per ciò, parlando a quelle che pesato non m'hanno, affermo che io non son grave, anzi son io sí lieve, che io sto a galla nell'acqua; e considerato che *le prediche fatte da' frati per rimorder delle lor colpe gli uomini, il piú oggi piene di motti e di ciance e di scede*, estimai che quegli medesimi non stesser male nelle mie novelle, scritte per cacciar la malinconia delle femine. Tuttavia, se troppo per questo ridessero, il lamento di Germia, la passione del Salvatore e il ramarichio della Maddalena ne le potrà agevolmente guerire. (Concl. Aut., 23–24)

I confess that I do have weight, and in my time I have been weighed on numerous occasions; but I assure those ladies who have never weighed me that I have little gravity. On the contrary, I am so light that I float on the surface of water. And considering that *the sermons preached by friars to chastise the faults of men are nowadays filled, for the most part, with jests and quips and raillery*, I concluded that the same sort of thing would be not out of place in my stories, written to dispel the woes of ladies. But if it should cause them to laugh too much, they can easily cure themselves by turning to the Lament of Jeremiah, the Passion of Our Lord, and the plaint of the Magdalen. (832; emphasis added)

As he argues the legitimacy of the use of jests and quips in his book, he produces a jest based on the ambiguity of the notion of gravity. He plays, that is, with the metaphorical and literal connotations of weight. He used in his book, he says, the same "motti," "ciance," and "scede" which the friars use in their sermons. Among these are precisely those that entail the degradation of the spiritual, and a playful manipulation of metaphor and letter in particular.

Aron Gurevich has reminded us that: "there was a tendency deeply inherent in medieval popular perception to translate the spiritual into the concretely sensible and the material. [. . .]. Vulgar popular grotesque, making material the spiritual and erasing the borders between abstraction and object, not only reduced the Other World to the earthly but also dissolved the earthly in the supernatural" (1988: 194). It may be useful to list here a number of Gurevich's examples:

Caesarius of Heisterbach tells without marvelling what took place in a church in which priests sang loudly and without piety, 'in a secular manner': one cleric noticed a demon standing on high and gathering the voices of the singers into a large sack. And they thus 'sang' a 'sack full'. Around a monk who habitually dozed off in the monastery choir demons scurried in the form of pigs. With grunts they picked up the words of the psalms, devoid of grace, that fell from the mouth of the sleepyhead. Prayers and psalms were conceived as material bodies. A rich citizen of Cologne, hearing from a priest that the Apostles will judge the universe, became thoughtful and decided to buy stones for the future, so that on Judgment Day, when his good and bad deeds are weighed, the Apostles can put these stones in the bowl with the good deeds. He acquired an entire ship of stones, which he unloaded near the Church of the Apostles in Cologne. Soon the church was enlarged and the stones used for its foundation. The course of this man's thought is extremely symptomatic. Giving stones to repair a church was itself a good deed to be taken into account in the Other World, but this citizen visually imagined his stones lying on the scales together with his other good deeds. A good deed in this system of consciousness possesses a physical body. As a result, we are not surprised to read that on a ship there was a man the weight of whose sins the sea could not support; or that fervent piety raised a priest into the air during prayer and that he soared in the church without touching his feet to the floor; or that demons failed to drag into hell the soul of the dying Charlemagne, since the stones put by St James on the scales outweighed the emperor's sins, the stones being understood in the vision of Bishop Turpin as the churches built by Charlemagne in honour of St James [. . .]. Nor is it surprising in this system of logic that during one deceased man's embalming no heart was discovered in his chest. After all, it says in Scripture: 'For where your treasure is, there will your heart be also' (Matt 6 : 21). They actually searched his moneybox and found his heart lying with his money [. . .] (Gurevich 1988: 194–95)

Indeed, we can safely state that everyday thinking, in the Medieval cultural and spiritual context, entailed a constant crossing and recrossing of the borders between the spiritual and the physical, between abstraction and concreteness, between metaphor and letter. An area of degradation — to use again Bakhtin's term — of the spiritual that certainly plays a central role in the conception of the *Decameron*, is the *contrafactum*, the parody of the sacred texts and of the liturgy of Christianity. Comical rewritings of the most popular prayers (*Pater, Credo, Ave Maria*), biblical and evangelical passages in which the moral message is subverted, *missae potatorum*, etc.: it is of this body of parodic cultural products that we are immediately reminded when we read the story of the "centuplum accipies" in Day I or that of Rustico and Alibech in Day III. But the mechanisms of comicality, and the philosophy of laughter of the *contrafactum*, leave clear traces in many other stories of the *Decameron*.

Boccaccio's poetics of realization must also be seen against the backdrop of the work of his two great *auctoritates*: Ovid and Dante. It has been observed that a typical contrivance by which Ovidian metamorphosis is made possible is the realization of a simile or a metaphor. A case in point is the story of Iphis and Anaxarete in *Metam.* XIV. Anaxarete's unremitting and cruel spurning of her suitor gives Vertumnus (the narrator of the story) the opportunity to speak about her as "harder than steel tempered in Noric fire, or living rock, which still holds firmly to its native bed" (351). The girl's

metaphorical hardness which is emphasized throughout the story, and
which drives Iphis to kill himself, is eventually punished with literal petri-
fication when she witnessess his funeral:

vixque bene inpositum lecto prospexerat Iphin:
deriguere oculi, calidusque e corpore sanguis
inducto pallore fugit, conataque retro
ferre pedes haesit, conata avertere vultus
hoc quoque non potuit, paulatimque occupat artus,
quod fuit in duro iam pridem pectore, saxum. (XIV 753–58)

Scarce had she gained a good look at Iphis, lying there upon the bier, when her eyes
stiffened at the sight and the warm blood fled from her pale body. She tried to step
back from the window, but she stuck fast in her place. She tried to turn her face
away, but this also she could not do; and gradually that stony nature took possession
of her body which had been in her heart all along. (355)

Given the story's premises, the metamorphosis becomes a symbolic monu-
ment to the woman's nature. As Joseph B. Solodow observed: "Ovid is
[. . .] enjoying a kind of literary joke here, in that he actualizes an image
familiar from Roman love elegy: the lover often complains that his mistress
is as hard as stone" (1988: 179).[19] This realization recalls what we said earlier
about Boccaccio's manipulation of the imagery of the heart which he found
in the tradition of courtly love poetry.

Dante's *Commedia*, at both the level of the general design (cf., for instance, Singleton 1980: 1–17) and that of canto-by-canto imagination, is
informed by oscillation between the allegorical-metaphorical and the literal.
One example of the remarkable effects achieved with such an oscillation,
may be gleaned from an episode of *Purgatorio*. At the beginning of
canto XVI, when Dante evokes the profound darkness in which the two
pilgrim poets find themselves on the terrace of the wrathful, the reader is
asked to re-experience, if only for a moment, the horror of the unremitting
night of Hell:

Buio d'inferno e di notte privata
d'ogne pianeto, sotto pover cielo,
quant'esser può di nuvol tenebrata,
   non fece al viso mio sì grosso velo
come quel fummo ch'ivi ci coperse,
né a sentir di così aspro pelo,

che l'occhio stare aperto non sofferse;
onde la scorta mia saputa e fida
mi s'accostò e l'omero m'offerse. (XVI 1–9)

Gloom of hell, or night bereft of every planet under a barren sky obscured by clouds as much as it can be, never made a veil to my sight so thick nor of stuff so harsh to the sense, as that smoke which covered us there, so that it did not let the eye stay open; wherefore my wise and trusty escort drew to my side and offered me his shoulder. (167)

In the lines that follow, the infernal impression is sustained by the presence of words and rhymes typical of the first canticle. The nature of this infernal smoke in Purgatory is clearly explained in Pasquini-Quaglio:

The punishment of the wrathful shows a simple and common application of the law of symbolic retribution: *evil wrath* (XVII 69) puts out or reduces the light of reason. A widely used metaphor, circulating in everyday language from time immemorial (it survives to this day in expressions such as "the fumes of wrath," "blinded by rage," etc.) is thus the source of the punishment inflicted upon this category of expiating souls. But in Dante's depiction the proverbial trope turns into a concrete narrative situation: hence the terrace immersed in infernal darkness, the pilgrim who procedes with difficulty in the dark leaning on his guide, the mysterious sounds of prayer which rend the darkness. (1990: 245)

This is the mechanism of retribution according to which the lustful in Hell are tossed about in a storm (the tempest of the senses, the storm of desire) and those in Purgatory are consumed by flames (the fire of passion). Indeed, setting and human landscape in the *Commedia* are often realizations of everyday-language metaphors. One must, however, observe more closely what Dante manages to accomplish in this case, thanks to his turning of the proverbial trope into a concrete narrative situation. The image of the blind man, already sketched out in lines 1–9, finds completion in the simile of lines 10–15:

Sì come cieco va dietro a sua guida
per non smarrirsi e per non dar di cozzo
in cosa che 'l molesti, o forse ancida,
    m'andava io per l'aere amaro e sozzo,
ascoltando il mio duca che diceva
pur: "Guarda che da me tu non sia mozzo." (XVI 10–15)

Even as a blind man goes behind his guide that he may not stray or knock against what might injure or perhaps kill him, so I went through that bitter and foul air, listening to my leader, who kept saying, "Take care that you are not cut off from me." (167)

Leaving aside possible references to the archetypal blind poet, Homer, we will concentrate our attention on the shift from the metaphorical universe to that of reality. More precisely, we must monitor the shift from the common notion of rage as a violent agitation which causes a blindness of rationality, to the figure of Dante, who really does find himself physically incapable of seeing in this episode of his journey. Dante's physical blindness, like that of the wrathful, is meant to represent metaphorical blindness. But if we think of a person blinded by rage, we conjure up an image of aggressive behavior. The metaphorically blind individual is hostile, violent, and out of control. Dante, instead, is a defenseless and harmless blind man, one "che va dietro a sua guida / per non smarrirsi e per non dar di cozzo / in cosa che 'l molesti, o forse ancida." He can be compared, therefore, to any literally blind person who tries to cope with the challenges of daily life. The image of the blind Dante is a "purged" image — purged of the signs of wrathful behavior — of the man blinded by wrath. It is, therefore, an image perfectly apt to represent the process of deliverance from sinful inclinations which the penitent Christian soul undergoes on the slopes of the mountain of Purgatory.[20] The device allows the collapse of sin and purgation in one memorable image.

It is virtually certain that Boccaccio fueled his own narrative work with the intriguing instances of rhetorical imagination he found in the works of writers such as Dante and Ovid. It is also beyond dispute that the whole of medieval mentality must be taken into consideration if we want to explore this field of Boccaccian *inventio*. The thirst for the literal was the inevitable by-product of a cultural context saturated with practices of allegorization.

5

Rhetoric and Narration in
the Story of Zima

Mario Baratto's excellent and neglected Boccaccian monograph reminds us eloquently that in the *Decameron* not only is action often a product of speech, but speech can be the only action of narrative interest. More precisely: "comedic rhetoric, technique of discourse, the articulation of a dialogue, may mark the turning point of a plot or define the nature of a character; but they also constitute at times the essential structural nucleus of a story" (Baratto 1970: 289). This certainly applies to the story of Zima (III 5), where essentially the only action is a function of the presence and absence of speech. Action proceeds and finds its completion through the protagonist's monologue, which develops into a dialogue of sorts when he must confront the silence of the woman he is pursuing. As one can clearly glean from the rubric, Zima's story is a comedy of speech and silence[1]:

Il Zima dona a messer Francesco Vergellesi un suo pallafreno, e per quello con licenza di lui parla alla sua donna; e ella tacendo, egli in persona di lei si risponde, e secondo la sua risposta poi l'effetto segue. (III 5, 1)

Zima presents a palfrey to Messer Francesco Vergellesi, who responds by granting him permission to converse with his wife. She is unable to speak, but Zima answers on her behalf, and in due course his reply comes true. (263)

Francesco Vergellesi, a wealthy and wise nobleman from Pistoia, is in need of a palfrey to show off in Milan during his coming term as *podestà* of that city. The finest horse in Pistoia is owned by Ricciardo, called il Zima, a young and rich commoner who is in love with Messer Francesco's beautiful wife. Ricciardo's nickname has to do with his being "azzimato," or foppish. (We will presently see that characteristic as not merely ornamental but structurally functional as well.) Tempted by *avarizia*, Messer Francesco asks the

young man to sell him the horse, hoping that he will be willing to part with
it for nothing out of love for the lady. Zima, who has been trying unsuc-
cessfully for quite some time to conquer the virtuous woman, replies that
his horse is not for sale, but he is prepared to give it to Messer Francesco
on one condition: "che io, prima che voi il prendiate, possa con la grazia
vostra e in vostra presenzia parlare alquante parole alla donna vostra, tanto
da ogni uom separato che io da altrui che lei udito non sia" (III 5, 7); "that
before you take possession of it, you allow me, in your presence, to address
a few words to your good lady in sufficient privacy for my words to be
heard by her and by nobody else" (264). Thinking that he can outsmart
him, the husband agrees and hastens to instruct his wife: she will have to
listen to whatever Zima has to say without uttering a single word in reply.
The woman, though mortified at being involved in such a transaction, feels
that she has no choice but to obey her husband. After the two men have
confirmed the terms of their agreement, Zima and the lady convene. The
young man reminds her of his unflagging love and begs her to abandon her
sternness. He does so with a richly textured rhetoric which reveals his familiarity with the notional and stylistic conventions of the medieval literature of praise and seduction from Andreas Capellanus through the
Provençals to the Stilnuovo. The woman is so moved by his words that she
begins to be stirred by love for the first time in her life. True to her husband's bidding, she speaks not a single word in response to his eleborate
plea, however: "non poté per ciò alcun sospiretto nascondere quello che
volentieri rispondendo al Zima avrebbe fatto manifesto" (III 5, 17); "she
was unable to restrain herself from uttering one or two barely perceptible
sighs, thus betraying what she would willingly have made clear to Zima,
had she been able to reply" (266).[2]

   After waiting in vain for a reply, Zima realizes the ruse, and proceeds
to employ a peculiar and clever counter strategy:

E cominciò in forma della donna, udendolo ella, a rispondere a se medesimo [. . .]
(III 5, 18)

And thus, mimicking the lady's voice whilst she sat and listened, he began to answer
his own plea, speaking as follows [. . .] (266)

She had been aware that Zima loved her but she had not yielded to his
courtship in the past in order not to damage her good name. However, this

does not mean that she does not reciprocate his feelings. Now that her husband is leaving town, the time has come for her to show just how much she loves him. This, in essence, is what the young man says in the lady's stead. After promising that their love will be brought to its "piacevole e intero compimento" (III 5, 21); "total and pleasurable consummation" (267), he continues to impersonate her, elaborating how they will meet on "her" husband's departure. This accomplished, he again assumes his own identity, thanks the lady for "her" words and promises to carry out "her" directions to the letter. The husband in due time leaves town on his new horse, his wife follows the directions Zima has given her, and the two manage to meet not once but several times. They are even able to continue their affair after Messer Francesco's return from Milan.

Is the device of the self-reply sound from the point of view of the logic of narrative? Is it a real functional nucleus or just a decorative element which while "making the story" — and making the story memorable — also makes it unsteady? Why does Zima impersonate his lady? Couldn't he express himself directly, even when confronted with the woman's silence? Is it not possible that the seduction might work even without impersonation? It is possible, not certain. He may think that by assuming her identity he will have a better chance. The strangeness, the whimsicality, the elegance — an elegance bordering upon affectation — of the theatrical antic may make for a winning strategy.[3] To say that he *thinks*, however, over-simplifies the picture of what is happening. Perhaps he only enacts an instinctive strategy, one which is in perfect accord with what we already know about his personality.

An unhappy love makes him similar, at the beginning, to a Federigo degli Alberighi or to a Gentile Carisendi. But the impeccable grooming in which his nickname originates [. . .] may bring to one's memory a character 'molto assettatuzzo' (I, 1, 9) ["and used to dress very neatly;" 70] such as Ser Cepperello, with whom he shares — although on a very different moral level — a fussy disposition to act. (Baratto 1970: 291)

Mario Baratto's observation is subtle and clearly applicable here. It is important not to lose sight of the fact that Boccaccio deliberately made his protagonist an "azzimato." He wanted to suggest, through smart clothes and fussy grooming, a narcissistic disposition and a preciosity of style from which the device of the self-reply could originate plausibly, and upon which the story could rest. A simple Ricciardo would not have been sufficient. A

Ricciardo called il Zima — a Ricciardo who is an exquisite fop — puts to rest immediately any doubts about the logico-narrative soundness of the re- cherché strategy of histrionics.[4]

It should be evident by now that this is a text in which narrative con- figuration must be studied with reference to rhetorical configuration. It is time, therefore, to review in a comprehensive way the structural discursive nucleus of the story. In the course of his courtly encounter, the young lover faces a violation of the so called "Cooperative Principle," which is at the core of human verbal exchanges.[5] Unexpectedly, the woman won't take her conversational turn. She breaches her conversational contract with Zima because of the previous agreement she has made, albeit unwillingly, with her husband.[6] Zima, who is smart and perceptive enough to understand both the reason behind the silence and his lady's real feelings, hastens to salvage the contract in an artificial, dramatic fashion.

This is certainly the turning point of the story. In fact, it is the point without which there would be no story. A key element for understanding this rhetorical and narrative construct must be sought in the first part of the speech, when Zima is still speaking as himself, unaware as yet that he is addressing someone who has been forbidden to reply. He tries to convince the lady to be merciful by telling her that his very survival is at stake. There is no doubt that unrequited love will kill him:

E lasciamo stare che la mia morte non vi fosse onore, nondimeno credo che, rimor- dendovene alcuna volta la coscienza, ve ne dorrebbe d'averlo fatto, e talvolta, meglio disposta, *con voi medesima direste: 'Deh, quanto mal feci a non aver misericordia del Zima mio!'* e questo pentere non avendo luogo, vi sarebbe di maggior noia cagione. (III 5, 14)

Now, leaving aside the fact that my death would not enhance your reputation, I believe, also, that your conscience would occasionally trouble you and you would be sorry for having been the cause of it, and sometimes, when you were even more favourably disposed, *you would say to yourself: "Alas, how wrong it was of me not to take pity on my poor Zima!"* But this repentance of yours, coming too late, would only serve to heighten your distress. (265; emphasis added)

It is essential not to overlook this first incursion of the pursuer in the locu- tory space of the pursued: "you would say to yourself: 'Alas, how wrong it was of me not to take pity on my poor Zima!'." It is a figure of presump- tion: the speaker formulates a hypothetical discourse, while attributing it to the interlocutor. It is a voice from the future skilfully captured in order to modify the present. In rhetorical terms, this is a case of *aversio ab oratore* or *sermocinatio*, a "detachment of the speaker from himself [. . .]; even though the words are the speaker's, he puts them in the mouth of another person" (Lausberg 1969: 240–41). The following definitions and examples of *sermocinatio* (sometimes translated into English as dialogue) are found in the *Rhetorica ad Herennium*, a text well known to Boccaccio:

Sermocinatio [. . .] consists in attributing to somebody speech in keeping with his character, in the following way [. . .]: "The wise man will maintain that for the good of the state he ought to brave every peril. Often he will say to himself: I was not born just for myself, rather, and much more, for the fatherland. [. . .]" (IV xliii, 55)

There are as well conjectural *sermocinationes*, such as: "Indeed, what do we think that they will say, if you have ruled this way? Will they not all say the following?" And then one adds the statement. (IV lii, 65)

Later, when Zima must face the unexpected obstacle of silence, the rhetorical figure of *sermocinatio* attains the rank of central narrative device through an unconventional, imaginative exploitation of its mimetic nature. In the previous segment he seized the voice of the silent interlocutor only for a moment, and within the boundaries of conventional oratory ("and sometimes [. . .] you would say to yourself: 'Alas, how wrong it was of me not to take pity on my poor Zima!' "). Now he *becomes* the interlocutor in a protracted game of seduction by dramatization. If previously the voice of the woman was presented as coming from a hypothetical future, now temporality is flattened into a framework of immediacy. Her voice is presented to her by her pursuer as present and real in a new and more ambitious strategy for the facilitation of an assent. Zima becomes the woman for more than one reason; one, however is certain: he wants to offer her a model of behavior, in the presumption that this will force her to relent. Part of his strategy is the detailed depiction of an ideal future for her. Everything is planned accurately and prudently by a dashing, dazzling and resourceful lover. She can (and she is supposed to) slip into it with ease and confidence. After all, this young man has clearly demonstrated that he wants her at any cost, while the husband to whom she has been faithful has used her to ac-quire a good horse for "nothing."

It is possible, therefore, to see the central device of the novella, the self-reply, as an instance of "inventive reading" of a rhetorical figure. I use the term in the technical sense proposed by Clayton Koelb in *Inventions of Reading*: "The invention of reading is the discovery process that can occur when a writer sensitive to the rhetorical complexities of even everyday language illustrates or elaborates those complexities poetically" (Koelb 1988: ix). Rather than considering *inventio* and *elocutio* as separate entities (*inventio* as something that precedes *elocutio*, according to the reasoning of classical rhetoric), we should always be alert to the possibility that *inventio* may take place with reference to *elocutio*, to the "inventive potential of tropes" (Koelb 1988: 18). Boccaccio in *Decameron* III 5 has exploited the inventive or narrative potential of the rhetorical figure of *sermocinatio*.

Let us go back to Zima's first incursion into the locutory space of the lady: "you would say to yourself: 'Alas, how wrong it was of me not to take pity on my poor Zima!'." This rhetorical posturing can also be classified as reported speech. In Bice Mortara Garavelli's words, "we have reported speech when a speaker L reproduces, on the verbal chain (e) in which he is producing a speech act of his own, E, another speech act, E_1, which belongs to a source L_2, not necessarily different from L" (Mortara Garavelli 1985: 21). We are used to thinking of reported speech as something that *comes from the past* (making present, as it were, something that was said in the past) but its realm, as Mortara Garavelli amply shows, is by no means bound to only one temporal reference. Indeed Chaïm Perelman and Lucie Olbrechts-Tyteca speak of *sermocinatio* and *dialogism* as «imaginary direct speech» (direct speech is, of course, one of the kinds of reported speech):

Imaginary direct speech increases the feeling of presence by the fictitious attribution of words to a person (*sermocinatio*) or to a group of persons engaged in conversation (*dialogism*). Imaginary direct speech can have a variety of purposes, but they all have to do with hypothesis. [. . .] The use of imaginary direct speech will reveal the intentions ascribed to a person, or what is thought to be the opinion of other people regarding those intentions. It can be presented as half spoken and half thought. (1969: 176)

Thus, in the first part of Zima's plea, rather than a reported speech of the documentary kind, we have a speech which comes (as we already observed) from a hypothetical future. Surely, the second part of the address, the one spoken in the lady's stead, can also fit the category of reported speech. But from where and when is it reported? My previous mention of a temporality flattened into a framework of immediacy is not completely satisfactory. The speech is reported from an alternative reality: the reality which the lover may believe would have materialized in the absence of the husband's prohibition. Let us recall the woman's reaction at the first part of the speech: "E quantunque, per seguire il comandamento fattole dal marito, tacesse, non poté per ciò alcun sospiretto nascondere quello che volentieri rispondendo al Zima avrebbe fatto manifesto" (III 5, 17); "And despite the fact that, in obedience to her husband's instructions, she said nothing, she was unable to restrain herself from uttering one or two barely perceptible sighs, thus betraying what she would willingly have made clear to Zima, had she been able to reply" (266). Of course the narrator at this point may know more of the woman's heart than her lover. Also, we will discover later in the story that at this point the lady has not yet decided to yield to her pursuer. Nonetheless, he is encouraged to build his scene by her sighs and glances. In more general terms, his speech is reported from the ideal scene of assent, a scene the young man may have played in his mind innumerable times during his long and unfruitful courtship.

There is at least one other instance in Boccaccio's work, where a character fashions a dialogue with a lover by speaking also in the lover's stead. This character is Fiammetta, in the novel that bears her name. Fiammetta's dialogue is an imaginary one, a hypothetical one — the only kind possible in her lover's absence:

Poi lui imaginava tornato e meco fingendolo, molte cose gli dicea, e di molte il dimandava, *e io stessa in suo luogo mi rispondea*; (*Eleg. Med. Fiamm.* III 12, 4)

Then I imagined that he had returned, and by making believe that he was with me, I told him and asked him many things, *answering myself in his place* [. . .] (50; emphasis added)

While Fiammetta's reply to herself in Panfilo's stead takes place in the course of a normal daydream, Zima seems to daydream aloud. He dramatizes his daydream for the beloved in order to persuade her and to give her the necessary instructions. As he dramatizes his own dream, he wants to believe, and with good reason, that he is also dramatizing the desires of the woman. He dreams aloud for her in order to show her that this is also *her* dream.

While we can say that our inquiry into the rhetorical make-up of the text has shed some light on its narrative make-up and its *inventio*, our work is far from complete. A different province of rhetoric must now be approached: that of intertextuality and interdiscursiveness.[7] The story's courtly cultural background has not received much critical attention. True, scholars continue to mention the name of Andreas Capellanus (see, for instance, Branca 370, n. 6). Boccaccio may have been thinking about Andreas's text, but he was not interested in producing a plain and straight-forward tribute to the great manual of courtly love. His story may be seen as poking fun at the model through exaggeration, distortion, and demotion. Francesco Vergellesi's character flaw is clearly and repeatedly condemned in Andreas's treatise: "Avaritiam sicut nocivam pestem effugias et eius contrarium amplectaris" (116); "Avoid miserliness as a harmful disease, and embrace its opposite" (117). The commercial transaction initiated by Francesco's avarice, though, belongs to a universe of imagination with which Andreas's stylized anthropology has little to do. Whereas Zima seems to embody all of the qualities of the perfect lover, amongst which is "copiosa sermonis facundia" (42); "eloquent speech" (43), his abundant and persuasive eloquence turns into an affected and zany aberration. It is worthwhile to remember Andreas's advice for the lover who faces the silence of the woman: "Sed si nimis ipsius mulieris loquendi differantur initia, post spatium moderatum sapienter in sermone prorumpas" (46); "But if the woman delays too long before beginning to speak, you must after a short pause cleverly break into conversation" (47). This is exactly what our lover does, with a very personal twist. All this, however, does not prove a direct connection between *De Amore* and *Decameron* III 5. Closer to hard evidence is the wording of Zima's moral blackmail:

[. . .] la quale [vita], se a' miei prieghi l'altiero vostro animo non s'inchina, senza alcun fallo verrà meno, e morrommi, *e potrete esser detta di me micidiale.* (III 5, 13)

[. . .] which [life of mine] will assuredly fail unless your proud spirit yields to my entreaties, *and then indeed people will be able to say that you have killed me.* (265; emphasis added)

In a passage from one of the speeches in the *De Amore* — a book made up largely of seductive speeches — we read:

[. . .] si me igitur tui amoris spe frustratum dimiseris, me protinus mortem subire compellis, cui tua postea nullatenus poterit prodesse medela, *et ita poteris homicida vocari.* (94)

[. . .] So if you dismiss me and cheat me of the hope of your love, you force me here and now to undergo death. No remedy of yours will later avail me, *so that you will justifiably be called a murderess.* (95; emphasis added)

A crucial formula in the amatory plea then ("e potrete esser detta di me micidiale") finds an almost identical antecedent in Andreas's Latin ("et ita poteris homicida vocari").

Both the language and the configuration of the story may be connected, therefore, either directly or indirectly to Andreas's book. We must also look beyond Andreas. With a certain degree of approximation it is possible, for instance, to identify the poetic voices of the lyric tradition in Italian vernacular upon which Zima seems to have fashioned his courtly language. There may be, as has been observed, a modicum of Cavalcanti: "riconforterete gli spiriti miei, li quali spaventati tutti trieman nel vostro cospetto" (III 5, 15); "thus restoring my failing spirits, which have turned quite faint with awe in your gracious presence" (265).[8] And there may be more of Cino da Pistoia than has been realized. It should not come as a surprise, however, that in his amatory plea the young fop from Pistoia should be using the love poetry of his fellow citizen Cino. If indeed Cino is reflected in Zima's speech, it may be due to an intentional move on Boccaccio's part. This seems a typically Boccaccian game of covert reference. Let us not forget that Cino's muse, Selvaggia, is a Vergellesi; Boccaccio's choice of a Francesco Vergellesi and his wife as co-protagonists of this story is probably connected to Cino's lyric autobiography.

Following are juxtaposed a few excerpts from Zima's amatory plea and from pleas found in Cino's poetry.

I.

Zima:

e sì come umilissimo servidor *vi priego* [. . .] che la vostra benignità sia tanta [. . .] che io [. . .] possa dire che, come per la vostra bellezza innamorato sono, così *per quella aver la vita*; (III 5, 13)

I beseech you, as your most humble servant, to show me some mercy [. . .]. Your compassion will console me, enabling me to claim that it is to your beauty that I owe, not only my love, *but also my very life* [. . .] (265; emphasis added)

Cino:

Vanne via, mia canzon, di gente in gente,
tanto che la più gentil donna trovi,
e priega che suoi novi
e begli occhi amorosi dolcemente
amici sian de' miei,
quando *per aver vita* guardan lei. (XCI 37–42)

Go, my song, circulate amongst all people, until you find the most gentle woman, *and beg her* that her loving wondrous eyes be sweet and merciful when mine — *in search of life* — meet them. (Emphasis added)

2.

Zima:

E lasciamo stare *che la mia morte non vi fosse onore* [. . .] (III 5, 14)

Now, leaving aside the fact *that my death would not enhance your reputation* [. . .] (265; emphasis added)

Cino:

   Dovunque sono, sto suo [di Amore] servitore,
e sempre pur mi fa di male in peggio;
ma se m'ancide, no·lli fie onore. (CXXXVII 12–14)

Wherever I am, I am his [Love's] servant, even though I am nothing but the worse for it; *but if he kills me, he will not enhance his reputation*. (Emphasis added)

3.

Zima:

[. . .] la quale [vita], *se a' miei prieghi l'altiero vostro animo non s'inchina*, senza alcun fallo verrà meno [. . .] (III 5, 13)

[. . .] my very life, which will assuredly fail *unless your proud spirit yields to my entreaties*. (265; emphasis added)

Cino:

Or inchinate a sì dolce preghiera; (CXXV 45)

Now yield to such a sweet entreaty. (Emphasis added)

A more striking Cinian subtext — one having to do with narrative structure rather then style — will be presented later. The possibility that Zima's "se a' miei prieghi l'altiero vostro animo non s'inchina" may have a direct antecedent in Cino's "Or inchinate a sì dolce preghiera" is doubly suggestive.

There Cino addresses not his beloved Selvaggia, but Dante, in a song intended to console his poet friend for the death of Beatrice, a song which rehearses guiding notions and language of Dante's *Vita nuova*. The *Vita nuova*, as we will see, provides another likely subtext for Zima's speech. More precisely, I believe that Dante's early work must be included amongst those which may have provided Boccaccio with the model for the central rhetorical device, the self-reply.

In the extant scholarship on the story, there seems to be no satisfactory source or analogue of this device. Branca reminds us that the motif of the husband who sells his wife to a pursuer is found in a number of oriental tales, but there is very little in those tales which aids in the understanding of the processes of *inventio* of *Decameron* III 5. Of greater interest, perhaps, is Branca's connecting the central dialogue of the story with the tradition of the "contrasto d'amore" (Branca 368, n. 1). It is easy to agree with the general notion that medieval poetic forms in dialogue must have stimulated Boccaccio's imagination.[9] When trying to build upon that notion, however, the nature and provenance of the rhetorical device of the self-reply remains largely unexplained, until one recalls that in some cases, poetic forms in dialogue underwent a sort of elementary staging.

Boccaccio may have perceived a narrative potential in a form of dramatization such as dialogic monologue: "With «dialogic mime» or «dialogic monologue» we indicate a dramatic genre which does not entail regular staging and which distinguishes itself from what we properly call drama less for the nature of the subjects than for the way of treating and representing them. It consists of works in which several characters are played by one actor who takes care by himself of all the needs of the representation and interprets in turn all the roles" (Faral 1910: 238). *Contrasti* were dramatized by professional entertainers. When representing a *contrasto*, the jongleur might be helped by a colleague, male or female. That help, however, was not essential: "It is virtually certain that in giving life to the form of the *contrasto* the jongleur would take a double role, modifying the timbre of the voice to suit the different characters he played. He would also modify accordingly countenance and gestures" (Suitner 1983: 140).[10]

There is another kind of dramatization which may help in assessing Zima's story. It is one which remains on paper, a purely textual one, a rhetorical convention which goes as far back as Homer. I refer to the representation of a character's mental activity in dialogic form. Let us turn, for example, to prose LXXII of the *Novellino*.

Cato filosofo, omo grandissimo di Roma, stando in pregione e in povertade, parlava
con la Ventura e doleasi molto, e dicea: — Perché m'hai tanto tolto? — *E poi si rispondea in luogo de la Ventura*, e dicea così: — Figliuolo mio, quanto dilicatamente t'hoe
allevato e nodrito! e tutto ciò che m'hai chesto t'ho dato. La signoria di Roma t'ho
data. Signore t'ho fatto di molte dilizie, di gran palazzi, di molto oro, gran cavalli,
molti arnesi. O figliuolo mio, perché ti rammarichi tue perch'io mi parta da te? — E
Cato rispondea: Sì, ramarico. — E la Ventura rispondea: — Figliuolo mio, tu se'
molto savio. Or non pensi tu ch'i' ho figliuoli piccolini, li quali mi conviene nutri-
care? vuo' tu ch'io l'abandoni? non sarebbe ragione. (860)

Cato the philosopher, one of the most prominent men in Rome, having lost everything and finding himself in jail, was very bitter and complained to Fortune. He
would say: "Why did you take everything from me?" *And then he replied to himself
in Fortune's stead*: "My son, I raised and nourished you in the most dainty way. I
gave you all that you asked. I made you lord of many treasures, of great mansions,
of gold, palfreys, furnishings. My son, why do you complain about my leaving
you?" And Cato would answer: "But I do." And Fortune would answer: "My son,
you are a wise man. Why don't you think about all the little children of mine whom
I must nourish? Do you want me to abandon them? That would not be right."
(Emphasis added)

Like Boethius in the *Consolatio*, Cato tries to come to terms with a ruinous
fall from happiness and plenty. Here too, we find an interlocutor in allegorical garb. However, while Boethius's text maintains a strong distinction
between the two characters (the Philosopher and Philosophia), in the *Novellino* Cato and Fortune tend to coincide not only essentially, but formally
as well. All thought refers clearly to only one mental source. There is a dialogue because Cato lends his voice to Fortune. The dramatic form remains,
but the scene becomes a mental one: Cato answers "si risponde," "answers
to himself."

The artifice is further reduced in the following instance of dramatization of thought, from Passavanti's *Specchio di vera penitenza* (X). The allegorical figure disappears and the interlocutors become a nobleman and his
thoughts (or a nobleman and himself, "se medesimo").

Leggesi che nel reame di Francia fu uno nobile uomo, il quale era vivuto molto
dilicatamente notrito, e amatore delle vanità del mondo. Costui un giorno cominciò
a pensare se e dannati, dopo mille anni, dovessono essere liberati; *e rispuose al suo
pensiero* che no. Appresso gli dicea i pensieri: — O dopo gli ottocento mille anni? —
e rispondea che mai no. E poi pensò se dopo mille migliaia d'anni fosse possibile la
loro liberazione, e dicea di no. — O dopo tante migliaia d'anni quante gocciole è in
mare d'acqua? — *E dicea di no a se medesimo.* Di tal pensiero conturbato e spaurito,

gli venne un dolore e un pianto di contrizione; e abbandonando la vanità di questo mondo, el peccatore disse: — Or come sono stolti e miseri gli uomini del mondo, che, per piccolo diletto che pìgliono nel mondo, vanno alle pene sanza fine! (95)

We read that in the kingdom of France there lived a nobleman who had had a sheltered and dainty life and who loved earthly pleasures. One day he fell to pondering whether the damned, after a thousand years could be freed; *and he replied to his own thought* that they could not. His thought insisted: "What about after eight hundred and a thousand years?" And the answer was still no. "What about after as many thousands of years as there are drops of water in the sea?" *And he replied no to himself.* He was perturbed and scared by that thought, and started to weep in grief and contrition. Deciding to abandon tha vain pleasures of this world, that sinner said: "Stupid indeed, and wretched, are humans, who pay with endless torment the modicum of pleasure they derive from their earthly lives." (Emphasis added)

Novellino LXXX and *Specchio di vera penitenza* X should not be considered direct sources of *Decameron* III 5.[11] In both only one real person is posited as interlocutor, while Zima speaks to and instead of a non-allegorical woman. The two former texts represent something happening in the mental space of the speaker (who is, therefore, simply a thinker), while in the latter the speaker dramatizes his thoughts in order to persuade his silent interlocutor. Zima's stratagem is an essential element in a narrative construct. Cato and the French nobleman, on the other hand, function as sources of thought in prose pieces of a meditative nature. It is impossible, however, to overlook the similarities linking Cato who "si rispondea in luogo de la Ventura," the French nobleman who "rispuose al suo pensiero," and "dicea di no a se medesimo," and Zima who "cominciò in forma della donna [. . .] a rispondere a se medesimo" (III 5, 18). The rhetorical convention of dramatized thought, one certainly fully assimilated by Boccaccio, may have been an elemental catalyst, an effective facilitator within the complex workings of *inventio*.

Boccaccio may have put to use, whether consciously or not, another rhetorical convention while fashioning his story-making device. It is a form of hypothetical speech of which Dante's *Vita nuova* offers at least two instances. The first is also a case of dramatized thought. In chapter XV, the poet-lover meditates on the recently experienced devastating effects that Beatrice's presence has had on his faculties:

Appresso la nuova trasfigurazione mi giunse uno pensamento forte, lo quale poco si partia da me, anzi continuamente mi riprendea, ed era di cotale ragionamento meco: «Poscia che tu pervieni a così dischernevole vista quando tu se' presso di questa donna, perché pur cerchi di vedere lei? Ecco che tu fossi domandato da lei: *che avrestù da rispondere, ponendo che tu avessi libera ciascuna vertude in quanto tu le rispondessi?*» E a costui rispondea un altro, umile, pensero, e dicea: «*S'io non perdessi le mie vertudi, e fossi libero tanto che io le potessi rispondere, io le direi* [. . .]» (XV 1–2)

After the strange transfiguration, there came to me a strong thought, which rarely left me. Rather, it would always return to occupy my mind. "Why do you still seek to see this woman, since you come to such a ridiculous appearance when you are near her? *Now, granting that your faculties were free to operate, what would your answer be if she asked you?*" And to this replied another, humble thought and said; "*If I didn't lose my faculties, and I were free enough that I could answer, I would tell her* [. . .]" (Emphasis added)

Keeping in mind both the psychological dynamics and the wording of this Dantean passage, let us turn to Boccaccio's story. After having spoken in his lady's stead, Zima resumes his own identity and replies:

"Carissima donna, *egli è per soverchia letizia della vostra buona risposta sí ogni mia vertú occupata, che appena posso a rendervi grazie formar la risposta; e se io pur potessi come io disidero favellare*, niun termine è sí lungo che mi bastasse a pienamente potervi ringraziare come io vorrei e come a me far si conviene; [. . .]" (III 5, 23)

'My dearest, [. . .] *your kind reply has filled all of my faculties with such a surfeit of happiness that I am scarcely able to express my gratitude. But even if I could go on talking for as long as I wished*, it would still be impossible for me to thank you as fully as my feelings dictate and your kindness deserves [. . .]' (267; emphasis added)

In both Dante and Boccaccio an overwhelming emotion caused by the beloved impedes the speech of the lover. In the first instance "ciascuna vertude" is not "libera"; in the other "ogni mia vertú" is "occupata." Both cases present a hypothesis about unimpeded speech ("s'io [. . .] fossi libero tanto che io le potessi rispondere"; "se io pur potessi come io disidero favellare"). However, for Dante the failing of the faculties, which is presented earnestly—as a fact, not as a rhetorical device—depends on his being in the presence of Beatrice. Boccaccio's character, on the other hand, has been able to withstand exceedingly well the presence of his lady. Far from being smitten, he has managed to enact an effective strategy of seduction, brilliantly employing glibness and histrionics. That is why the statement to his lady that he can barely articulate a reply appears to be carrying ironic overtones. Why is he purportedly just barely able to speak? Because he is too happy.

Why is he so happy? Because his lady, or rather his own impersonation of his lady, has shown him mercy and he is no longer in danger of dying of unrequited love. In chapter XV of the *Vita nuova* and in neighboring chapters, on the other hand, we witness Dante's unsuccessful attempt to obtain Beatrice's mercy. The baring of his soul, the confession of his being brought close to death by the intensity of his love, are of no avail. These are the chapters where for Dante poet-protagonist, the possibility of using poetry as a means of amatory persuasion, or, more generally, of making poetry with a self-centered mental disposition fades forever. He will realize very soon (chapters XVII and XVIII) that there is only one solution to his plight, that of turning to a new and nobler subject matter: the disinterested praise of Beatrice. One may argue that in Boccaccio's story we must look for traces of an intentional response, a jocular, lighthearted, perhaps irreverent one, to Dante's *Vita nuova*.[12]

Mario Baratto brought to bear Dante's *prosimetrum* on III 6, the Neapolitan story of the seduction of Catella by Ricciardo, which immediately follows Zima's. Baratto pointed out that in Dante the chorus of women is "instrumental in his choosing a solely poetic relationship with Beatrice — one, that is, of objective praise" (1970: 276). In *Decameron* III 6, on the other hand, the women, including a "donna dello schermo," a "lady-screen,"[13] act as facilitators in the scheme of seduction of the beloved. In other words, Boccaccio uses the Dantean courtly material only on a demoted level of "erotic comedy." Similar considerations seem in order for our *novella*. Even in our case the "courtly ethic" of Dantean — but not only Dantean — extraction "is transferred into an erotic adventure" (1970: 278). But it is in Zima's story that Dante makes his presence felt more intensely and pervasively.

At issue in *Vita nuova* XXII is, among other things, a prohibition to speak. After the death of Beatrice's father, the poet encounters a group of mourning women; overhearing them comment upon the pitiful sight of Beatrice in tears, he is overcome with grief. The poet himself, then, places himself in the position of the object of the women's commiseration. He would like to speak to them, but is prevented from doing so by the social convention which requires strict separation of the sexes on occasions such as this. At any rate, the comments he hears about her grief and his response to it begin to stimulate the creative process:

Onde io poi, pensando, propuosi di dire parole, acciò che degnamente avea cagione di dire, ne le quali parole io conchiudesse tutto ciò che inteso avea da queste donne;

e però che volentieri l'averei domandate se non mi fosse stata riprensione, *presi tanta matera di dire come s'io l'avesse domandate ed elle m'avessero risposto. E feci due sonetti; che nel primo domando, in quello modo che voglia mi giunse di domandare; ne l'altro dico la loro risponsione, pigliando ciò ch'io udio da loro sì come lo mi avessero detto rispondendo.* (XXII 7–8)

Therefore, I proposed to say words—since it was a seemly and worthy poetic matter—to relate all that I had heard from these ladies; and, since I would willingly have questioned them, if that had not been reproachable, *I decided to write as if I had questioned them and they had replied. And I made two sonnets. In the first I ask, in the manner that it occurred to me to ask. In the other I report their answer, taking what I had heard from them as they would have said to me in reply.* (Emphasis added)

Both Dante and Zima face an obstacle in communication. Dante, unable to address the women about his lady, contrives an imaginary (hypothetical) dialogue in verse. He posits the question and then furnishes the answer. Zima gives the form of a dialogue to his monologue responding in his woman's stead. In both cases we are in the realm of the "as if" (De Robertis 1978: 165–74). Dante overcomes the obstacle by projecting the event to the level of imagination, transforming it into poetry. Zima succeeds by dramatizing his own fantasy.[14] Dante's operation is essentially retrospective: the sonnets are an idealized rewriting of the past. Zima's belongs to the present. His fantasizing aloud is intended to bring about a modification in immediate reality. At the same time it is a prescription for the future inspired by desire.

Judging by the previously examined evidence, it seems only reasonable to connect the story-making dramatic device, Zima's self-reply, to the instances of hypothetical speech which one finds in Dante's *Vita nuova*. Even so, I would not suggest that we must consider Dante's text *the* privileged source. It is Cino who, in my opinion, may have a greater influence on the structure of our story. A close examination of his sonnet *Ora che rise lo spirito mio*, to which we have not yet referred, provides clues of exceptional interest.

Ora che rise lo spirito mio,
doneava il pensero entro lo core,
e con mia donna parlando d'amore,
sotto pietate si covria 'l disio:
   perché là il chiama la follia ched io
vo i[n]seguendo, e mostrone dolore,
e par ch'i' sogni, e sia com'om ch'è fòre
tutto del senno, e se stesso ha'n oblio.

Per questo donear che fa 'l pensero,
fra me medesmo vo parlando, e dico
che 'l suo sembiante non mi dice vero
    quando si mostra di pietà nemico,
ch'a forza par ched el si faccia fero:
perch'io pur di speranza mi nutrico. (XLVII)

A smile came upon my spirit as thought, inside my heart, was lost in contemplation; and while I was speaking of love to my woman, my desire took shelter by her mercy. Indeed, the folly I chase entices it there, which I regret; and I am hallucinating, and I am like one who has lost his mind and forgotten his nature. As this gallant courting of thought goes on, I talk to myself and say that her merciless countenance is a lie — the cruel mask is self-imposed. *Therefore I can feed on hope.* (Emphasis added)

A first and decisive tie between the texts can be found in the strong verbal analogue of the last line of the sonnet which marks the first part of Zima's plea:

[. . .] e sí come umilissimo servidor vi priego, caro mio bene e sola *speranza* dell'anima mia, che nell'amoroso fuoco *sperando in voi si nutrica*, che la vostra benignità sia tanta [. . .]. (III 5, 13)

Dearest beloved, since I am yours and you alone have the power *to fortify my soul with some vestige of hope* as I languish in the fiery flames of love, I beseech you, as your most humble servant [. . .]. (265; emphasis added)

Boccaccio, however, seems to have done more than appropriate a line.[15] In fact, his story can be seen as a free rearrangement of the content of the whole sonnet in narrative fashion. This rearrangement entails the transposition of the "doneare" from a mental ("doneava il pensero entro lo core") to a physical space. Zima's is a "doneare" taking place in concrete reality. The Cinian mental conversation with the woman ("e con mia donna parlando d'amore") becomes a real conversation in Boccaccio. Zima speaks of love to his woman in her presence. Concretization of imaginative stimuli, a device akin to that of demotion (in this case, from the ideal to the real), is constantly present in Boccaccio's narrative work (cf. Chapter 4).

As we well know, the conversation turns out to be a monologue because Zima is compelled to answer to himself ("E cominciò in forma della donna, udendolo ella, a *rispondere a se medesimo*"). His speaking to the woman, therefore, resembles a speaking to himself. Thus it relates to what

Cino does ("*fra me medesmo vo parlando*") in his sonnet. And what does Cino do when he speaks to himself?

fra me medesmo vo parlando, e dico
che 'l suo sembiante non mi dice vero
    quando si mostra di pietà nemico,
ch'a forza par ched el si faccia fero [. . .] (10–13)

Cino tries to persuade himself that his woman's merciless appearance may just be a façade.[16] This distinction between appearance and reality, between behavior and heart, is one that Zima as well makes while tendentiously interpreting past and present for his woman during the process of seduction. Having assumed the female identity in the second part of his plea, he cunningly states:

Tuttafiata, se dura e crudele paruta ti sono, non voglio che tu creda che io nell'animo stata sia quel che nel viso mi son dimostrata; anzi, t'ho sempre amato e avuto caro innanzi a ogni altro uomo, ma cosí m'è convenuto fare e per paura d'altrui e per servare la fama della mia onestà. (III 5, 20)

[. . .] *and I would not wish you to suppose, because I have seemed harsh and cruel, that my outward appearance reflected my true feelings towards you.* On the contrary, I have always loved you and held you higher than any other man in my affection, but I was obliged to behave as I did for fear both of my husband and of damaging my good name. (266; emphasis added)

Finally, one wonders whether and to what extent lines 7–8 of Cino's sonnet may have stimulated Boccaccio's imagination. It would not be uncharacteristic for him to transform conventional erotic folly into a highly unusual form of crazy behavior (Zima's antics). Indeed, "se stesso ha'n oblio" can describe Zima's loss of his own identity and the assumption of that of his beloved.

Here it is necessary to speak one last time of the inclination towards demotion. Not only can one argue that the *Vita nuova* was instrumental in the fashioning of *Decameron* III 5, but one can make a persuasive case for relevance of the *Convivio* as well. Toward the end of the story, when the dialogue/monologue is over and Zima is taking his leave, Boccaccio inserts a final exchange of words between husband and lover. Messer Francesco, gloating over his conviction that he has cheated his rival out of his horse with no loss to himself, asks Zima whether he believes that he, Francesco, has kept his promise. Zima answers that no, he has not, since the agreement was that he, Zima, would speak to his wife and not to a marble statue. A delighted Messer Francesco then proceeds to remind his opponent that the horse now belongs to him:

A cui il Zima rispose: 'Messer sí, ma se io avessi creduto trarre di questa grazia ricevuta da voi tal frutto chente tratto n'ho, *senza domandarlavi ve l'avrei donato*: e or volesse Idio che io fatto l'avessi, per ciò che *voi avete comperato il pallafreno e io non l'ho venduto*'. (III 5, 28)

'Quite so,' Zima replied. 'And for all the good it did me to insist on this favour of yours, *I might as well have pesented it to you without conditions in the first place.* Indeed, I wish to God I had, because now *you have bought the palfrey and I have got nothing to show for it* [lit.: and I have not sold it].' (268; emphasis added)

The immediate meaning of "voi avete comperato il pallafreno e io non l'ho venduto" is simple enough. Messer Francesco was able to buy the horse — the price being the permission to speak to his wife; Zima, on the other hand, has nothing to show for the sacrifice of the prized animal, therefore he has not sold it. This final reasoning in terms of buying and selling contrasts with the contents of Zima's proposal at the beginning of the story. In that case, Zima had refused to look at the transaction in commercial terms: "Messer, se voi mi donaste ciò che voi avete al mondo, voi non potreste per via di vendita avere il mio pallafreno, ma in dono il potreste voi bene avere, quando vi piacesse, con questa condizione: che io, prima che voi il prendiate, possa con la grazia vostra e in vostra presenzia parlare alquante parole alla donna vostra" (III 5, 7); "Sir, [. . .] if you were to offer me everything you possess in the world you could not buy my palfrey: but you could certainly have it as a gift, whenever you liked, on this one condition, that before you take possession of it, you allow me, in your presence, to address a few words to your good lady" (264). According to what Zima says here, the transaction must be seen as a gift — one that comes with a problematic condition, but a gift nonetheless.

How can we explain the switch between the lexicon of giving at the beginning of the story to that of buying and selling at the end? I will provide one possible explanation with the help of Dante's *Convivio*. In chapter I viii of his philosophical *prosimetrum*, a chapter on the notion of giving, Dante speaks about the characteristics of true liberality. One of them is "sanza essere domandato lo dono, dare quello" (I viii, 3); "to give without being asked." It is more than likely, in my opinion, that Boccaccio was thinking of this chapter while fashioning the general configuration of his story. Dante argues, towards the end of his chapter:

La terza cosa, ne la quale si può notare la pronta liberalitade, si è dare non doman-dato: acciò che 'l domandato è da una parte non vertù ma mercatantia, *però che lo ricevitore compera, tutto che 'l datore non venda.* Per che dice Seneca che "nulla cosa più cara si compera che quella dove i prieghi si spendono." Onde acciò che nel dono sia pronta liberalitade e che essa si possa in esso notare, allora, s[e] conviene esser netto d'ogni atto di mercatantia, conviene esser lo dono non domandato. (I viii, 16–17)

The third feature of true liberality is giving without being asked: indeed, anything that is solicited has to do with commerce and not virtue, *since the recipient buys even though the giver does not sell.* This is why Seneca says that "nothing is more expensive than what one buys with entreaties." Therefore, in order for true liberality to be present and manifest in the gift, the gift must be free of any act of commerce, it must be unsolicited. (Emphasis added)

Let us begin with the obvious textual correspondence. It is indeed reason-able to suggest that Boccaccio's "voi avete comperato il pallafreno e io non l'ho venduto" may be patterned after Dante's "però che lo ricevitore com-pera, tutto che 'l datore non venda."[17] Immediate evidence always encour-ages a search for covert aspects of the process of appropriation. It is true that we find a conceptualization of the transaction between the two men in the terms of "free giving" at the beginning of the story and in commercial terms at the end. The contrast, however, is more apparent than real. Through his final statement ("voi avete comperato il pallafreno e io non l'ho venduto"), Zima covertly unmasks, as it were, the true nature of Mes-ser Francesco's initiative. By quoting a passage where Dante speaks about solicited gifts, he implicitly dismisses Messer Francesco's initial offer to buy the horse. It was not a real offer, but rather an indirect request for a gift. In order to achieve a richer understanding of Boccaccio's free use of Dante's text we must not forget Seneca, the *auctoritas*, upon whom Dante bases his argument. Let us ricapitulate the argument. When a gift is solicited, we are not in the realm of "vertù" but rather in that of "mercatantia," because even though the giver technically does not sell, the receiver nevertheless buys, and buys at a very dear price. "Nulla cosa più cara si compera che quella dove i prieghi si spendono" (I viii, 16); "Nothing is more expensive than what one buys with entreaties," says Seneca in Dante's voice. One wonders whether Zima, by quoting Dante, is not also covertly telling Messer Francesco: "certainly you have paid a very high price for your asking; you, fool that you are, have given me you wife."

There may be, however, another dimension to the game of covert reference played by Boccaccio. Why should it be that nothing is so dearly bought as what is bought with "prieghi?" The reader of Dante who expects a gloss of Seneca's statement will not find it in chapter I viii: "Perché sí caro costa quello che si priega, non intendo qui ragionare, perché sufficientemente si ragionerà ne l'ultimo trattato di questo libro" (I viii, 18); "I do not intend to illustrate here why what is acquired by entreaties is so costly. The last book of this work will address this issue exhaustively." As a matter of fact, the reader will not find this gloss anywhere, since Dante never completed the promised final segment of his book. I would like to suggest the possibility that Boccaccio could not resist the temptation to do what Dante never got around to doing. He may have thought of his *novella* as coming close to an illustration of Seneca's truth and as a completion of *Convivio* I viii. Zima's story does not show exactly why nothing is more costly than that which is acquired by plea. It shows, rather, how dearly one can pay: Messer Francesco's expenditure was his wife. Boccaccio's is, of course, a jocular illustration, one entailing a lowering of the level of discourse. Dante and Seneca speak of moral cost: hurt pride, the inevitable mortification involved in asking. In Boccaccio the issue of cost appears within a context of commercial transaction, where the objects to be gained and lost are concrete ones: a woman and a horse.

As it pertains to the issue of gift-giving, a look in a completely different direction is also in order. Not enough attention has been given, by readers of III 5, to the connection between women and silence elaborated by Christian thought. A thorough investigation of these issues with reference to the Old and New Testaments, to devotional and exemplary sources, and to books of practical precepts may prove fruitful. "A silent wife is a gift from the Lord" we read, for instance, in the Siracides (26. 14). A jocular reading of this sentence may have contributed to the *inventio* of the story.

Increasingly in recent years, the notion of parody, together with that of ironization,[18] has been used to define recurrent phenomena of intertextuality and interdiscursiveness in the *Decameron*. As we saw in Chapter 2, a number of scholars have highlighted Boccaccio's widespread practice of parodic writing. It is a widely accepted notion, for instance, that a central object (if not *the* central one) of his parodic games (which can be assisted by both jocular and serious intentions) is Dante's *Commedia*. Not only can one detect in the *novelle* the reworking of single Dantean textual segments; the view that the whole *Decameron* is patterned, in a parodic mode, after Dante's divine poem can and has been supported.[19] Dante's great poem, however, is far from monopolizing Boccaccio's parodic strategies. A concise assessment of the spectrum of his objects of rewriting appears in Carlo Delcorno's essay on irony and parody in the *Decameron*:

Indeed, Boccaccio's *novella* is firstly an act of rewriting—always tendentially a parody of the most diverse literary genres, ancient and medieval, oral and written, in prose and in verse. Boccaccio puts to use first of all the short forms of narrative which the author of the *Novellino* had already begun to rework. He is interested both in the lay ones (*fabliau, lai,* the provençal *vida*) and the edifying ones (*exemplum, legenda,* vision). He also takes his inspiration from episodes of ancient and medieval romances. Furthermore, he makes the object of his parody lyric stilnovistic poetry, homiletic and political oratory, books of good behaviour, and travel literature. Finally, he is particularly keen on producing parodies of vulgarized religous texts and of all of the multifarious expressions of pietistic literature, and ends up touching the realms of folklore and magic. (1995: 174)[19]

Zima's story is certainly a good example of Boccaccio's taste—or need—for parody and for games of more or less covert reference. It is an example of multiple parody, one in which different genres are put to work at the same time.[20] Obviously not every reference, or unsettled model must appear in the text, Boccaccian or otherwise, thanks to a conscious authorial choice. Boccaccian parodic rewriting, whether conscious or not, entails essentially three modes of intervention on a textual model: inversion, demotion and concretization. Inversion of course can imply demotion, and so can concretization. All of these modes, or processes, recurring with exceptional frequency in the *inventio* of the *Decameron*, are present in Zima's enigmatic and fascinating story.

While the exceptional variety of Boccaccio's parodic spectrum is well documented, a good amount of work remains to be done on the techniques he employs and on the meaning, in each case and in general, of his parodic maneuvers. Certainly, the ongoing debate between those who uphold an epistemological seriousness of the book and those who underplay or deny it, would acquire more substance if pivotal philosophical questions about the parodic components were answered unequivocally. As far as our assessment of Zima's story is concerned, however, a final consideration must be given to the issue of self-parody. The self-parodic element in the *Decameron* has been documented by several of the critics who have addressed the issue of parody. The essential distinction to be made is between a self-parody which looks outside the book (the rewriting of segments of works such as *Teseida, Filocolo, Comedia delle Ninfe, Amorosa Visione*, briefly but eloquently illustrated in Branca 1976: XXXV–XXXVIII), and one which involves segments of the book itself. To this second kind belongs Dioneo's practice of presenting in most Days a story which is a parody either of a specific story or of the theme of the same Day (Giannetto 1981: 14–18). A case of self-parody involving tales of different Days is the narrative response which Filostrato gives in Day V to the story presented by Fiammetta in Day IV (cf. Chapter 2, 34–39).

In Part V of Boccaccio's *Filostrato* an extraordinary act of rewriting takes place. In order to lessen the pains of love, Troiolo composes a song in honor of his beloved Criseida. The song is an adaptation of four stanzas of Cino's *canzone La bella vista e 'l bel guardo soave*. It is debatable whether this procedure should be considered a parody, but one can certainly argue that demotion is involved. The *canzone*, the noblest of metrical forms in vernacular, is broken and forced into the humble grid of the octave, the traditional metre of popular narrative poetry. On the other hand, it was part of Boccaccio's agenda, in writing the *Filostrato*, to ennoble the narrative material of the *cantari*. One must consider the possibility that the transformation of a Cinian sonnet into a *novella* may be connected to that earlier transformation of a Cinian *canzone* into octaves. The turning of a mental encounter into a real one, of a lyric, stilnovistic abstraction into an erotic comedy: with respect to Cino's sonnet *Ora che rise lo spirito mio* these are the parodic contours of Zima's story we have already observed. Boccaccio's earlier use of Cino in the *Filostrato* adds a new dimension. The turning of a Cinian sonnet into a *novella* may be seen as a parody of the turning of a Cinian *canzone* into narrative octaves. Amongs the many things Boccaccio is doing with Zima's story there may be an act of self-parody, one concerning the very issue of his own practice of rewriting.

Afterword

I HOPE THAT THIS STUDY has managed to indicate with sufficient clarity a number of fruitful ways in which the notion of rhetoric may be applied to the critical assessment of Boccaccio's *Decameron*. It should be apparent that the *cornice* occupies a much more relevant place in the conception of the work than previously acknowledged. Closely observing the contexture of the discursive-narrative ritual upon which the book is built, and that of the stories' *inventio*, has made it possible to shed light on the complex connections between the two. That the study of Boccaccio's realism may benefit from an attention to the narrators' discursive patterns is a further result. We observed the realistic import of typical colloquial segments, showing their function in narrative structuring. Finally, a good portion of the book is about a radical re-evaluation of the notion of source with regard to Boccaccio's writing practice. Such re-evaluation entailed identifying the rhetorical basis of a number of acts of *inventio*. With reference to these phenomena, we spoke of a poetics of realization.

Our survey of the forms of realization in the *Decameron* allows us now to draw two fundamental preliminary conclusions. 1) Mimesis and rhetorical construction should not be seen as separate entities. Rhetorically constructed stories are never exclusively such; addressing the rhetorical component of their narrative construction does not exhaust their critical predicability. 2) The oscillation between the metaphorical and the literal is only one aspect of Boccaccio's imaginative use of rhetoric in the conception of his stories. A narrative structure can be construed out of speech without being rhetorical in the senses illustrated by Koelb. *Filocolo* IV 67, which reappears as *Decameron* X 4, is a clear case in point; another is *Decameron* III 5.

Perhaps the best way of summarizing the findings of this study is the following: the testing and forcing of rhetorical boundaries between *sententia* and *eventum* is a recurring aspect of Boccaccio's *inventio*. We have only begun to survey the phenomenology of realization in the *Decameron*, but what we have found allows us to enlarge the notion of realism which for centuries, in one form or another, has been the cornerstone of Boccaccio criticism. When we think of Boccaccian realism we must think, among other things, of acts of the imagination which entail reaching the sphere of *res* through the sphere of *verba*. This is the kind of realism which Boccaccio criticism will have to investigate in years to come in order to arrive at a comprehensive evaluation of the writer's narrative poetics.

Appendix: *Horror of Incest and Seduction of Literature in Boccaccio's* Decameron

EVEN A CURSORY SURVEY of the history of criticism of Boccaccio's *Decameron* reveals a consistent tendency to define this founding work of European narrative prose in terms of adherence to truth and reality.[1] One could mention, for instance, the radical attempt of the eighteenth-century erudite Domenico Maria Manni to demonstrate the factual truth of the contents — all contents — of the book. But the winning notion of truth in the field of Boccaccio studies is a different one, one whose point of reference is not what *happened* in real life, but rather what *happens* in it, what reality *is*. Let us turn to the comprehensive evaluation given by another eighteenth-century scholar, Giovanni Bottari:

> He [Boccaccio] indeed set out, with a magnanimous disposition, to paint from truth the whole world, and all customs, and the innermost and hidden characteristics of humans. He did so being true to their social status, age, interests, occupations, attachments, ruses and passions. The falsehood of many popular opinions, which are held as true either on account of ignorance or of malice, is thus unveiled. Rather than stopping at the surface of appearances, he strove to show clearly the innermost feelings, the sincere opinions, the machinations and guiles of men, and to paint them as they are in truth, with no alteration. (Bottari 1818: I. 12)

While Manni tries to guarantee Boccaccio's moral integrity by proclaiming the documentary truth of his contents — the stories are what they are because things really occurred that way in the real world — Bottari, who in turn claims that Boccaccio is a moralist, adopted a more complex notion of imitation:

> It is clear, then, that in his great wisdom Messer Gio. Boccaccio extracted all of the wonderful events which he left us from the inexhaustible mine of his most fertile genious [. . .]. Also, by inventing with his fertile creative mind those stories, he was better able to shape them in such a way that he could reap from them, for the common good, a more generous crop of the teachings which he set out to impart. (Bottari 1818: II. 74–75)

According to Bottari, the writer took from real events of his time "the seeds, and themes of his wondrous inventions" (75), but they remain, nevertheless, inventions. The shift, with respect to Manni, is from a perspective of factual to one of essential reality. Thus we enter the field of Boccaccio's realism as it is commonly delineated. It is precisely this non-documentary reality which constitutes the main interest of all of the most prominent students of the realistic components in the *Decameron*, from De Sanctis to Auerbach, from Branca to Getto.

An inexhaustible interest in reality in all its manifestations, "a sense of the variety of life" (Tateo 1960: 171) — is how realism is often conceptualized with reference to Boccaccio's work. Bottari does not simply state that the *Decameron* mirrors certain aspects of the world, of life, but rather *all* of the world, *all* of life. This is one of the first times that this enormously resilient notion is proposed in a detailed and consciously critical fashion. However, at the onset of Boccaccio criticism, Lorenzo de' Medici had stated that the *Decameron* contains "all of the trials and tribulations that might befall human beings," and details "every kind of human nature and passion in the world" (1991: 148). Francesco De Sanctis, in his still fundamental Boccaccian essay in the *Storia della letteratura italiana*, published in the second half of the nineteenth century, spoke of the *Decameron* as "an immense picture of life in all its varieties of characters and occurrences, calculated to provoke wonder" (1968: 357). Around the middle of this century, Giovanni Getto reformulated the argument in his influential Boccaccian monograph: "One of the most typical aspects of Boccaccio's realism is found in the multiplication of life's presences and of the world's aspects, in the variety of human occurences and, consequently, in the lack of selection and exclusion — criteria which in Petrarch, on the other hand, function as an essential law of his lyrical universe" (1986: 194–95). Of particular interest is Auerbach's version of the argument, in which Dante's influence is fully exposed:

Yet there is no mistaking the fact that Dante's work was the first to lay open the panorama of the common and multiplex world of human reality. [. . .] Without the *Commedia* the *Decameron* could not have been written. [. . .] What he [Boccaccio] owes to Dante is the possibility of making such free use of his talent, of attaining the vantage point from which it is possible to survey the entire present world of phenomena, to grasp it in all its multiplicity, and to reproduce it in a pliable and expressive language. (Auerbach 1974: 220)

It would be easy to list more testimonies. Across the centuries, the argument of variety and totality has been repeated to the point of becoming the most common of the critical commonplaces on the work. This does not mean, of course, that there should be no place for it in contemporary criti-

cal discourse. It is not sufficient, however, that we rediscover today Boccaccio's openness towards reality in all its forms (his empiricism, to use the
category proposed by Salinari). Rather, we should focus on the different
textual forms assumed by this inclination. Since it is impossible to literally
predicate all reality, the writer must convey a sense of totality, which he can
achieve in a number of ways. One of these is the contrivance of structures
of opposition and complementarity (Cf. Chapter 1). Thus we observe vice
and sundry moral weaknesses derided and chastised in Day I, and virtue
and liberality triumphant in Day X. To a Day in which human beings are at
the mercy of fortune, another Day is juxtaposed in which human resource-
fulness succeeds in determining the course of events (II–III). A balance is
established between loves with a tragical ending in Day IV and loves happily fulfilled in Day V. And so on. Innumerable, then, are the instances of
correspondence and inversion involving individual stories, such as the one
observed by Getto concerning Day II, where a story of complex vicissitudes centered around the figure of a mother (Madonna Beritola) must find
its necessary complement in an equally adventurous story centered around
the figure of a father (the Count of Anguersa) (Getto 1986: 202). Getto
assessed the phenomenon more felicitously than others:

These symmetrical, or rather bipolar situations seem to be due, at least in part, to
the intention of collecting all of reality, in its contrasting or complementary aspects.
At the same time, they reveal the strategy with which the book as a whole was conceived: a processing and ordering in well balanced patterns of the material offered
by experience. Indeed, it has been noted that the *Decameron* is "the masterpiece of
order and pattern," and that in Boccaccio every detail shows how "order and pattern
are the writer's most significant concern" [Apollonio 1943: 371]. It is not a reality
fastidiously picked that which Boccaccio relished, but neither is one chaotically assembled. His formula is instead that of a total reality arranged according to a perspective which conveys the sense of a most varied totality. (Getto 1986: 202)[2]

When it comes to bipolar situations, a most interesting case in point is
offered by IV 1 and V 4. With the story in which Lizio di Valbona catches
his daughter Caterina as she lies in bed with her lover Ricciardo (V 4),
Filostrato responds to Fiammetta's tragic first story of Day IV (at the core
of which lies Prince Trancredi's witnessing of his daughter's illicit intercourse with her Guiscardo). On Day IV, Fiammetta had reluctantly ad-
hered to Filostrato's tragic theme. Now, under Fiammetta's reign, on the
Day of happily fulfilled loves, unhappy lover Filostrato accepts the challenge
of the new genre. He does so, as we saw in Chapter 1, by presenting a

retelling, in a comedic mode, of Fiammetta's tragic story. Elsewhere I have examined in detail correspondences and inversions characterizing the two stories, and focused on the theme of father-daughter love upon which much of this textual unit of the *Decameron* pivots.[3] It is to this latter component that I would like to return in these pages, in order to present an expanded version of my previously stated argument with the support of new data.

Any study of Boccaccio's effort to give an illusion of totality, to produce the sense of a complete record of human experience, cannot ignore his treatment of the erotic. Our perception of the book is defined, to a large extent, by its extremely varied and crowded erotic phenomenology. In the *Decameron*, love rules over all humankind, from king all the way down to pauper. The book presents us with the first stirring of desire in the young and the permanence of it in the old, with the young pining for the young, and the old coveting the young, with men pursuing women as well as women pursuing men. Men and women of the cloth are as actively and imaginatively engaged in erotic pursuits as the laity. Love may appear in the guise of tender yearning, nobilitating influx, robust natural drive, or insatiable lust. It may be reciprocated and it may be extorted. Day III is an *Ars Amatoria* of sorts, a merry survey of strategies of seduction. Marital bliss is the attained goal of the stories in Day V, but adultery and fornication are ubiquitous. While the rule is that the object of one's desire must be of the opposite sex, at least one story (V 10) makes a clear allusion to homosexual erotic activities of the protagonists. Although there is no systematic exploration of perversion, the range of erotic situations includes a case of necrophilia (X 4). As we contemplate this rich and varied erotic mosaic, we may wonder where the author locates incestuous love, if at all.

The only explicit reference to incest in the *Decameron* appears in X 8, in the course of Titus's distressed soul-searching at the onset of the story. The Roman youngster, who has fallen in love with his friend Gisippus's wife, attempts to cope with the moral demands of the situation by contrasting the erotic transgression which he is contemplating with others of graver nature:

Le leggi d'amore sono di maggior potenzia che alcune altre: elle rompono non che quelle della amistà ma le divine. Quante volte ha già il padre la figliuola amata, il fratello la sorella, la matrigna il figliastro? Cose piú monstruose che l'uno amico amar la moglie dell'altro, già fattosi mille volte. (X 8, 16)

The laws of Love are more powerful than any others; they even supplant divine laws, let alone those of friendship. How often in the past have fathers loved their daughters, brothers their sisters, or mothers their stepsons? These are far more reprehensible than the man who loves the wife of his friend, for he is only doing what a thousand others have done before him. (778)

Incest, however, does not enter the plot of the story.[4] As Branca duly observes in his gloss (1184, n. 6), Titus's rationalizing move is akin to that of Fiammetta in the *Elegia*. As she ponders her old nurse's wise advice to resist at all costs her passion for Panfilo, which would lead her to betray her husband, Venus appears to her and eloquently goads her to yield to it. It is futile, the goddess argues, to try to oppose the dictates of love:

Egli [Amore], sí come più forte, l'altrui leggi, non curando, anullisce, e dà le sue. Pasife similmente aveva marito, e Fedra, e noi ancora, quando amammo. Essi medesimi mariti amano le più volte avendo moglie: riguarda Iansone, Teseo e il forte Ettore e Ulisse. [. . .] Ecco, se tu al potente Amore non vuoi soggiacere, fuggire ti conviene; e dove fuggirai tu, ch'e' non ti séguiti e non ti giunga? Egli ha in ogni luogo iguale potenzia [. . .]. Bastiti sommamente, o giovane, che di non abominevole fuoco, come Mirra, Semiramis, Biblìs, Cannace e Cleopatra fece, ti molesti. (I 23–26)

Since he is the strongest, he annuls the laws of others by disregarding them and gives his own. Pasiphae, Phaedra, and I too still had a husband when we fell in love. Husbands themselves most of the time fall in love while they have a wife; look at Jason, Theseus, the strong Hector, and Ulysses. [. . .] In sum, if you do not wish to be subjected to this powerful Love, you should run away, but where will you run so that he may not follow you and reach you? He has the same power everywhere; [. . .] Be it enough for you, young woman, that he did not molest you with a wicked fire as he did with Myrrha, Semiramis, Byblis, Canace, and Cleopatra. (20–21)

Venus's speech in the *Elegia di Madonna Fiammetta* provides a handy reminder of the archetypal references behind Titus's mention of the monstrous deeds of incest in *Decameron* X 8. Phaedra lusted after her stepson. In turn, Byblis, Canace, and Cleopatra all forced the bounds of nature in loving their own brothers, and so did Semiramis, known to have had carnal knowledge of her son, as did Myrrha—the main case of interest for our purposes—seducer of her father. Boccaccio's fascination with these archetypes of abominable love is already evident in the *Filocolo*, the romance which launched his literary career. In Book II, as Florio argues with his father that love is a natural thing, and that to love a virtuous and virtue-inspiring woman such as Biancifiore cannot be shameful, he indignantly states:

— [. . .] Sieno del loro amore ripresi la trista Mirra e lo scelerato Tireo e la lussuriosa Semiramis, i quali sconciamente e disonestamente amarono, e me più non riprendete, se la mia vita v'aggrada —. (II 15, 14)

'[. . .] Let wretched Myrrha and wicked Tereus and lustful Semiramis be blamed for their loves, for they loved obscenely and unchastely; but do not blame me any further, if you value my life.' (61)

Later, in Book III, Fileno fills his indictment of the second sex with references to the canon of lustful female evil-doers:

E in cui si trovò mai tanto tracutato amore quanto in Mirra, la quale con sottili ingegni adoperò tanto che col propio padre più fiate si giacque? E la dolente Biblis non si vergognò di richiedere il fratello a tanto fallo, e la lussuriosa Cleopatra d'adoperarlo. [. . .] E qual diabolico spirito avrebbe potuto pensare quello che fece Fedra, la quale non potendo avere recato Ipolito suo figliastro a giacere con lei, con altissima voce gridando e stracciandosi i vestimenti e' capelli e 'l viso, disse sé essere voluta isforzare da lui e, lui preso, consentì che dal propio padre fosse fatto squartare? (III 35, 7–8)

And where can one ever find such unbridled lust as in Myrrha, who devised cunning snares so that she might lie repeatedly with her own father? And the grieving Byblis did not blush to ask her brother for such a thing, or the lustful Cleopatra to carry it out. [. . .] And what diabolic spirit could have conceived what Phaedra did, when she could not persuade her stepson Hippolytus to lie with her, and cried out loudly and tore her garments and hair and face, and said that he had tried to force her? And when he was taken, she consented that his own father should have him torn apart. (187–88)

A famed catalogue of instances of extreme and transgressive female lust which certainly makes its presence felt in these passages is the one in book I of Ovid's *Ars Amatoria* (269–341). But the primary source toward which Boccaccio would turn to find fully developed versions of several of these characters' vicissitudes is Ovid's *Metamorphoses*. See, for instance, Phaedra (XV 500 ff.), Byblis (IX 453 ff.), and Myrrha (X 312 ff.) Far from being occasional, references to the codified tradition of loathsome love surface along the entire course of Boccaccio's literary production. Further mentions of Myrrha, in particular, may be found in *Teseida* (glosses) VI 42, *Comedia Ninfe* II 12, XVI 70, and XXVI 36, and *Amorosa visione* XXII. In this latter instance, we have a brief retelling of the entire myth:

Era di dietro a lei, con gli occhi fissi
sopra 'l suo padre, *Mirra scellerata*,
né da lui punto li teneva scissi.
   Riguardando io costei lunga fiata,
quivi la vidi poi di notte oscura
esser con lui in un letto colcata.
   Correndo poi fuggir l'aspra figura
del padre la vedea, che conosciuta
avea l'abominevole mistura.
   Albero la vedeva divenuta
che 'l suo nome ritien, sempre piangendo
o 'l fallo o forse la gioia compiuta. (43–54)

Behind her, with her eyes fixed / on her father, was *criminal Myrrha*, / nor did she ever take them off him. / Gazing upon her for a long time, / I saw her there then, in the dark of night, / lying in bed with him. / Then I saw her running to escape the fierce figure / of her father; he had come to understand / the abomination of their amorous embrace. / I then saw that she had become the tree / which keeps her name, still weeping for her fault, / perhaps because of the joy she had taken from it. (93; emphasis added)

Myrrha is "scellerata" not only because Ovid uses repeatedly "scelus" in his text, but as an homage to Dante, who gave his compact version of the story in *Inferno* XXX:

Ed elli a me: "Quell'è l'anima antica
   di *Mirra scellerata*, che divenne
   al padre, fuor del dritto amore, amica.
Questa a peccar con esso così venne,
   falsificando sé in altrui forma [. . .]" (37–41)

And he to me, "That is the ancient spirit of *infamous Myrrha*, who became loving of her father beyond rightful love. She came to sin with him by falsifying herself in another's form [. . .]" (317; emphasis added)

Later Boccaccian mentions of the myth in works of erudition, include *De casibus virorum illustrium* I xii, 4 and *Genealogie deorum gentilium* II li-lii. We will return later to this last instance. Although Boccaccio deemed unsuitable for the *Decameron* an overt use of the materials inherited from classical antiquity, that unsettling body of knowledge left a significant trace in the book. Indeed, it is with reference to it that decisive progress may be obtained in our critical awareness of *Decameron* IV 1, one of the most famous, most admired, and, inevitably, most analyzed stories in the book.

It was not until the 1960s that critical discourse on the story of Tancredi and Ghismonda began to address with utter frankness the issue of incest. Carlo Muscetta was among the very first to explicitly link the story's tragic events to the morbid connotations of Tancredi's tender love for his daughter. In his essay "Giovanni Boccaccio e i novellieri," written for the volume on the Trecento of the *Storia della letteratura italiana* edited by Cecchi and Sapegno, we read:

> [Tancredi's killing of his daughter's lover] is not just a question of a point of honor, as De Sanctis believed. [. . .] Tancredi is essentially a good man. Why, then, does he sully his hands with the "blood of passion?" Some critics, unable to fathom his tragedy, say that he is a badly developed character. Russo says that he is "a miserable wretch," and that his character is that of not having one. But I believe that "blood of passion" means blood shed for love — not only the love of the two victims, but above all his own, the father's. Tancredi's tragedy is in his own tenderness, and he will lose himself in the crime because the fates willed that he and his only daughter should be prematurely widowed. Having made Ghismonda the object of all of his affections, he represses a charge of morbid passion in his innermost self, without being aware of it. (Muscetta 1965: 412)

Leaving aside the complex question of the awareness that the father and daughter may have of the nature of the father's affection, it is not at all farfetched to suggest that such affection may have an incestuous component.[5] Both what we are told about it (Boccaccio never tires of stressing its unusual intensity and tenderness) and what we witness of Tancredi's behavior, seem to point in this direction. In particular, as Almansi has observed, Tancredi's actions in the second part of the story resemble only superficially those of other Boccaccian fathers who discover their daughter's affairs: "The Salernitan Prince does not react as Boccaccian *father*, but rather like a *man* in the throes of a jealous rage which assumes in his mind the connotations of a sweeping affection, unknown and unconfessable" (1980: 174).

It is not my intention here to review the body of circumstantial evidence which has been used by Muscetta, Almansi, and those who have followed them, to argue for a thematic presence of incest in *Decameron* IV 1.

Suffice it to reiterate that one can build a rather strong case on the basis of that material. My suggestion is that there is a different body of evidence, intertextual evidence, which it would be unwise to ignore. To give a stronger basis to our claims of incest, and to gain a clearer understanding of its thematic significance, we must take a close look at the problem of the story's *inventio*. In particular, I believe that we must connect the story of Tancredi and Ghismonda to that of Cinyras and Myrrha as it is presented in Ovid's *Metamorphoses*.

This is how Fiammetta opens her narration in the *Decameron*:

Tancredi, prencipe di Salerno, fu signore assai umano e di benigno ingegno, se egli nell'amoroso sangue nella sua vecchiezza non s'avesse le mani bruttate, il quale in tutto lo spazio della sua vita non ebbe che una figliuola, *e piú felice sarebbe stato se quella avuta non avesse.* (IV 1, 3)

Tancredi, Prince of Salerno, was a most benevolent ruler, and kindly of disposition, except for the fact that in his old age he sullied his hands with the blood of passion. In all his life he had but a single child, a daughter, *and it would have been better for him if he had never had any at all.* (332; emphasis added)

And this is the beginning of the story of Cinyras and Myrrha in the *Metamorphoses*:

Editus hac ille est, *qui si sine prole fuisset,*
inter felices Cinyras potuisset haberi. (X 297–98; emphasis added)

Cinyras was her [Paphos's] son and, had he been without offspring, might have been counted fortunate. (85)

Focus on the figure of the father, the hypothetical segment, foreshadowing of the tragic outcome: these essential elements seem to indicate that Boccaccio patterned his rhetoric of beginning after Ovid's. Of course the story of incest in the *Metamorphoses* differs in many ways from the one which opens the Day of tragic loves in the *Decameron*. In Ovid it is the daughter who covets the father, incest is consummated, the girl gives birth to a child, etc. There seems to be little doubt, however, that this mythical archetype is very much active in Boccaccio's imagination. Myrrha is supposed to choose a husband from among her many worthy suitors:

[. . .] undique lecti
te cupiunt proceres, totoque Oriente iuventus
ad thalami certamen adest: *ex omnibus unum*
elige, Myrrha, virum, dum ne sit in omnibus unus. (X 315–18)

From every side the pick of princes desire you; from the whole Orient young men are here vying for your couch; *out of them all choose one for your husband, Myrrha,* only let not one be among them all. (87; emphasis added)

But she shows no interest in the young men, having already made her ill-fated choice. Ghismonda, on the other hand, prevented from marrying by her loving father, does indeed choose among the available youths in Tancredi's court. Her choice was a rational and wise one, she reminds her father in the course of her long speech in the second part of the story:

Guiscardo non per accidente tolsi, come molte fanno, ma con diliberato consiglio *elessi innanzi a ogni altro* [. . .] (IV 1, 37)

I did not take a lover at random, as many women do, but deliberately *chose Guiscardo in preference to any other* [. . .] (338; emphasis added)

The segment "elessi innanzi a ogni altro" may be an echo of Ovid's "ex omnibus unum elige." Ghismonda's is a rational choice based on a natural need. It is indeed with reference to the demands of nature that she justifies her actions. Her speech finds an antecedent in the soliloquy with which Myrrha attempts to convince herself that her illicit passion finds its justification in nature:

illa quidem sentit foedoque repugnat amori
et secum 'quo mente feror? quid molior?' inquit
'di, precor, et pietas sacrataque iura parentum,
hoc prohibete nefas scelerique resistite nostro,
si tamen hoc scelus est. sed enim damnare negatur
hanc Venerem pietas: coeunt animalia nullo
cetera dilectu, nec habetur turpe iuvencae
ferre patrem tergo, fit equo sua filia coniunx,
quasque creavit init pecudes caper, ipsaque, cuius
semine concepta est, ex illo concipit ales.
felices, quibus ista licent! humana malignas
cura dedit leges, et quod natura remittit,
invida iura negant. (X 319–31)

She, indeed, is fully aware of her passion and fights against it and says within herself: 'To what is my purpose tending? What am I planning? O gods, I pray you, and piety and the sacred rights of parents, keep this sin from me and fight off my crime, *if indeed it is a crime*. But I am not sure, for piety refuses to condemn such love as this. Other animals mate as they will, nor is it thought base for a heifer to endure her sire, nor for his own offspring to be a horse's mate; the goat goes in among the flocks which he has fathered, and the very birds conceive from those from whom they were conceived. Happy they who have such privilege! Human civilization has made spiteful laws, and what nature allows, the jealous laws forbid. (87; emphasis added)

The tension between *natura* and *iura* is at the core of the two stories. While Myrrha, yielding to her "natural" desire, breaks the law prohibiting incest, Ghismonda breaks the one prohibiting non-marital intercourse. Furthermore, she defies the rules of society by choosing a lover of humble origins. By connecting their infraction to a natural drive, both Myrrha and Ghismonda question the nature of the infraction. Myrrha's "si tamen hoc scelus est" becomes "se peccato è" at the apex of Ghismonda's peroration in front of her father:

[. . .] se tu nella tua estrema vecchiezza a far quello che giovane non usasti, cioè a incrudelir, se' disposto, usa in me la tua crudeltà, la quale a alcun priego porgerti disposta non sono, sí come in prima cagion di questo peccato, *se peccato è*; (IV 1, 44)

If you are intent, in your extreme old age, upon behaving as you never behaved in your youth, and resorting to cruelty, then let your cruelty be aimed at me, for it was I who caused *this so-called sin* to be committed. (339; emphasis added)

These instances of intertextuality are sufficient, I believe, to suggest that Boccaccio found in Ovid's story of Cinyras and Myrrha essential elements for the configuration of *Decameron* IV 1. In what appears to be a rewriting of that story, he conceived of Ghismonda, in part, as a new Myrrha. She is a new Myrrha whose sexual transgression is not with her father, but the responsibility of which belongs to her father, who inherits the incestuous drive of the old Myrrha. The new Myrrha is the object of the desire which defined the destiny of the old one. It is certainly possible that Boccaccio's response to Ovid was accurately planned as a complex game of allusive parallels and inversions. On the other hand, the result may have been achieved with minimal or no conscious reference to the Latin model. I believe the former possibility to be more likely.

We know for certain that Boccaccio knew Ovid's Cinyras and Myrrha's story very well; that it became for him the archetype of father-daughter incestuous love; that he mentioned it explicitly in almost all of his works. In the *Genealogie deorum gentilium*, where he dedicates a chapter to Cinyras (II li) and one to Myrrha (II lii), he even quotes the original beginning of the story in Ovid's text, the beginning which, as we have seen, he appears to have adapted for use in *Decameron* IV 1:

Cinara filius fuit Paphi, prout ostendit Ovidius dum dicit: Editus hac ille est, qui, si sine prole fuisset, Inter felices Cynaras potuisset haberi. (II li)

Cinara was son of Paphus, as Ovid shows when he says: Cynaras was his son, and, had he been without children, might have been deemed fortunate.

We do not know for certain that he conceived of *Decameron* IV 1 as a re-writing of Ovid's story, but it seems likely. On the basis of all that we have said thus far, we may suggest with a good degree of confidence that the story of Tancredi and Ghismonda is the story of incestuous love in the *Decameron*. Incest is allowed in the book, but only as desire (there is no consummation), desire with no explicit tag. The abnormal desire is located in a man, rather than a woman, as in the case in the Latin archetype. Did Boccaccio consider an overt treatment of incest only to rule it out as unsuitable for the audience of women which he identifies in the Proem? Did he make the bearer of incestuous desire a man rather than a woman with that audience in mind? Was consummated incest too horrible to contemplate for the youngsters of the *brigata*? We don't know. What we do know is that the story functions on two levels, like many others in the *Decameron*: a level for the access of general readers, and a level for the "intendenti," the readers who can read beneath the surface. Those in this latter category are supposed, in this case, to discern the Ovidian contexture in the text, and to appreciate the complex set of attending implications I have presented.

I hope that the evidence I have presented in this appendix will suffice to show that it is legitimate to claim that there is more to *Decameron* IV 1 than what De Sanctis saw in it—that one may detect an incestuous component in Tancredi's love for his daughter. The critical notion that Tancredi's actions are simply the product of the social conventions of the late Middle Ages, according to which a daughter is the property of her father, seems inadequate to do justice to the story; indeed, it has been challenged oftentimes in the past few decades (cf. Forni 1992: 119–46). This notion still finds, however, the occasional endorsement, among readers who seem to believe that the theme of incest may be detected only with recourse to psychoanalytical clichés (cf. Marti 1992). In fact, I do not believe that there is any need for psychoanalytic enlightenment to detect an incestuous component in the story of Tancredi and Ghismonda — this is one of the points that I tried to make in *Forme complesse*. What is needed is, first of all, a willingness to entertain the notion that something new can be found in old, venerable, and extensively interpreted texts, and then, a modicum of common sense, an average acquaintance with Boccaccio's work and his *modus operandi* in *inventio*, and a little familiarity with the work of Ovid, Boccaccio's great Latin idol.

Notes

Chapter 1. Configurations of Discourse

1. Cf. Maria Corti's definition: "This concept is applicable, in determined conditions only, to a group of poetic or prose texts by the same author; in other words, a collection of poems or stories may be simply a group of texts gathered together for diverse reasons, or that collection may be in itself the configuration of a large unitary text, or macrotext. In this second case, every single poetic or prose text is a microstructure that is articulated inside a macrostructure, hence the functional and informative character of the collection. It is like saying that the total meaning does not coincide with the sum of the partial meanings of the single texts, but goes beyond it. [. . .] The functionality and information possibility of a collection as such occurs when at least one of the following conditions is present: (1) if there exists a combination of thematic and/or formal elements that runs through all the texts and produces the unity of the collection; (2) if there is a progression to the discourse for which each single text can occupy only one place. Clearly, the second condition presupposes the first, but the reverse is not true" (Corti 1978: 112). Cf. also Segre 1988: 31–33. On the *Decameron* as macrotext, cf. Forni 1992: 15–26 and passim.

2. In the *Libro dei sette savi*, which Boccaccio may have used, the young son of a Roman emperor finds himself in mortal peril having been wrongly accused by his stepmother of attempting sexual violence against her. The seven sages, then, in order to save the boy, take turns narrating in the sovereign's presence exemplary stories, while the stepmother responds with her own narratives intended to persuade her husband to order the execution. Contrary to what happens in the *Sette savi*, in the *Decameron* the narrative ritual has a prominent connotation of *ludus*, of recreation. The wisdom-narrative connection (narrative born of wisdom, or illustrating wisdom) is present in both works, but in Boccaccio's text the moral yield of the narrative is meant to be a permanent acquisition for the listeners' lives. There is no immediate, practical task (like the life-saving attempt in the *Sette savi*) to be accomplished through eloquence and narration. An essential element of innovation in the *Decameron* is the contemporary setting of the frame-story. A detailed contrast between *Sette savi* and *Decameron* can be found in Picone 1988b: 97–99.

3. For the juridical components of the *Decameron* cf. Chiappelli 1988. Although the framing chosen for the *Decameron* was innovative in Boccaccio's time, the mere ordering of topics which it features was commonplace. At this elementary level Boccaccio's book may be compared to compilations such as Valerius Maximus's *Factorum et Dictorum Memorabilium*, Petrus Alfonsi's *Disciplina Clericalis*, Iacobus de Vitry's *Sermones de Tempore*, Stephanus de Borbone's *Tractatus de Diversis*

Materiis Predicabilibus, Jacobus de Varagine's *Legenda aurea*, or the *Novellino* itself. In all of these collections the stories (anecdotes, *exempla, novelle*) are ostensibly or discreetly ordered by topic.

4. On the *cornice* cf. Cerisola 1975, Marino 1979, Potter 1982, Shklovsky 1990: 52–71, Getto 1986: 1–33, Bevilacqua 1978, Prete 1970, Römhild 1974, Barberi Squarotti 1983, Picone 1988b and c, Plaisance 1989, Olson 1986: 164–204, Surdich 1987.

5. This connection is one of the core issues discussed in Forni 1992.

6. For a discussion on the likelihood of this link cf. Forni 1992: 89–96.

7. On the recommendations of medieval rhetoricians about use of *sententia* and *proverbium*, cf. Vecchi 1954 and Chiecchi 1975–76. Chiecchi's is to date the most comprehensive study of Boccaccio's use of maxims and proverbs in the *Decameron*.

8. Elsewhere, I have shown how difficult it is to extract from this final page of the Preface a clearly defined causal connection between the workings of *diletto-consiglio* and the eventual *passamento di noia* (Forni 1992: 31–32). Of paramount interest, however, is the insistence on pedagogical intent.

9. On the notions of *noia* and *malinconia* in the *Decameron*, cf. Ciavolella 1976 and Zago 1992.

10. Cf. *Remedia Amoris* 13–22: "Siquis amat quod amare iuvat, feliciter ardens / Gaudeat, et vento naviget ille suo. / At siquis male fert indignae regna puellae, / Ne pereat, nostrae sentiat artis opem. / Cur aliquis laqueo collum nodatus amator / A trabe sublimi triste pependit onus? / Cur aliquis rigido fodit sua pectora ferro? / Invidiam ceadis, pacis amator, habes. / Qui, nisi desierit, misero periturus amore est, / Desinat; et nulli funeris auctor eris" (13–22); "If any lover has delight in his love, let him rejoice in his happy passion and sail on with favouring wind. But if any endures the tyranny of an unworthy mistress, lest he perish, let him learn the help my art can give. Why has some lover cast the noose about his neck, and hung, a sad burden, from a lofty beam? Why has one pierced his breast with the unyielding sword? Lover of peace, thou bearest the reproach of that murder" (179).

11. For a first critical assessment cf. Forni 1991.

12. Cf. I Intr., 114 and passim.

13. Social harmony characterizes life in the Decameronian *cornice*: "In the *Decameron* there is an astonishingly high degree of obedience and agreement among the ten narrators involved. They agree without any discussion with the proposal concerning the story-telling as a very useful pastime during their deliberate exile in Paradise on earth. They agree also in a remarkable way with the anthropological views underlying the stories. [. . .] the reactions of the listeners can be summarized in such terms as agreement and consent. [. . .] Still one more proof of the striking consent within the group is their unconditional obedience to the prescriptions of the queen or king, especially with regard to the observation of the theme of the day" (Janssens 1977: 139–40).

14. "La reina, la quale lui e sollazzevole uomo e festevole conoscea e ottimamente s'avisò questo lui non chieder se non per dovere la brigata, se stanca fosse del ragionare, rallegrare con alcuna novella da ridere, col consentimento degli altri lietamente la grazia gli fece" (I Concl., 14); "The queen, knowing what a jovial and entertaining fellow he was, and clearly perceiving that he was only asking this favour

so that, if the company should grow weary of hearing people talk, he could enliven the proceedings with some story that would move them to laughter, cheerfully granted his request, having first obtained the consent of the others" (112).

15. "Fiera materia di ragionare n'ha oggi il nostro re data, pensando che, dove per rallegrarci venuti siamo, ci convenga raccontar l'altrui lagrime, le quali dir non si possono che chi le dice e chi l'ode non abbia compassione. Forse per temperare alquanto la letizia avuta li giorni passati l'ha fatto: ma che che se l'abbia mosso, poi che a me non si conviene di mutare il suo piacere, un pietoso accidente, anzi sventurato e degno delle nostre lagrime, racconterò" (IV 1, 2); "Cruel indeed is the topic for discussion assigned to us today by our king, especially when you consider that, having come here to fortify our spirits, we are obliged to recount people's woes, the telling of which cannot fail to arouse compassion in speaker and listener alike. Perhaps he has done it in order to temper in some degree the gaiety of the previous days; but whatever his motive, it is not for me to alter his decree, and I shall therefore relate an occurrence that was not only pitiful, but calamitous, and fully worthy of our tears" (332).

16. "Pampinea, a sé sentendo il comandamento venuto, più per la sua affezione cognobbe l'animo delle compagne che quello del re per le sue parole: e per ciò, più disposta a dovere alquanto recrear loro che a dovere, fuori che del comandamento solo, il re contentare, a dire una novella, senza uscir del proposto, da ridere si dispose" (IV 2, 4); "On hearing herself singled out as the next speaker, Pampinea, knowing that her own feelings were a better guide than the king's words to the mood of her companions, was more inclined to amuse them than to satisfy the king in aught but his actual command; and so she decided that without straying from the agreed theme, she would narrate a story to make them laugh" (342–43).

17. Similar views are rehearsed in a much less blatant fashion during the two weeks of narration by the narrators themselves (see below). Only a servant, however, will be allowed to champion them so explicitly, vehemently, and earnestly.

18. Licisca has a kindred soul in the old woman who presents a reversal of traditional morality in the last tale of the previous Day.

19. In a characteristic twist, Dioneo will not conform to the topic he has given as king (cf. VII 10).

20. On Dioneo "roi pour rire," cf. Grimaldi 1987: 243–56.

21. For a full account of the sources of this story, cf. Pastore Stocchi 1963.

22. Following is Horace's pertinent passage: "quid refert, uri virgis ferroque necari / auctoratus eas, an turpi clausus in arca, / quo te demisit peccati conscia erilis, / contractum genibus tangas caput?" (58–61); "What matters it, whether you go off in bondage, to be scourged and slain with the sword, or whether, shut up in a shameful chest, where the maid, conscious of her mistress's sin, has stowed you away, you touch your crouching head with your knees?" (229). Just as in Horace we find the lover "clausus in arca" thanks to the servant's intervention, in the Boccaccian story it is the maid who suggests to her lady that he be "messo nell'arca" (IV 10, 19); "stuffed inside the trunk" (395). The notion of being killed by the sword found in the satire may be responsible for the servant's further suggestion (overruled by the lady) that they stab the body. IV 10 is not the only Boccaccian story featuring a chest or trunk, but it is the only one in which the chest is called an

"arca," a term usually employed in the *Decameron* with the meaning of tomb or sarcophagus.

23. Although Muscetta (1989: 303) connects the Licisca and Tindaro episode with the *Saturnalia*, he does so with reference to his central argument of the importance of Macrobius's work for the conception of the *Decameron*. He does not entertain the possibility of a Horatian input.

24. Several of the stories narrated by Dioneo (II 10, III 10, IV 10, VII 10) prominently feature sexual demands of women.

25. "Carissime donne mie, elle son tante le beffe che gli uomini vi fanno, e spezialmente i mariti, che, quando alcuna volta avviene che donna niuna alcuna al marito ne faccia, voi non dovreste solamente esser contente che ciò fosse avvenuto o di risaperlo o d'udirlo dire a alcuno, ma il dovreste voi medesime andar dicendo per tutto, acciò che per gli uomini si conosca che, se essi sanno, e le donne d'altra parte anche sanno: il che altro che utile esser non vi può, per ciò che, quando alcun sa che altri sappia, egli non si mette troppo leggiermente a volerlo ingannare. Chi dubita dunque che ciò che oggi intorno a questa materia diremo, essendo risaputo dagli uomini, non fosse lor grandissima cagione di raffrenamento al beffarvi, conoscendo che voi similemente, volendo, ne sapreste beffare? E' adunque mia intenzion di dirvi ciò che una giovinetta, quantunque di bassa condizione fosse, quasi in un momento di tempo per salvezza di sé al marito facesse" (VII 2, 3–6); "Adorable ladies, so numerous are the tricks that men, and husbands in particular, play upon you, that whenever any woman happens to play one on her husband, you should not only be glad to hear about it but you should also pass it on to as many people as you can, so that men will come to see that women are just as clever as they are. All of which is bound to work out to your own advantage, for when a man knows that he has clever people to deal with, he will think twice before attempting to deceive them. Who can be in any doubt, therefore, that when husbands come to learn of what we shall be saying today on this subject, they will have every reason to refrain from trifling with you, knowing that if you so desired you could do the same to them? And for this reason, it is my intention to tell you about the trick which a young woman, though she was of lowly condition, played on the spur of the moment upon her husband, in order to save her own skin" (527–28).

26. Similar statements of modesty can be found in the *exordia* of II 4, VI 8, and VII 3.

27. The controversial story of the widow and the scholar told by Pampinea in Day VIII continues to stir the *brigata*'s imagination well into the narrative session of the following Day. In the *exordium* of IX 8, Lauretta will connect her story to Pampinea's, making a point of defining in detail her *variatio* in *inventio*.

28. Cf. also Forni 1992: 109–11 and, here, the Appendix.

29. I outlined for the first time this manipulation of the notion of truth in Forni 1995: 308–9.

30. Cf. Bruni 1990, Forni 1991, Barolini 1983–91, Markulin 1983. Stories such as that of Melchisedech and Saladin (I 3) are usually brought forward to exemplify this dimension of Boccaccio's work. Melchisedech, with the parable of the three rings shows the Sultan that it is impossible to determine which is the true law

(among the Christian, the Jewish, and the Saracen). "Boccaccio here," Markulin extrapolates, "rejects absolute answers and definitive solutions outright in favor of open-endedness. [. . .] There is no final, eternal truth accessible to the mind of man and capable of being expressed in fiction. The only absolutely correct interpretation is that there are no correct interpretations, the only definite answer that there are no definite answers, and as Melchisedech aptly concludes his tale, 'ancora ne pende la quistione' (I, 3, 16)" (Markulin 1983: 190).

Chapter 2. Pleasure and Response

1. "Donne, il vostro senno piú che il nostro avvedimento ci ha qui guidati; io non so quello che de' vostri pensieri voi v'intendete di fare: li miei lasciai io dentro dalla porta della città allora che io con voi poco fa me ne usci' fuori: e per ciò o voi a sollazzare e a ridere e a cantare con meco insieme vi disponete (tanto, dico, quanto alla vostra dignità s'appartiene), o voi mi licenziate che io per li miei pensier mi ritorni e steami nella città tribolata" (I Intr., 92–93); "It is not our foresight, ladies, but rather your own good sense, that has led us to this spot. I know not what you intend to do with your troubles; my own I left inside the city gates when I departed thence a short while ago in your company. Hence you may either prepare to join with me in as much laughter, song and merriment as your sense of decorum will allow, or else you may give me leave to go back for my troubles and live in the afflicted city" (64).

2. "E ciascun generalmente, per quanto egli avrà cara la nostra grazia, vogliamo e comandiamo che si guardi, dove che egli vada, onde che egli torni, che che egli oda o vegga, niuna novella altra che lieta ci rechi di fuori" (I Intr., 101); "And unless they wish to incur our royal displeasure, we desire and command that each and every one of the servants should take good care, no matter what they should hear or observe in their comings and goings, to bring us no tidings of the world outside these walls unless they are tidings of happiness" (66).

3. A detailed comparison appears in Marcus 1979b: 55–56. Cf. also Forni 1992: 104 and Smarr 1986: 165–204.

4. Cf. Chapter 4.

5. It is as though Ricciardo, a character of the *Decameron*, had read the *Decameron*. Cf. Forni 1992: 106.

6. For the rhetorical complexities of these pages cf. Marcus 1979b: 44–63 and Mazzotta 1986: 131–58. My present reading is based in part on observations which I recorded in Forni 1992: 94 and 105–6. A different focus, however, has allowed me to reach new conclusions.

7. On the symbology of these birds cf. Davy 1992.

8. The complexity of the game of response makes us aware, once more, of the fact that in many instances Boccaccio availed himself of what we could call workshop sources: of imaginative elements, that is to say, made available by stories which he had already written or readied for writing. It is virtually certain that he worked on different stories at the same time, or, more precisely, that while fashioning a story he represented to himself the configuration of connections in which that story

would participate. As I have observed elsewhere, the work on a story may have generated, at times, not only an element to be used in another story, but also the architecture of a Day, or a part of a Day (Forni 1992: 25–26).

9. Cf. Branca 1986, Delcorno 1995, Hollander 1981–82 and 1983–84, L. Rossi 1989, Bettinzoli 1983–84, Bruni 1990, Giannetto 1981.

Chapter 3. Realism and the Needs of the Story

1. Cf. Propp 1984: 24–26; Weinrich 1978: 125–46; Longacre and Chenoweth 1986: 126; Longacre 1983: 21; Staples 1990: 35–36.

2. These segments have been noticed by scholars such as Branca (1986: 349) and Padoan (1978: 20–22), who have remarked on their realistic import, without bringing to the fore their rhetorical and narrative complexities.

3. In addition to the anticlerical polemic, we find here the theme, so dear to Boccaccio, of an inferior cleverly chastising an unworthy superior. For this type of confrontation, cf. Chiappelli 1984: 21–40.

Chapter 4. The Poetics of Realization

1. For the notion of lightness applied to literary texts, cf. Calvino 1988: 3–29.

2. Umberto Eco refers to this story in a study of rhetoric in the visual language of publicity. After pointing out that visualization or literalization of metaphor is a characteristic of that kind of language, he adds: "The literalization of metaphor is on the other hand unusual in verbal language: so much so that Massimo Bontempelli has made this transgression the basis of an amusing tale in which the metaphors of common language suddenly materialize. Reality imitates language and gives a surreal impression that we do not experience at all when images imitate language" (1968: 172, n. 10).

3. Severe objections to Todorov's theory of the fantastic are found in Lem 1974 and Philmus 1980.

4. On the literature of the fantastic cf. also: Finne 1980, Rabkin 1976, Penzoldt 1952, Brooke-Rose 1981, Bonifazi 1982, S. Albertazzi 1993.

5. Cf. also the following observations by Olbrechts-Tyteca: "Metaphor, as a daughter of analogy, is always the result of the comparison of two different fields. It is creative, but creative of what? Of relationships, evidently. Born of an analogy, it can also suggest other analogies, since nothing guarantees that the listener will interpret it in the same way as the speaker. We must however avoid taking it as a new object belonging to the one or the other of the two fields. Metaphor is a meeting place, not a real object—whatever our conception of reality may be. To forget this may give rise to the comic. We would laugh, for example, at the person who asks a

junk dealer to sell him 'one of those iron curtains that they talk about all the time.' "
(1977: 278).

6. This passage in Bontempelli is studied, from a different perspective, in Guidi 1992: 66. For the relation between materialization and the comic cf. Dorfles 1977: 97–116. Dorfles's essay is particularly useful for its references to the visual arts.

7. Cf. Sokel's assessment: "German usage applies the term *Ungeziefer* (vermin) to persons considered low and contemptible, even as our usage of 'cockroach' describes a person deemed a spineless and miserable character. The traveling salesman Gregor Samsa, in Kafka's *The Metamorphosis*, is 'like a cockroach' because of his spineless and abject behavior and parasite wishes. However, Kafka drops the word 'like' and has the metaphor become reality when Gregor Samsa wakes up finding himself turned into a giant vermin. With this metamorphosis, Kafka reverses the original act of metamorphosis carried out by thought when it forms metaphor; for metaphor is always 'metamorphosis.' Kafka transforms metaphor back into his fictional reality, and this counter-metamorphosis becomes the starting point of this tale" (Sokel 1966: 5). A very persuasive case for a similar connection to the sphere of the commonplace can be made with regard to the worm which antagonizes the protagonist Roberto Coracaglina in Tommaso Landolfi's *Il Mar delle Blatte*. Cf. Vittori 1988: 58.

8. "Et omnis qui reliquerit domum, vel fratres, aut sorores, aut patrem, aut matrem, aut uxorem, aut filios, aut agros propter nomen meum, centuplum accipiet, et vitam aeternam possidebit." (19.29); "And he who in my name will have left his house, or his brothers, or sisters, or his father, his mother, his wife and children, or his land, will receive a hundredfold, and will have eternal life."

9. Boccaccio uses a similar image in the *Trattatello in laude di Dante*: "ancor che fanciul fosse, con tanta affezione la bella imagine di lei ricevette nel cuore, che da quel giorno innanzi, mai, mentre visse, non se ne dipartí" (33); "even though he was just a child, he received in his heart her beautiful image with so much affection that, from that day on, as long as he lived, he never separated himself from it."

10. Connections between Boccaccio's story and the Dantean episode are observed in Forni 1992: 73–75.

11. Cf. Chapter 2, 36–37. For the distinction between eyes of the body and eyes of the mind cf. also VII 5, 53 and VII 9, 78. An oscillation between the physical and the spiritual as it regards the heart can be found in the story of Nastagio degli Onesti: "e quante volte io la giungo, tante con questo stocco, col quale io uccisi me, uccido lei e aprola per ischiena, e quel cuor duro e freddo, nel qual mai né amor né pietà poterono entrare, con l'altre interiora insieme, sí come tu vedrai incontanente, le caccio di corpo e dolle mangiare a questi cani" (V 8, 24); "Every time I catch up with her, I kill her with this same rapier by which I took my own life; then I slit her back open, and (as you will now observe for yourself) I tear from her body that hard, cold heart to which neither love nor pity could ever gain access, and together with the rest of her entrails I cast it to these dogs to feed upon" (460). For the rhetoric of the heart in early Romance literatures cf. Bruni 1988, Mancini 1988, and L. Rossi 1983.

12. Cf. Bellomo 1992: 202–3.

13. "The protagonist's spiritual fall is now matched by two other falls, one physical, as he leaps from the bedroom window into the canal, and one dramatic, as his fortunes take a turn for the worse" (Marcus 1979a: 17).

14. Cf. the anthology of Senecan sentences included in the *Fiori e vita di filosafi e d'altri savi e d'imperatori*: "Ozio sanza lettera è morte e sepultura dell'uomo vivo" (195).

15. On the *inventio* of Guido's story cf. also Watson 1989.

16. Cf. Usher 1986: 630: "For Boccaccio, as indeed for his contemporaries, the boundary between life and death was not clear-cut. Diagnostic problems could be considerable: both Salvestra (IV,8,24–25) and Andriuola (IV,6,22) have to make distressing and repeated tactile examinations before slowly coming to the conclusion that their companions are dead. Even medical practitioners were ill-equipped: Catalina's collapse during pregnancy is wrongly interpreted, and premature burial ensues (X,4,6–7). Luckily for her, Gentile decides to open her tomb, and his manual exploration which establishes Catalina's heartbeat is exactly analogous to Salvestra's less-fortunate diagnostic attempt (X,4,9–12). In each of the above cases, the indistinct physiological boundary between life and death allows Boccaccio to indulge in one of his more persistent fantasies: erotic experiences with totally passive partners. Cimone's intent perusal of the sleeping Efigenia is another variant on the same theme (V,1,7–10)." Cf. also Michel David's essay on voyeurism in Boccaccio.

17. As it is in the Epitaph of Omonea, Boccaccio's main source for the elegy. The latin part of the epitaph can be found in Velli's edition of the elegy (467).

18. For the dependance of the elegy on the story of Pyramus and Thisbe, cf. Velli 1979: 102–3.

19. Cf. also, among a large number of examples, Lichas's transformation into a rock as he is hurled by Hercules into the Euboean sea: "[. . .] tremit ille, pavetque / *pallidus*, et timide verba excusantia dicit. / dicentem genibusque manus adhibere parantem / corripit Alcides, et terque quaterque rotatum / mittit in Euboicas tormento fortius undas. / ille per aërias pendens *induruit* auras: / [. . .] illum validis iactum per inane lacertis / *exanguemque metu* nec quicquam umoris habentem / in rigidos versum silices prior edidit aetas" (IX 214–25; emphasis added); "The young man trembled, grew pale with fear, and timidly attempted to excuse his act. But while he was yet speaking and striving to clasp the hero's knees, Alcides caught him up, and, whirling him thrice and again about his head, he hurled him far out into the Euboean sea, like a missile from a catapult. The youth stiffened as he yet hung in air; [. . .] hurled by strong arms through the empty air, bloodless with fear, his vital moisture dried, he changed, old tradition says, to flinty rock." (19) The rhetorical basis of the narrative is apparent. Psychological and physiological phenomena ("pallidus," "induruit," "exanguis metu") prepare the metamorphosis. Petrified by terror, having become *like* a stone in the brief course of his ordeal, Lychas *is* now a stone. The common hyperbolic expression "exanguis metu," which normally does not imply the total loss of vital fluids, acquires a radical meaning as the flesh and blood human being crosses the treshold of inorganic eternity. On metaphor as generator of metamorphosis in Ovid's poem cf. also Pianezzola 1979.

20. The "purged" image heralds the arrival of the penitent wrathful whose behavior is now purged of wrath: "Io sentia voci, e ciascuna pareva / pregar per pace e

per misericordia / l'Agnel di Dio che le peccata leva. / Pur *'Agnus Dei'* eran le loro essordia; / una parola in tutte era e un modo / sí che parea tra esse ogni concordia" (XVI 16–21); "I heard voices, and each one seemed to pray for peace and for mercy to the Lamb of God that takes sins away" (167).

Chapter 5. Rhetoric and Narration in the Story of Zima

1. On the relevance of silence in Day III, cf. Ferrante: "Since deception and the exchange of rôles necessitate discretion on the part of the conscious participants, silence is a recurrent theme through the day: The gardener in 1 pretends to be a mute and the abbess maintains a discreet silence when she learns he is not; the groom in 2 must not speak when he visits the queen in the dark, and the king chooses not to speak about the affair; the lady in 3 tells no one but her confessor what is supposedly going on; the husband in 4 is enjoined to keep his special penance a secret; the wife in 5 is forbidden by her husband to speak; the wife in 6 cannot talk without revealing her identity, and the lover disguises his voice for the same reason; in 7, the dangers of speaking are disclosed—the wife says too much in her confession, and the murderers are discovered when they are overheard discussing the need to keep quiet about what they have done; in 8, the wife is told to keep her husband's trip to Purgatory a secret; in 9, as in 6, the wife must be silent to conceal her identity" (Ferrante 1978: 593).

2. Zima will be able to assess the woman's feelings noticing her telling glances in his direction as well (III 5, 18). Cf. Ovid, *Ars Am.* I 574: "Saepe tacens vocem verbaque vultus habet"; "There are often voice and words in a silent look" (53).

3. With his strategy Zima introduces into his plea an element of play which may further weaken the woman's resistance. The psychological dynamics at work are those outlined by Freud with reference to the joke: "The thought seeks to wrap itself in a joke because in that way it recommends itself to our attention and can seem more significant and more valuable, but above all because this wrapping bribes our powers of criticism and confuses them. We are inclined to give the *thought* the benefit of what has pleased us in the *form* of the joke; and we are no longer inclined to find anything wrong that has given us enjoyment and so to spoil the source of a pleasure. If the joke has made us laugh, moreover, a disposition most unfavourable for criticism will have been established in us; [. . .] Where argument tries to draw the hearer's criticism over on to its side, the joke endeavors to push the criticism out of sight" (Freud 1966: 132–33); cf. also Olbrechts-Tyteca 1977: 11. The persuasive power of playfulness and the comic was well known to antiquity. Cf. the famous section *de risu* in Quintilian's *Institutio Oratoria* (VI iii). The use of playing and joking in the process of seduction was theorized by Ovid (*Ars Am.* III 367–68).

4. On the connection between narcissism and need to seduce, cf. Roccato 1989: 43–55.

5. "Make your conversational contribution such as is required, at the stage at which it occurs, by the accepted purpose or direction of the talk exchange in which you are engaged" (Grice 1989: 26). Grice distinguishes four categories "under one

or another of which will fall certain more specific maxims and submaxims, the following of which will, in general, yield results in accordance with the Cooperative Principle" (ibid.). The first of these categories is that of "Quantity," which "relates to the quantity of information to be provided" (ibid.). The first maxim pertaining to it is: "Make your contribution as informative as is required (for the current purposes of the exchange)" (ibid.). Zima's lady appears to be opting out of the conversation. In Grice's words, a speaker "may say, indicate, or allow it to become plain that he is unwilling to cooperate in the way the maxim requires. He may say, for example, *I cannot say more; my lips are sealed*" (Grice 1989: 30). Our case, of course, presents a radical version of this option. The quantity of verbal information is reduced to zero; the indication is: *I will not, or cannot say anything*, or: *I am choosing not to be engaged in a conversational exchange*.

6. It is still Grice who invites us to think of the observance of the Cooperative Principle and the maxims as a "quasi-contractual matter" (Grice 1989: 29).

7. On these notions cf. Segre 1982: 15–28.

8. Cf. Branca 372, n. 1, 3, 8; cf. also Balduino 1984: 141–206.

9. On the poetic forms in dialogue cf. Zumthor 1992: 357–74.

10. The narrator's modification of countenance according to the different roles was and is, of course, commonplace; cf., for example, Martelli 1989: 225–27.

11. For the *Specchio*, which is a record of sermons given in 1354, there might be a chronological difficulty; but cf. De Luca's introduction to the *Specchio* in Passavanti 1984: 83.

12. To my knowledge the possibility of a connection between Zima's story and Dante's *Vita nuova* was entertained for the first time in Forni 1986.

13. The reference is to the lady whom Dante uses to conceal his love for Beatrice.

14. For the theatrical connotations of the story cf. Baratto: "Zima sublimates a passion and at the same time instrumentalizes a culture: he is forced to contrive a clever comedy of courtly and stilnovistic language" (Baratto 1970: 290). Muscetta speaks of a "comedic courtly one-act" (Muscetta 1981: 214). Assessments of the theatricality of the *Decameron* may be found in Baratto 1970: 239–69, and 271–322; Borsellino 1974: 11–50; Padoan 1973: 335–36; V. Russo 1983: 11–88.

15. For this line cf. also Dante's *Fiore*: "E di buona speranza il mi notrico" (iii 13).

16. This is not the only possible way to interpret these lines, but it seems to me more Boccaccian than the one (cf. Orlando 1987: 103–4) in which the "sembiante" is that of "pensero."

17. The connection did not escape Franco Fido's attention (Fido 1988: 106, n. 4). He simply recorded it as something never noticed before without surmising as to its significance.

18. "Branca uses the term 'ironization', rather than the term 'parody', because it seems better suited to render the idea of the type of parody that characterizes the *Decameron*, which, in general, is something somewhat hazy, and which never extends to unrestrained comedy or caustic sarcasm. Viewed in this light, literary ironization, in particular, is seen by Branca not as a desecration of *auctoritates*, but as a

simple 'forcing of linguistic and structural codes', that has as its aim the 'renewal from within of worn-out and consecrated themes and plots' " (Giannetto 1981: 19, n.2). The term "parody" will be used here in a sense which includes Branca's.

19. This is not the place to review the various aspects of Boccaccio's use of the masterpiece which he greatly admired and against which he could not help measuring his own. Three examples will suffice. In recent years, both Hollander and L. Rossi have given new circulation to the idea that the Dantean figure of Brunetto Latini was the model, or at least one of the models, for ser Cepparello da Prato, the comedic protagonist of the first story of Day I. According to Rossi, Boccaccio, struck by the praise that Dante lavished upon his old "maestro" who, after all, is damned in Hell, took the liberty of making him a "saint" in his first *novella*, introducing thus "the problem of the relationship between truth and appearance, which will be one of the Leitmotives of the *Decameron*" (L. Rossi 1989: 388). Rossi sees in the important, pivotal, identification of real women, rather than the Muses, as sources of inspiration (IV Intr.) an "invocazione alla rovescia," an "inverted invocation," responding to Dante's invocation to the Muses in *Purg*. I (L. Rossi 1989: 394–95). One need not agree completely with the following sweeping statement by the same scholar in order to recognize its critical usefulness. "What has been turned upside-down in the hundred *novelle* is above all perspective. Dante's characters appeared to the poet in their intimate and immutable essence. They presented themselves as they *must* have been, so that it was possible 'to punish their sins' and 'reward virtue.' Boccaccian 'heroes,' on the other hand, are as they appear, and in each case appearances determine their essence: think of Cepparello, Alatiel, Griselda" (L. Rossi 1989: 382).

20. Cf. also Branca 1976: XXXIV–XXXV, on which Delcorno relies.

21. Cf. Delcorno 1995: 174–75.

Appendix

1. Cf. Forni 1995.

2. On these aspects of the book, cf. also Ferrante 1978 and Smarr 1986.

3. Cf. Forni 1992: 104 and passim; cf. also Chapter 2, 34–39.

4. The word "incesto" does not appear in the *Decameron*. A definition of it, however, can be found in the *Esposizioni sopra la Comedia di Dante*. There, Boccaccio presents "incesto" as one of the kinds of lust. A sexual act is called incest when at least one of the lovers is a member of the clergy, or when it involves relatives: "Alcuni a questa spezie aggiungono il commettere questo peccato tra congiunti, il quale di sopra fu nominato 'stupro'; e per avventura non senza sentimento s'aggiugne, per ciò che questo pare male da non potere in alcun tempo con futuro matrimonio risarcire, per ciò che, come la monaca sacrata mai maritar più non si puote, così né tra congiunti può mai intervenire matrimonio, dove nell'altre spezie potrebbe intervenire" (V ii 74); "Some add to this kind the sin committed by relatives, which above we called rape ["stupro"]; and there is a good reason for that, since this is an

evil which can never be redressed with a future marriage. Indeed, just as a consecrated nun can never be given in marriage, marriage is impossible between relatives, while it could happen in the other cases."

5. On the question of the father's and daughter's awareness of the nature of the father's affection, cf. Forni 1992: 121–46.

Works Consulted

Primary Sources

Andreas Capellanus. *On Love*. Ed. P. G. Walsh. London: Duckworth, 1982.

Apuleius. *Metamorphoses*. Ed. and trans. J. Arthur Hanson. 2 vols. Cambridge, Mass.: Harvard University Press, 1989.

Boccaccio, Giovanni. *Amorosa Visione*. Trans. Robert Hollander, Timothy Hampton, and Margherita Frankel. Hanover, N.H. and London: University Press of New England, 1986.

———. *The Elegy of Lady Fiammetta*. Ed. and trans. Mariangela Causa-Steindler and Thomas Mauch. Chicago and London: University of Chicago Press, 1990.

———. *Il Filocolo*. Trans. Donald Cheney with the collaboration of Thomas G. Bergin. New York and London: Garland, 1985.

———. *Genealogie deorum gentilium libri*. Ed. Vincenzo Romano. 2 vols. Bari: Laterza, 1951.

Bontempelli, Massimo. *Racconti e romanzi*. Ed. Paola Masino. 2 vols. Milano: Mondadori, 1961. Vol. I.

Buzzati, Dino. *Il Colombre e altri cinquanta racconti*. Milano: Mondadori, 1992.

Calvino, Italo. *I nostri antenati: Il visconte dimezzato, Il barone rampante, Il cavaliere inesistente*. Milano: Garzanti, 1985.

Cavalcanti, Guido. *Rime. Con le Rime di Iacopo Cavalcanti*. Ed. Domenico De Robertis. Torino: Einaudi, 1986.

Cino da Pistoia. *Poeti del Dolce stil nuovo*. Ed. Mario Marti. Firenze: Le Monnier, 1969. 421–923.

Contini, Gianfranco, ed. *Poeti del Duecento*. 2 vols. Milano: Ricciardi, 1960.

Cornificius. *Rhetorica ad C. Herennium*. Ed. Gualtiero Calboli. Bologna: Pàtron, 1969.

Dante Alighieri. *Il Convivio*. Ed. Giovanni Busnelli and Giuseppe Vandelli. 2 vols. Firenze: Le Monnier, 1968.

———. *The Divine Comedy*. Ed. and trans. Charles S. Singleton. 3 vols. Princeton, N.J.: Princeton University Press, 1970.

———. *Il fiore*. Ed. Gianfranco Contini. *Opere minori*. Ed. Domenico De Robertis and Gianfranco Contini. Milano-Napoli: Ricciardi, 1984. I, I: 553–798.

———. *Vita nuova*. Ed. Domenico De Robertis. Milano: Ricciardi, 1980.

Evangelia Apocrypha. Ed. Costantin von Tischendorf. Leipzig: Mendelssohn, 1876.

Fiori e vita di filosafi e d'altri savi e d'imperadori. Ed. Alfonso D'Agostino. Firenze: La Nuova Italia, 1979.

Historia Apollonii Regis Tyri. Archibald, Elizabeth. *Apollonius of Tyre: Medieval and*

Renaissance Themes and Variations. Including the text of the *Historia Apollonii Regis Tyri* with an English translation. Cambridge: Brewer, 1991.

Horace. *Satires, Epistles and Ars Poetica*. Trans. H. Rushton Fairclough. Cambridge, Mass.: Harvard University Press, 1991.

Jacobus de Voragine. *Legenda Aurea Vulgo Historia Lombardica Dicta*. Ed. Theodor Graesse. Bratislava: Koebner, 1890.

Juvenal. *Juvenal and Persius*. Trans. G. G. Ramsay. Cambridge, Mass.: Harvard University Press, 1993.

Landolfi, Tommaso. *Il Mar delle Blatte e altre storie*. Milano: Rizzoli, 1975.

Il libro dei sette savi[. . .]. Ed. Antonio Cappelli. Bologna: Romagnoli, 1865.

Lidia. La «Comédie» Latine en France au XIIe Siècle. Gen. ed. Gustave Cohen. 2 vols. Paris: Les Belles-Lettres, 1931. 1: 211–46.

Morovich, Enrico. *Miracoli quotidiani*. Palermo: Sellerio, 1988.

———. *Piccoli amanti*. Milano: Rusconi, 1990.

Il «Novellino». *La prosa del Duecento*. Ed. Cesare Segre and Mario Marti. Milano: Ricciardi, 1959. 793–881.

Ovid. *The Art of Love and Other Poems*. Trans. J.H. Mozley. Cambridge, Mass.: Harvard University Press, 1985.

———. *Metamorphoses*. Trans. Frank Justus Miller. 2 vols. Cambridge, Mass.: Harvard University Press, 1984.

Passavanti, Iacopo. *«Molti begli esempli»* [. . .] *nel libro dello «Specchio della vera penitenzia»*. *Prosatori minori del Trecento. I. Scrittori di religione*. Ed. Giuseppe De Luca. Milano: Ricciardi, 1954. 83–102.

Petrarca, Francesco. *Rerum Memorandarum Libri*. Ed. Giuseppe Billanovich. Firenze: Sansoni, 1945.

Petrus Alfonsi. *The Disciplina Clericalis*. Ed. and trans. Eberhard Hermes. English trans. P. R. Quarrie. Berkeley: University of California Press, 1977.

Quintilian. *The Institutio Oratoria*. Trans. H. E. Butler. 4 vols. Cambridge, Mass.: Harvard University Press, 1976–80.

Rabelais. *Oeuvres complètes*. 2 vols. Paris: Garnier, 1962. Vol. I.

Salimbene de Adam. *Cronica*. Ed. Giuseppe Scalia. 2 vols. Bari: Laterza, 1966.

Seneca. *Ad Lucilium Epistulae Morales*. Trans. Richard M. Gummere. 3 vols. Cambridge, Mass.: Harvard University Press, 1989.

Seneca. *Epistles*. 66–92. Trans. Richard M. Gummere. Cambridge, Mass.: Harvard University Press, 1991.

Valerius Maximus. *Factorum et Dictorum Memorabilium Libri Novem cum Iulii Paridis et Ianuarii Nepotiani Epitomis*. Ed. C. Kempf. Stuttgart: Teubner, 1966.

Secondary Sources

Albertazzi, Adolfo. *Parvenze e sembianze*. Bologna: Zanichelli, 1892.

Albertazzi, Silvia, ed. *Il punto su: La letteratura fantastica*. Roma: Laterza, 1993.

Alessandri, Maria Rita. *Manuale del fantastico*. Scandicci: La Nuova Italia, 1992.

Almansi, Guido. *L'estetica dell'osceno*. Torino: Einaudi, 1980.

————. *The Writer as Liar: Narrative Technique in the* Decameron. London: Routledge and Kegan Paul, 1975.

Anders, Günther. *Franz Kafka*. London: Bowes & Bowes, 1960.

Apollonio, Mario. *Uomini e forme nella cultura italiana delle origini*, Firenze: Sansoni: 1934.

Arieti, Silvano. *Creativity: The Magic Synthesis*. New York: Basic Books, 1976.

Auerbach, Erich. *Mimesis: The Representation of Reality in Western Literature*. Princeton, N.J.: Princeton University Press, 1974.

Bajoni, Maria Grazia. "La novella del *dolium* in Apuleio *Metamorfosi* IX, 5–7 e in Boccaccio, *Decameron* VII, 2." *Giornale Storico della Letteratura Italiana* 171 (1994): 217–25.

Bakhtin, Mikhail. *Rabelais and His World*. Cambridge, Mass. and London: MIT Press, 1968.

Balduino, Armando. *Boccaccio, Petrarca e altri poeti del Trecento*. Firenze: Olschki, 1984.

Baratto, Mario. *Realtà e stile nel* Decameron. Vicenza: Pozza, 1970.

Barberi Squarotti, Giorgio. *Il potere della parola: Studi sul «Decameron»*. Napoli: Federico and Ardia, 1983.

————, ed. *Prospettive sul Decameron*. Torino: Tirrenia, 1989.

Barkan, Leonard. *The Gods Made Flesh: Metamorphosis & the Pursuit of Paganism*. New Haven, Conn. and London: Yale University Press, 1986.

Barolini, Teodolinda. "Giovanni Boccaccio (1313–1375)." *European Writers: The Middle Ages and the Renaissance*. Ed. William T. H. Jackson and George Stade. 14 vols. New York: Scribner, 1983–91. II: 509–34.

Battaglia, Salvatore. *La coscienza letteraria del Medioevo*. Napoli: Liguori, 1965.

————. *Esemplarità e antagonismo nel pensiero di Dante*. 2nd ed. Napoli: Liguori, 1967.

————. *Mitografia del personaggio*. Napoli: Liguori, 1991.

Battaglia Ricci, Lucia. *Ragionare nel giardino: Boccaccio e i cicli pittorici del "Trionfo della morte."* Roma: Salerno Editrice, 1987.

Bellomo, Saverio. "La caduta dell'agnolo Gabriello: Da Dante a Boccaccio (*Decameron* IV 2)." *L'angelo dell'immaginazione*. Ed. Fabio Rosa. Trento: Dipartimento di Scienze Filologiche e Storiche, 1992. 195–214.

Benkov, Edith Joyce. "Language and Women: From Silence to Speech." Wasserman and Roney 1989: 245–65.

Bergson, Henri. *Laughter. Comedy*. Ed. Wylie Sypher. Baltimore: Johns Hopkins University Press, 1984. 61–190.

Bernardo, Aldo S. and Anthony L. Pellegrini, eds. *Dante, Petrarch, Boccaccio: Studies in the Italian Trecento in Honor of Charles S. Singleton*. Binghamton, N. Y.: Medieval and Renaissance Texts and Studies, 1983.

Bettinzoli, Attilio. "Per una definizione delle presenze dantesche nel *Decameron*. I. I registri 'ideologici', lirici, drammatici." *Studi sul Boccaccio* 13 (1981–82): 267–326.

————. "Per una definizione delle presenze dantesche nel *Decameron*. II. Ironizzazione ed espressivismo antifrastico-deformatorio." *Studi sul Boccaccio* 14 (1983–84): 209–40.

Bevilacqua, Mirko. *L'ideologia letteraria del Decameron*. Roma: Bulzoni, 1978.

Billanovich, Giuseppe. *Restauri boccacceschi*. Roma: Edizioni di "Storia e Letteratura," 1947.

Bonciani, Giovanni. *Lezione sopra il comporre delle novelle. Trattati di poetica e retorica del Cinquecento*. Ed. Bernard Weinberg. 4 vols. Bari: Laterza, 1970–74. III: 135–73.

Bonifazi, Neuro. *Teoria del fantastico e il racconto fantastico in Italia: Tarchetti, Pirandello, Buzzati*. Ravenna: Longo, 1982.

Borsellino, Nino. *Rozzi e intronati: esperienze e forme di teatro dal «Decameron» al «Candelaio»*. Roma: Bulzoni, 1974.

Bosco, Umberto. *Il "Decameron": Saggio*. Rieti: Bibliotheca, 1929.

Bottari, Giovanni. *Lezioni sopra il Decamerone*. 2 vols. Firenze: Ricci, 1818.

Bragantini, Renzo. *Il riso sotto il velame: La novella cinquecentesca tra l'avventura e la norma*. Firenze: Olschki, 1987.

Bragantini, Renzo and Pier Massimo Forni, eds. *Lessico critico decameroniano*. Torino: Bollati Boringhieri, 1995.

Branca, Vittore. *Boccaccio Medievale e nuovi studi sul Decameron*. Firenze: Sansoni, 1986.

———. "Introduzione." *Tutte le opere di Giovanni Boccaccio. Decameron*. Ed. Vittore Branca. Milano: Mondadori, 1976. 4: XI- XXXVIII.

Brooke-Rose, Christine. *A Rhetoric of the Unreal: Studies in Narrative and Structure, Especially of the Fantastic*. Cambridge: Cambridge University Press, 1981.

Bruni, Francesco. *Boccaccio: L'invenzione della letteratura mezzana*. Bologna: il Mulino, 1990.

———, ed. *Capitoli per una storia del cuore: Saggi sulla lirica romanza*. Palermo: Sellerio, 1988.

Caillois, Roger. *Nel cuore del fantastico*. Milano: Feltrinelli, 1984.

Calvino, Italo. *Six Memos for the Next Millennium*. Cambridge, Mass.: Harvard University Press, 1988.

Cardini, Franco. "Il banchetto del falcone, ovvero l'amante mangiato." *Quaderni medievali* 17 (1984): 45–71.

Cerisola, Pier Luigi. "La questione della cornice del *Decameron*." *Aevum* 49 (1975): 137–56.

Cherchi, Paolo and Michelangelo Picone, eds. *Studi di Italianistica: In onore di Giovanni Cecchetti*. Ravenna: Longo, 1988.

Chiappelli, Fredi. "Discorso o progetto per uno studio sul «Decameron»." Cherchi and Picone 1988: 105–11.

———. *Il legame musaico*. Ed. Pier Massimo Forni with the collaboration of Giorgio Cavallini. Roma: Edizioni di Storia e Letteratura, 1984.

Chiecchi, Giuseppe. "Sentenze e proverbi nel «Decameron»." *Studi sul Boccaccio* 9 (1975–76): 119–68.

Ciavolella, Massimo. *La "malattia d'amore" dall'Antichità al Medioevo*. Roma: Bulzoni, 1976.

Comolli, Giampiero. "Visione, genesi del narrare." *aut-aut* n.s. 231 (1989): 9–23.

Corngold, Stanley. "Kafka's *Die Verwandlung*: Metamorphosis of the Metaphor." *Mosaic* 3, 4 (1970): 91–106.

Corti, Maria. *An Introduction to Literary Semiotics*. Bloomington: Indiana University Press, 1978.

Costantini, Aldo Maria. "Studi sullo *Zibaldone Magliabechiano*. II. Il florilegio senechiano." *Studi sul Boccaccio* 8 (1975): 79–126.

Cottino-Jones, Marga. "Saggio di lettura della prima giornata del *Decameron*." *Teoria e critica* 1 (1972): 111–38.

Cottino-Jones, Marga and Edward F. Tuttle, eds. *Boccaccio: Secoli di vita*. Ravenna: Longo, 1977.

Curtius, Ernst Robert. *European Literature and the Latin Middle Ages*. Princeton, N.J.: Princeton University Press, 1990.

D'Andrea, Antonio. *Il nome della storia: Studi e ricerche di storia e letteratura*. Napoli: Liguori, 1982.

Dardano, Maurizio. *Lingua e tecnica narrativa nel Duecento*. Roma: Bulzoni, 1969.

David, Michel. "Boccaccio pornoscopo?" *Medioevo e Rinascimento Veneto con altri studi in onore di Lino Lazzarini*. 2 vols. Padova: Antenore, 1979. 1: 215–43.

Davis, Walter R. "Boccaccio's *Decameron*: The Implications of Binary Form." *Modern Language Quarterly* 42 (1981): 3–20.

Davy, Marie-Madeleine. *L'oiseau et sa symbolique*. Paris: Michel, 1992.

Degani, Chiara. "Riflessi quasi sconosciuti di *exempla* nel *Decameron*." *Studi sul Boccaccio* 14 (1983–84): 189–208.

Delcorno, Carlo. *Exemplum e letteratura: Tra Medioevo e Rinascimento*. Bologna: Il Mulino, 1989.

———. "Ironia/parodia." Bragantini and Forni 1995: 162–91.

Delcorno Branca, Daniela. *Boccaccio e le storie di Re Artù*. Bologna: Il Mulino, 1991.

Del Lungo, Andrea. "Pour une poétique de l'incipit." *Poétique* 94 (1993): 131–52.

De Michelis, Cesare. *Contraddizioni nel Decameron*. Milano: Guanda, 1983.

de' Negri, Enrico. "The Legendary Style of the *Decameron*." *Romanic Review* 43 (1952): 166–89.

De Robertis, Domenico. "Storia della poesia e poesia della propria storia nel XXII della «Vita Nuova»." *Studi danteschi* 51 (1978): 153–77.

De Sanctis, Francesco. *Storia della letteratura italiana*. Torino: UTET, 1968.

Di Girolamo, Costanzo and Ivano Paccagnella, eds. *La parola ritrovata: Fonti e analisi letteraria*. Palermo: Sellerio, 1982.

Dorfles, Gillo. *Artificio e natura*. Torino: Einaudi, 1977.

Durling, Robert M. "Boccaccio on Interpretation: Guido's Escape (*Decameron* VI.9)." Bernardo and Pellegrini 1983: 273–304.

Easthope, Antony. *Literary into Cultural Studies*. London: Routledge, 1991.

Eco, Umberto. *The Limits of Interpretation*. Bloomington: Indiana University Press, 1990.

———. *La struttura assente: Introduzione alla ricerca semiologica*. Milano: Bompiani, 1968.

Falassi, Alessandro. "Il Boccaccio e il folklore di Certaldo." Cottino-Jones and Tuttle 1975: 265–92.

Faral, Edmond. *Les arts poétiques du XIIe et du XIIIe siècle: recherches et documents sur la technique littéraire du moyen âge*. Paris: Champion, 1924.

———. *Les jongleurs en France au moyen âge*. Paris: Champion, 1910.

Ferrante, Joan M. "The Frame Characters of the *Decameron*: A Progression of Virtues." *Romance Philology* 19 (1965): 212–26

———. "Narrative Patterns in the *Decameron*." *Romance Philology* 31 (1978): 585–604.

Fido, Franco. *Il regime delle simmetrie imperfette: Studi sul "Decameron."* Milano: Angeli, 1988.

Finné, Jacques. *La littérature fantastique: essai sur l'organisation surnaturelle*. Bruxelles: Université de Bruxelles, 1980.

Forni, Pier Massimo. "Appunti sull'intrattenimento decameroniano." *Passare il tempo* 1993 2: 529–40.

———. "Boccaccio retore." *MLN* 106 (1991): 189–201.

———. "Come cominciano le novelle del *Decameron*." *La novella italiana* 1989 2: 689–700.

———. *Forme complesse nel Decameron*. Firenze: Olschki, 1992.

———. "Realtà/verità." Bragantini and Forni 1995: 300–319.

———. "Zima sermocinante (*Decameron*, III 5)." *Giornale Storico della Letteratura Italiana* 163 (1986): 63–74.

Forster, E.M. *Aspects of the Novel*. New York: Harcourt Brace, 1927.

Freud, Sigmund. *Jokes and Their Relation to the Unconscious*. New York: Norton, 1963.

Friedman, Michael D. "'Hush'd on purpose to grace harmony': Wives and Silence in *Much Ado About Nothing*." *Theatre Journal* 42 (1990): 350–63.

Getto, Giovanni. *Vita di forme e forme di vita nel Decameron*. 4th ed. Torino: Petrini, 1986.

Giannetto, Nella. "Parody in the *Decameron*: A 'Contented Captive' and Dioneo." *The Italianist* 1 (1981): 7–23.

Gibaldi, Joseph. "The *Decameron* Cornice and the Responses to the Disintegration of Civilization." *Kentucky Romance Quarterly* 24 (1977): 349–57.

Gilman, Sander L. *The Parodic Sermon in European Perspective: Aspects of Liturgical Parody from the Middle Ages to the Twentieth Century*. Wiesbaden: Steiner, 1974.

Goldin, Daniela. "I detti, le sentenze e i florilegi medievali." *Quaderni di Retorica e Poetica* 2 (1986): 21–31.

Gorni, Guglielmo. "Parodia e scrittura in Dante." *Dante e la Bibbia*. Atti del Convegno Internazionale promosso da 'Biblia.' Firenze, 26–28 settembre 1986. Ed. Giovanni Barblan. Firenze: Olschki, 1988. 323–40.

Gorni, Guglielmo and Silvia Longhi. "La parodia." *Letteratura italiana*. Ed. Alberto Asor Rosa. 9 vols. Torino: Einaudi 1986. 5: 459–87.

Greene, Thomas M. "Forms of Accommodation in the *Decameron*." *Italica* 45 (1968): 296–313.

Grice, Paul. *Studies in the Way of Words*. Cambridge, Mass.: Harvard University Press, 1989.

Grimaldi, Emma. *Il privilegio di Dioneo. L'eccezione e la regola nel sistema Decameron*. Napoli: Edizioni Scientifiche Italiane, 1987.

Gross, Nicolas P. *Amatory Persuasion in Antiquity: Studies in Theory and Practice.* Newark: University of Delaware Press, 1985.

Guidi, Stefano. "Comicità e retorica nella 'Vita intensa' di Massimo Bontempelli." *Autografo* 9, 27 (1992): 47–69.

Gurevich, Aron. *Medieval Popular Culture: Problems of Belief and Perception.* Cambridge: Cambridge University Press, and Paris: Maison des Sciences de l'Homme, 1988.

Hansen, Patrizia C. "I racconti di Enrico Morovich (1942–1985)." *La Rassegna della Letteratura Italiana* 91 (1987): 459–68.

Hauvette, Henri. *La "morte vivante:" Étude de littérature comparée.* Paris: Boivin, 1933.

Holland, Eugene W. "Boccaccio and Freud: A Figural Narrative Model for the *Decameron*." *Assays* 3 (1985): 85–97.

Hollander, Robert. "Boccaccio's Dante: Imitative Distance (*Dec.* I,1; *Dec.* VI,10)." *Studi sul Boccaccio* 13 (1981–82): 169–98.

———. "*Decameron*: The Sun Rises in Dante." *Studi sul Boccaccio* 14 (1983–84): 241–55.

Irwin, William Robert. *The Game of the Impossible: A Rhetoric of Fantasy.* Urbana: University of Illinois Press, 1976.

Janssens, Marcel. "The Internal Reception of the Stories Within the *Decameron*." Tournoy 1977: 135–48.

Jaworski, Adam. *The Power of Silence: Social and Pragmatic Perspectives.* Newbury Park, Calif.: Sage, 1993.

Kern, Edith G. "The Gardens in the *Decameron* Cornice." *PMLA* 66 (1951): 505–23.

Kirkham, Victoria. *The Sign of Reason in Boccaccio's Fiction.* Firenze: Olschki, 1993.

Koelb, Clayton. *The Incredulous Reader: Literature and the Function of Disbelief.* Ithaca, N.Y.: Cornell University Press, 1984.

———. *Inventions of Reading: Rhetoric and the Literary Imagination.* Ithaca, N.Y.: Cornell University Press, 1988.

Lausberg, Heinrich. *Elementi di retorica.* Bologna: Il Mulino, 1969.

Lavagetto, Mario, ed. *Il testo moltiplicato. Lettura di una novella del "Decameron."* Parma: Pratiche, 1982.

Lem, Stanislaw. "Todorov's Fantastic Theory of Literature." *Science-Fiction Studies* 1 (1974): 227–37.

Longacre, Robert E. *The Grammar of Discourse.* New York: Plenum, 1983.

Longacre, Robert E. and Vida Chenoweth. "Discourse as Music." *Word* 37, 1–2 (1986): 125–39.

Lorenzo de' Medici. *Comento de' miei sonetti.* Ed. Tiziano Zanato. Firenze: Olschki, 1991.

Mancini, Franco. *La figura nel cuore fra cortesia e mistica: Dai Siciliani allo Stilnuovo.* Napoli: Edizioni Scientifiche Italiane, 1988.

Mann, Jill. "La poesia satirica e goliardica." *Lo spazio letterario del Medioevo. 1 Il Medioevo latino.* 5 vols. Ed. Guglielmo Cavallo, Claudio Leonardi, and Enrico Menestò. Roma: Salerno, 1993. 1, 2: 73–109.

Manni, Domenico Maria. *Istoria del Decamerone.* Firenze: Ristori, 1742.

Marcus, Millicent J. "The Accommodating Frate Alberto: A Gloss on *Decameron* IV, 2." *Italica* 56 (1979): 3–21. a

————. *An Allegory of Form: Literary Self-Consciousness in the "Decameron."* Saratoga: Anma Libri, 1979. b

Markulin, Joseph. "Emilia and the Case for Openness in the *Decameron.*" *Stanford Italian Review* 3 (1983): 183–99.

Marino, Lucia. *The Decameron «Cornice»: Allusion, Allegory, and Iconology.* Ravenna: Longo, 1979.

Martelli, Mario. "Considerazioni sulla tradizione della novella spicciolata." *La novella italiana* 1989 1: 215–44.

Marti, Mario. *Dante Boccaccio Leopardi: Studi.* Napoli: Liguori, 1980.

————. "Rassegna di studi sul Boccaccio." *Giornale Storico della Letteratura Italiana* 169 (1992): 424–39.

Mazzotta, Giuseppe. "The *Decameron*: The Literal and the Allegorical." *Italian Quarterly* 18 (1975): 53–73.

————. *The World at Play in Boccaccio's* Decameron. Princeton, N.J.: Princeton University Press, 1986.

Meneghello, Luigi. *Libera nos a malo.* Milano: Rizzoli, 1975.

Moravia, Alberto. *L'uomo come fine e altri saggi.* Milano: Bompiani, 1964.

Mortara Garavelli, Bice. *La parola d'altri: Prospettive di analisi del discorso.* Palermo: Sellerio, 1985.

Muscetta, Carlo. "Giovanni Boccaccio e i novellieri." *Storia della Letteratura Italiana.* Ed. Emilio Cecchi and Natalino Sapegno. 9 vols. Milano: Garzanti, 1965. 2: 315–558.

————. *Giovanni Boccaccio.* Bari: Laterza, 1989.

Nemesio, Aldo. *Le prime parole: L'uso dell' «incipit» nella narrativa dell'Italia unita.* Alessandria: Edizioni dell'Orso, 1990.

Nencioni, Giovanni. "Lettura linguistica." *Il testo moltiplicato: lettura di una novella del Decameron.* Ed. Mario Lavagetto. Parma: Pratiche 1982. 87–102.

Novati, Francesco. *Studi critici e letterari.* Torino: Loescher, 1889.

La novella italiana. Atti del Convegno di Caprarola. 19–24 settembre 1988. 2 vols. Roma: Salerno Editrice, 1989.

Nuttall, A. D. *Openings: Narrative Beginnings from the Epic to the Novel.* Oxford: Clarendon Press, 1992.

Olbrechts-Tyteca, Lucie. *Il comico del discorso: un contributo alla teoria generale del comico e del riso.* Milano: Feltrinelli, 1977.

Olson, Glending. *Literature as Recreation in the Later Middle Ages.* Ithaca, N.Y.: Cornell University Press, 1986.

Orlando, Sandro. *Appunti sul Dolce stil nuovo: Testi commentati ad uso dell'esame di Filologia romanza a.a. 1986–1987.* Alessandria: Edizioni dell'Orso, 1987.

Padoan, Giorgio. *Il Boccaccio le Muse il Parnaso e l'Arno.* Firenze: Olschki, 1978.

————. "Il senso del teatro nei secoli senza teatro." *Concetto, storia, miti e immagini del Medio Evo.* Ed. Vittore Branca. Firenze: Sansoni, 1973. 325–38.

Parodi, Ernesto Giacomo. "La miscredenza di Guido Cavalcanti e una fonte del Boccaccio." *Bullettino della Società Dantesca Italiana* n.s. 22 (1915): 37–47.

————. *Lingua e Letteratura: Studi di Teoria linguistica e di Storia dell'italiano antico.* 2 vols. Venezia: Pozza, 1957.

Pasquini, Emilio and Antonio Quaglio. Commentary. Dante Alighieri. *La Divina*

Commedia. Purgatorio. Ed. Emilio Pasquini and Antonio Quaglio. Milano: Garzanti, 1990.

Passare il tempo. La letteratura del gioco e dell'intrattenimento dal XII al XVI secolo. Atti del Convegno di Pienza. 10–14 settembre 1991. 2 vols. Roma: Salerno Editrice, 1993.

Pastore Stocchi, Manlio. "Un antecedente latino-medievale di Pietro di Vinciolo (*Decameron,* V 10)." *Studi sul Boccaccio* 1 (1963): 349–62.

Penzoldt, Peter. *The Supernatural in Fiction.* London: Nevill, 1952.

Perelman, Chaïm and Lucie Olbrechts-Tyteca. *The New Rhetoric: A Treatise on Argumentation.* Notre Dame, Ind.: University of Notre Dame Press, 1969.

Perrus, Claude. "Lecture de la nouvelle III, 5 du «Décaméron»." *Revue des Études Italiennes* 18 (1972): 235–44.

Petronio, Giuseppe. *I miei Decameron.* Roma: Editori Riuniti, 1989.

Philmus, R. M. "Todorov's Theory of 'The Fantastic': The Pitfalls of Genre Criticism." *Mosaic* 13 (1980): 71–82.

Pianezzola, Emilio. "La metamorfosi ovidiana come metafora narrativa." *Retorica e Poetica.* Atti del III Convegno italo-tedesco (Bressanone, 1975). Ed. Daniela Goldin. Padova: Liviana, 1979. 77–91.

———. "Personificazione e allegoria. Il topos della contesa." *Simbolo, metafora, allegoria.* Atti del IV convegno italo-tedesco (Bressanone 1976). Ed. Daniela Goldin. Padova: Liviana, 1980. 61–72.

Picone, Michelangelo, ed. *Il giuoco della vita bella: Folgore da San Gimignano.* Studi e testi. San Gimignano: Città di San Gimignano, 1988. a

———. "Preistoria della cornice del *Decameron.*" Cherchi and Picone 1988: 91–111. b

———. "Tre tipi di cornice novellistica: modelli orientali e tradizione narrativa medievale." *Filologia e Critica* 13 (1988): 3–26. c

Picone, Michelangelo, Giuseppe Di Stefano, and Pamela D. Stewart, eds. *La nouvelle: Formation, codification et rayonnement d'un genre médiéval.* Actes du Colloque International de Montréal (McGill University, 14–16 octobre 1982). Montréal: Plato Academic Press, 1983.

Plaisance, Michel. "Funzione e tipologia della cornice." *La novella italiana* 1989. 1: 103–18.

Potter, Joy Hambuechen. *Five Frames for the* Decameron: *Communication and Social Systems in the Cornice.* Princeton, N.J.: Princeton University Press, 1982.

Prete, Antonio. *La distanza da Croce.* Milano: CELUC, 1970.

Prince, Gerald. *Narratology: The Form and Functioning of Narrative.* Berlin: Mouton, 1982.

Propp, Vladimir. *Morphology of the Folktale.* Austin: University of Texas Press, 1984.

Rabkin, Eric S. *The Fantastic in Literature.* Princeton, N.J.: Princeton University Press, 1976.

Richardson, Brian. "La moglie di Sicofante." *Lingua nostra* 34 (1973): 42–4.

Roccato, Paolo. "La seduzione come relazione collusiva." Saraval 1989: 43–55.

Rømhild, Lars Peter. "Osservazioni sul concetto e sul significato della cornice nel *Decameron.*" *Analecta Romana Instituti Danici* 7 (1974): 157–204.

Rose, Margaret A. *Parody: Ancient, Modern, and Post-modern.* Cambridge: Cambridge University Press, 1993.

Rossi, Aldo. "Modularità e composizione." *Attualità della retorica*. Atti del I Convegno italo-tedesco. Padova: Liviana, 1975. 55–64.

Rossi, Luciano. "Il cuore, mistico pasto d'amore: dal 'Lai Guirun' al 'Decameron.'" *Studi provenzali e francesi* 82 (1983): 28–128.

———. "Ironia e parodia nel *Decameron*: da Ciappelletto a Griselda." *La novella italiana* 1989 1: 365–405.

Russo, Luigi. *Letture critiche del Decameron*. Bari: Laterza, 1956.

Russo, Vittorio. *"Con le muse in Parnaso": tre studi su Boccaccio*. Napoli: Bibliopolis, 1983.

Sanguineti White, Laura. *La scena conviviale e la sua funzione nel mondo del Boccaccio*. Firenze: Olschki, 1983.

Sapegno, Natalino. *Il Trecento*. Milano: Vallardi, 1960.

Saraval, Anteo. *La seduzione: saggi psicoanalitici*. Milano: Cortina, 1989.

Segre, Cesare. "Intertestuale-interdiscorsivo: Appunti per una fenomenologia delle fonti." Di Girolamo and Paccagnella 1982: 15–28.

———. *Introduction to the Analysis of the Literary Text*. With the collaboration of Tomaso Kemeny. Bloomington: Indiana University Press, 1988.

———. *Le strutture e il tempo*. Torino: Einaudi, 1974.

Shklovsky, Viktor. *Theory of Prose*. Elmwood Park, Ill.: Dalkey Archive Press, 1990.

Singleton, Charles S. *Dante's* Commedia: *Elements of Structure*. Baltimore: Johns Hopkins University Press, 1980.

Smarr, Janet. *Boccaccio and Fiammetta: The Narrator as Lover*. Urbana and Chicago: University of Illinois Press, 1986.

Sokel, Walter. *Franz Kafka*. New York: Columbia University Press, 1966.

Solodow, Joseph B. *The World of Ovid's* Metamorphoses. Chapel Hill: University of North Carolina Press, 1988.

Staples, Max. "Discursive Structure in Boccaccio's *Decameron*." *Esperienze Letterarie* 15, 1 (1990): 31–45.

Stassi, Maria Gabriella. "Amore e «industria»: III Giornata." Barberi Squarotti 1989: 39–58.

Staüble, Antonio. "La brigata del *Decameron* come pubblico teatrale." *Studi sul Boccaccio* 9 (1975–76): 103–17.

Stewart, Pamela D. *Retorica e mimica nel «Decameron» e nella commedia del Cinquecento*. Firenze: Olschki, 1986.

Suitner, Franco. *La poesia satirica e giocosa nell'età dei comuni*. Padova: Antenore, 1983.

Surdich, Luigi. *La cornice di amore: Studi sul Boccaccio*. Pisa: ETS, 1987.

Tarquini, Tarcisio. *Landolfi libro per libro*. Alatri: Hetea, 1988.

Tateo, Francesco. *Retorica e poetica fra Medioevo e Rinascimento*. Bari: Adriatica, n. d. [1960].

Terracini, Benvenuto. *Analisi stilistica: teoria, storia, problemi*. Milano: Feltrinelli, 1966.

Thorne, Barrie and Nancy Henley, eds. *Language and Sex: Difference and Dominance*. Rowley, Mass.: Newbury House, 1975.

Todorov, Tzvetan. *The Fantastic: A Structural Approach to a Literary Genre*. Ithaca, N.Y.: Cornell University Press, 1975.

Tournoy, Gilbert, ed. *Boccaccio in Europe*. Proceedings of the Boccaccio Conference. Louvain, December 1975. Leuven: Leuven University Press, 1977.

Traversetti, Bruno and Stefano Andreani. *Incipit: Le tecniche dell'esordio nel romanzo europeo*. Roma: Nuova ERI, 1988.

Usher, Jonathan. "Boccaccio's *Ars Moriendi* in the *Decameron*." *Modern Language Review* 81, 3 (1986): 621–32.

———. "Discorso d'oltretomba nel *Decameron*." *Paragone* 36 (1985): 48–57.

———. "Le rubriche del *Decameron*." *Medioevo romanzo* 10 (1985): 391–418.

Valency, Maurice and Harry Levtow, eds. *The Palace of Pleasure: An Anthology of the Novella*. New York: Capricorn, 1960.

Valesio, Paolo. *Ascoltare il silenzio: la retorica come teoria*. Bologna: Il Mulino, 1986.

Vax, Louis. *L'art et la littérature fantastique*. Paris: Presses Universitaires de France, 1960.

Vecchi, Giuseppe. "Il «proverbio» nella pratica letteraria dei dettatori della scuola di Bologna." *Studi Mediolatini e Volgari* 2 (1954): 283–302.

Velli, Giuseppe. *Petrarca e Boccaccio: Tradizione Memoria Scrittura*. Padova: Antenore, 1979.

———. "Seneca nel «Decameron»." *Giornale Storico della Letteratura Italiana* 168 (1991): 321–34.

Viarre, Simone. *L'image et la pensée dans les «Métamorphoses» d'Ovide*. Paris: Presses Universitaires de France, 1964.

———. *Ovide: essai de lecture poétique*. Paris: Les Belles Lettres, 1976.

Vittori, Maria Vittoria. "Il mar delle blatte." Tarquini 1988: 55–67.

Wasserman, Julian N. and Lois Roney, eds. *Sign, Sentence, Discourse: Language in Medieval Thought and Literature*. Syracuse, N.Y.: Syracuse University Press, 1989.

Watson, Paul F. "On Seeing Guido Cavalcanti and the Houses of the Dead." *Studi sul Boccaccio* 18 (1989): 301–18.

Weinrich, Harald. *Tempus: Le funzioni dei tempi nel testo*. Bologna: il Mulino, 1978.

Yaguello, Marina. *Les mots et les femmes: Essai d'approche socio-linguistique de la condition féminine*. Paris: Payot, 1978.

Zago, Esther. "Gender and Melancholy in Boccaccio's 'Decameron'." *Lingua e Stile* 27 (1992): 235–249.

Zumthor, Paul. *Toward a Medieval Poetics*. Minneapolis: University of Minnesota Press, 1992.

Index

The entries under Boccaccio include mention of individual works and *novelle* of the *Decameron*, not occurrences of the author's name.

University of Pennsylvania Press
MIDDLE AGES SERIES
Ruth Mazo Karras and Edward Peters,
General Editors

F. R. P. Akehurst, trans. *The* Coutumes de Beauvaisis *of Philippe de Beaumanoir.* 1992

Peter L. Allen. *The Art of Love: Amatory Fiction from Ovid to the* Romance of the Rose. 1992

David Anderson. *Before the Knight's Tale: Imitation of Classical Epic in Boccaccio's* Teseida. 1988

Benjamin Arnold. *Count and Bishop in Medieval Germany: A Study of Regional Power, 1100–1350.* 1991

Mark C. Bartusis. *The Late Byzantine Army: Arms and Society, 1204–1453.* 1992

Thomas N. Bisson, ed. *Cultures of Power: Lordship, Status, and Process in Twelfth-Century Europe.* 1995

Uta-Renate Blumenthal. *The Investiture Controversy: Church and Monarchy from the Ninth to the Twelfth Century.* 1988

Gerald A. Bond. *The Loving Subject: Desire, Eloquence, and Power in Romanesque France.* 1995

Daniel Bornstein, trans. *Dino Compagni's* Chronicle *of Florence.* 1986

Maureen Boulton. *The Song in the Story: Lyric Insertions in French Narrative Fiction, 1200–1400.* 1993

Charles R. Bowlus. *Franks, Moravians, and Magyars: The Struggle for the Middle Danube, 788–907.* 1995

Kevin Brownlee and Sylvia Huot, eds. *Rethinking the* Romance of the Rose*: Text, Image, Reception.* 1992

Matilda Tomaryn Bruckner. *Shaping Romance: Interpretation, Truth, and Closure in Twelfth-Century French Fictions.* 1993

Otto Brunner (Howard Kaminsky and James Van Horn Melton, eds. and trans.). Land *and Lordship: Structures of Governance in Medieval Austria.* 1992

Robert I. Burns, S.J., ed. *Emperor of Culture: Alfonso X the Learned of Castile and His Thirteenth-Century Renaissance.* 1990

David Burr. *Olivi and Franciscan Poverty: The Origins of the* Usus Pauper *Controversy.* 1989

David Burr. *Olivi's Peaceable Kingdom: A Reading of the Apocalypse Commentary.* 1993

Thomas Cable. *The English Alliterative Tradition.* 1991

Anthony K. Cassell and Victoria Kirkham, eds. and trans. *Diana's Hunt/Caccia di Diana: Boccaccio's First Fiction.* 1991

John C. Cavadini. *The Last Christology of the West: Adoptionism in Spain and Gaul, 785–820.* 1993

Brigitte Cazelles. *The Lady as Saint: A Collection of French Hagiographic Romances of The Thirteenth Century.* 1991

Karen Cherewatuk and Ulrike Wiethaus, eds. *Dear Sister: Medieval Women and the Epistolary Genre.* 1993

Anne L. Clark. *Elisabeth of Schönau: A Twelfth-Century Visionary.* 1992

Willene B. Clark and Meradith T. McMunn, eds. *Beasts and Birds of the Middle Ages: The Bestiary and Its Legacy.* 1989

Richard C. Dales. *The Scientific Achievement of the Middle Ages.* 1973

Charles T. Davis. *Dante's Italy and Other Essays.* 1984

William J. Dohar. *The Black Death and Pastoral Leadership: The Diocese of Hereford in the Fourteenth Century.* 1994

Judith Ferster. *Fictions of Advice: The Literature and Politics of Counsel in Late Medieval England.* 1996

Katherine Fischer Drew, trans. *The Burgundian Code.* 1972

Katherine Fischer Drew, trans. *The Laws of the Salian Franks.* 1991

Katherine Fischer Drew, trans. *The Lombard Laws.* 1973

Nancy Edwards. *The Archaeology of Early Medieval Ireland.* 1990

Richard K. Emmerson and Ronald B. Herzman. *The Apocalyptic Imagination in Medieval Literature.* 1992

Theodore Evergates. *Feudal Society in Medieval France: Documents from the County of Champagne.* 1993

Felipe Fernández-Armesto. *Before Columbus: Exploration and Colonization from the Mediterranean to the Atlantic, 1229–1492.* 1987

Pier Massimo Forni. *Adventures in Speech: Rhetoric and Narration in Boccaccio's Decameron.* 1996

Jerold C. Frakes. *Brides and Doom: Gender, Property, and Power in Medieval Women's Epic.* 1994

R. D. Fulk. *A History of Old English Meter.* 1992

Peter Heath. *Allegory and Philosophy in Avicenna (Ibn Sînâ), with a Translation of the Book of the Prophet Muhammad's Ascent to Heaven.* 1992

John Bell Henneman. *Olivier de Clisson and Political Society Under Charles V and Charles VI.* 1996

J. N. Hillgarth, ed. *Christianity and Paganism, 350–750: The Conversion of Western Europe.* 1986

Richard C. Hoffman. *Land, Liberties, and Lordship in a Late Medieval Countryside: Agrarian Structures and Change in the Duchy of Wrocław.* 1990

John Y. B. Hood. *Aquinas and the Jews.* 1995

Edward B. Irving, Jr. *Rereading* Beowulf. 1989

Richard A. Jackson, ed. Ordines Coronationis Franciae: *Texts and Ordines for the Coronation of Frankish and French Kings and Queens in the Middle Ages, Vol. I.* 1995

C. Stephen Jaeger. *The Envy of Angels: Cathedral Schools and Social Ideals in Medieval Europe, 950–1200.* 1994

C. Stephen Jaeger. *The Origins of Courtliness: Civilizing Trends and the Formation of Courtly Ideals, 939–1210.* 1985

Richard W. Kaeuper and Elspeth Kennedy, trans. *Geoffroi de Charny and his* Livre de Chevalerie: *Study, Text, and Translation.* 1996

Donald J. Kagay, trans. *The Usatges of Barcelona: The Fundamental Law of Catalonia.* 1994

Richard Kay. *Dante's Christian Astrology.* 1994

Ellen E. Kittell. *Fron* Ad Hoc *to Routine: A Case Study in Medieval Bureaucracy.* 1991

Alan C. Kors and Edward Peters, eds. *Witchcraft in Europe, 1100–1700: A Documentary History.* 1972

Barbara M. Kreutz. *Before the Normans: Southern Italy in the Ninth and Tenth Centuries.* 1992

Michael P. Kuczynski. *Prophetic Song: The Psalms as Moral Discourse in Late Medieval England.* 1995

E. Ann Matter. *The Voice of My Beloved: The Song of Songs in Western Medieval Christianity.* 1990

Shannon McSheffrey. *Gender and Heresy: Women and Men in Lollard Communities, 1420–1530.* 1995

A. J. Minnis. *Medieval Theory of Authorship.* 1988

Lawrence Nees. *A Tainted Mantle: Hercules and the Classical Tradition at the Carolingian Court.* 1991

Lynn H. Nelson, trans. *The Chronicle of San Juan de la Peña: A Fourteenth-Century Official History of the Crown of Aragon.* 1991

Barbara Newman. *From Virile Woman to WomanChrist: Studies in Medieval Religion and Literature.* 1995

Thomas F. X. Noble. *The Republic of St. Peter: The Birth of the Papal State, 680–825.* 1984

Joseph F. O'Callaghan. *The Learned King: The Reign of Alfonso X of Castile.* 1993

Odo of Tournai (Irven M. Resnick, trans.). *Two Theological Treatises:* On Original Sin *and* A Disputation with the Jew, Leo, Concerning the Advent of Christ, the Son of God. 1994

David M. Olster. *Roman Defeat, Christian Response, and the Literary Construction of the Jew.* 1994

William D. Paden, ed. *The Voice of the Trobairitz: Perspectives on the Women Troubadours.* 1989

Edward Peters. *The Magician, the Witch, and the Law.* 1982

Edward Peters, ed. *Christian Society and the Crusades, 1198–1229: Sources in Translation, including* The Capture of Damietta *by Oliver of Paderborn.* 1971

Edward Peters, ed. *The First Crusade: The* Chronicle of Fulcher of Chartres *and Other Source Materials.* 1971

Edward Peters, ed. *Heresy and Authority in Medieval Europe.* 1980

James M. Powell. *Albertanus of Brescia: The Pursuit of Happiness in the Early Thirteenth Century.* 1992

James M. Powell. *Anatomy of a Crusade, 1213–1221.* 1986

Susan A. Rabe. *Faith, Art, and Politics at Saint-Riquier: The Symbolic Vision of Angilbert.* 1995

Jean Renart (Patricia Terry and Nancy Vine Durling, trans.). *The Romance of the Rose or Guillaume de Dole*. 1993

Michael Resler, trans. *Erec by Hartmann von Aue*. 1987

Pierre Riché (Michael Idomir Allen, trans.). *The Carolingians: A Family Who Forged Europe*. 1993

Pierre Riché (Jo Ann McNamara, trans.). *Daily Life in the World of Charlemagne*. 1978

Jonathan Riley-Smith. *The First Crusade and the Idea of Crusading*. 1986

Joel T. Rosenthal. *Old Age in Medieval England: The Search for Lived Experience*. 1996

Joel T. Rosenthal. *Patriarchy and Families of Privilege in Fifteenth-Century England*. 1991

Teofilo F. Ruiz. *Crisis and Continuity: Land and Town in Late Medieval Castile*. 1994

James A. Rushing, Jr. *Images of Adventure: Ywain in the Visual Arts*. 1995

James A. Schultz. *The Knowledge of Childhood in the German Middle Ages, 1100–1350*. 1995

John A. Scott. *Dante's Political Purgatory*. 1996

Pamela Sheingorn, ed. and trans. *The Book of Sainte Foy*. 1995

Robin Chapman Stacey. *The Road to Judgment: From Custom to Court in Medieval Ireland and Wales*. 1994

Sarah Stanbury. *Seeing the* Gawain-*Poet: Description and the Act of Perception*. 1992

Robert D. Stevick. *The Earliest Irish and English Bookarts: Visual and Poetic Forms Before A.D. 1000*. 1994

Thomas C. Stillinger. *The Song of Troilus: Lyric Authority in the Medieval Book*. 1992

Susan Mosher Stuard. *A State of Deference: Ragusa/Dubrovnik in the Medieval Centuries*. 1992

Susan Mosher Stuard, ed. *Women in Medieval History and Historiography*. 1987

Susan Mosher Stuard, ed. *Women in Medieval Society*. 1976

Jonathan Sumption. *The Hundred Years War: Trial by Battle*. 1992

Ronald E. Surtz. *The Mothers of Saint Teresa of Avila: Female Religious Voices from Late Medieval to Early Modern Spain*. 1995

Del Sweeney, ed. *Agriculture in the Middle Ages: Technology Practice, and Representation*. 1995

William H. TeBrake. *A Plague of Insurrection: Popular Politics and Peasant Revolt in Flanders, 1323–1328*. 1993

Patricia Terry, trans. *Poems of the Elder Edda*. 1990

Hugh M. Thomas. *Vassals, Heiresses, Crusaders, and Thugs: The Gentry of Angevin Yorkshire, 1154–1216*. 1993

Mary F. Wack. *Lovesickness in the Middle Ages: The* Viaticum *and Its Commentaries*. 1990

Benedicta Ward. *Miracles and the Medieval Mind: Theory, Record, and Event, 1000–1215*. 1982

Suzanne Fonay Wemple. *Women in Frankish Society: Marriage and the Cloister, 500–900*. 1981

Kenneth Baxter Wolf. *Making History: The Normans and Their Historians in Eleventh-Century Italy*. 1995

Jan M. Ziolkowski. *Talking Animals: Medieval Latin Beast Poetry, 750–1150*. 1993